RYA Manual of Seamanship

Written by Tom Cunliffe

Illustrations by Andrew Simpson

2007

Reprinted April 2010

First Published 2007
The Royal Yachting Association
RYA House, Ensign Way, Hamble
Southampton SO31 4YA
Tel: 0844 556 9555
Fax: 0844 556 9516
Email: publications@rya.org.uk
Web: www.rya.org.uk
ISBN: 978-1-905104079
RYA Order Code: G36

Totally Chlorine Free *Sustainable Forests*

A CIP record of this book is available from the British Library

Cover Design: Pete Galvin
Photographic credits: Jon Nash, US Coastguard, Andrew Simpson, Lewmar, Mike Golding Racing. All other photographs by the author.
Acknowledgements: Firemaster Extinguisher Ltd, Ocean Safety Ltd. The author acknowledges the assistance of Andrew Simpson, seaman and surveyor, who has been so much more than an illustrator in the preparation of this book.
Typeset: Creativebyte
Proofreading and glossary: Alan Thatcher
Printed through: World Print

Tom Cunliffe's Manual of Seamanship

Tom Cunliffe is a lifelong sailor who has served before the mast in small sailing ships, skippered yachts for private owners, raced offshore been to sea as mate on a British-registered coasting vessel and taught sailing, seamanship and navigation at all levels. He is one of the UK's senior Yachtmaster examiners and has acted as a consultant for the governing body of sailing in the USA.

The author of many nautical text books on subjects as diverse as astro-navigation and the global history of pilotage in the days of sail. He is also the compiler of The Shell Channel Pilot and writes regular columns for Yachting Monthly, Yachting World and SAIL.

www.tomcunliffe.com

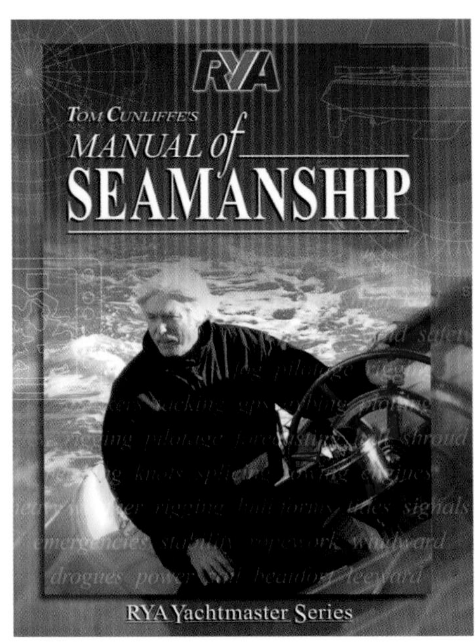

Foreword to the Manual of Seamanship

You can spot a seamanlike yacht from a cable away. Actually it's easier to identify an unseamanlike one. Skippers unaware of seamanship have slack halyards and guardrails, the traveller and jib cars are in the wrong position, the jib sheets are frayed and attached to the wrong sail for the job. The crew is unhappy because the whole trip is taking longer than it should and below a cascade of clothing, coffee mugs and sleeping bags slide across the cabin at every tack. The chart table is a dumping ground for tools, lunch and other kit and last week's soup provides an adhesive surface in the galley. Such skippers urgently need this book.

For many years I worked with Tom Cunliffe training and assessing Yachtmaster Instructors. We sailed with some outstanding masters of the craft of seamanship. In the hands of these experts the whole job of taking charge seems easy. It isn't, but they made it look that way by being one jump ahead. I think that they are all secret worriers wondering what they are going to do if the visibility drops, the wind veers or the hull strikes a semi-submerged container. They take the pragmatic view that seamanship is about saving yourself work. It is much less effort to prepare for the storm before it arrives.

My wife regularly reminds me that no one has to go sailing. We do so for work or pleasure because we love the sport. A seamanlike yacht is a happy ship and a "seaman's eye" greatly enhances safety and efficiency on board. This book provides a wealth of information for both newcomers and experienced hands who wish to improve their knowledge, understanding and enjoyment.

There can be few authors better qualified to write on this subject than Tom Cunliffe who has a lifetime not only of skippering yachts but also imparting those skills in a clear informative and inimitable style.

James Stevens FRIN

RYA Training Manager and Chief Examiner

Contents

	Foreword by James Stevens FRIN	3
	Preface	6
1	Hull Forms	8
2	Speed in theory and practice	12
3	Motive Force – Sail	18
4	Power units	29
5	Ropes and ropework	40
6	Boat handling	56
7	Anchoring	76
8	Mooring	84
9	Heavy Weather	86

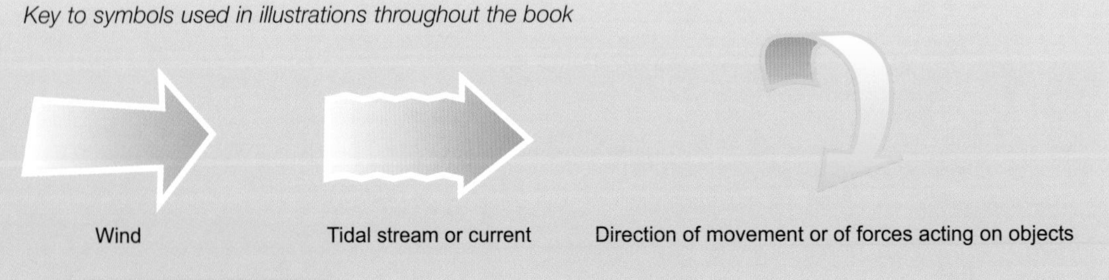

10	Storm Survival	100
11	Emergencies	110
12	Crew care and watchkeeping	124
13	Fog and poor visibility	128
14	Manners and customs of the sea	132
15	Dinghy Work	138
16	River seamanship	140
17	Grounding	144
18	Wind and wave	148
	Glossary	156
	Index	163
	Membership pages	170

Preface

The Shorter Oxford English Dictionary defines seamanship as, 'Skill in the art of working a ship or boat'. Taken literally, this could mean absolutely everything nautical, including navigation, communications, chipping rust, and rigging a Nelsonian frigate for church on a trade-wind Sunday morning. Any manual of seamanship would therefore run to so many volumes that stowing it aboard a small vessel could create major trim problems.

Fortunately, the dictionary's categorisation represents a landsman's simplified impression. Sailors view the matter differently. How many times have we heard remarks such as, 'Old Baines is a fine seaman but he can't navigate to save his life,' or, 'Tosher's great with a paint brush but he's a shocking seaman.' These throw-away comments offer an insight, even if only by default, but it does seem that salt-water people don't consider navigational skills to be an essential part of the seaman's makeup. However, dealing with rope and rigging, the sailor's primary tools, would surely ride high on any list. Other aspects of ship's husbandry might also figure, but the ability to paint a yacht to a mirror finish probably wouldn't. An arbitrary distinction, you might think; but is it?

The 1932 edition of The Admiralty Manual of Seamanship, Volume 1 shamelessly shirks any attempt to define its subject. Instead, the writer wades straight in with an exposition of how to sling a hammock, then goes on with a clear diagram of how 1st and 2nd class boys should lay out their kit for inspection. Such issues were critical to the success of any naval rating of those days, and were thus very much part of seamanship. The book's chapters on traditional knotting are timeless and have yet to be beaten, but much of the contents of its three volumes remain less than relevant to non-military small-craft operators in the 21st century.

Much closer to the mark is Admiral Smyth's definition of 1867. 'The noble practical art of rigging and working a ship, and performing with effect all her various evolutions at sea.' This description can be readily brought up to date by including under 'rigging' all the machinery and necessary adjuncts to it that make up the modern vessel.

While noting with satisfaction that the Admiral considered the art of seamanship to be a noble one, the reassuring choice of words for the writer of this manual was 'practical'. Since the book is published by the RYA, it must be seen as carrying official approval. Much consideration went into the scope, but the recurring theme was, 'let's keep it hands-on'. A clear gap existed between what could realistically be taught on a course and the actuality of all the skills required to operate a boat safely and smoothly in any conditions at sea and in harbour. Originally conceived to take up that slack, the manual moved on to establish a more general position extending beyond the RYA course programmes.

A glance through the contents list will indicate those subjects the writer and the RYA feel should be incorporated into a modern definition of small-craft seamanship. They begin with an analysis of the commonest hull configurations, because without this knowledge it is impossible to predict how a specific vessel may behave. This is followed by a section on what Admiral Smyth called 'rigging'. In his day, a ship's motive force was delivered by natural fibre cordage, wood and canvas. Today, the job may be done by the diesel engine, or perhaps a sailing rig of stainless steel, polyester sailcloth and ropes whose qualities would have boggled the mind of an 1860s' rigger. The 21st century seaman must know how to work with them all. In addition to what remains essentially ship's husbandry, however, he or she must be able to berth and unberth vessels of widely varying characteristics, then confidently handle the same boats offshore in a storm. And when the tempest is past, good seamen can rub shoulders with others of their calling without attracting attention by some embarrassing slip-up in conventional behaviour or unwitting bad manners.

Late 20th century developments in navigation and communication revolutionized seafaring to an extent only previously achieved by the engine. Those of us who deal with small craft are now in far closer touch with the sea's elemental nature than professionals in powerful ships. Our seamanship should be our pride as well as our joy.

Notes on gender

A matter of gender

'Seaman' – Back in ancient history when the term 'seaman' was coined, the salt-water calling was largely confined to the male of the species. Things have changed, but the name remains as a quaint reminder of a different world. The author has consulted his wife, his adult daughter and a number of ladies of his acquaintance, all seafarers of wide experience, and none find the word sexually offensive. In search of political correctness, such bodies as the National Union of Seamen have switched to 'seafarer', but to say, 'the normal practice of seafarers', or 'Jemima is a grand seafarer', sounds so strained and lame that the author has decided to stick to the old ways. As for 'seapersonship', or any other such gobbledegook, let us have none of it. For the purposes of this book, 'seaman' does not mean 'a male who goes on a boat', it means 'a man or woman who is master or mistress of the way of a vessel on salt water'.

'She' – Throughout the text, boats, ships and all vessels are generally referred to by the traditional 'she'. The author makes no apology for this. Seamen still do it, and if non-specialist journalists and government officials choose to substitute this ancient choice of pronoun with the neuter, 'it', that is their privilege. This is a manual written by a seaman for seamen and, 'she', a boat emphatically remains.

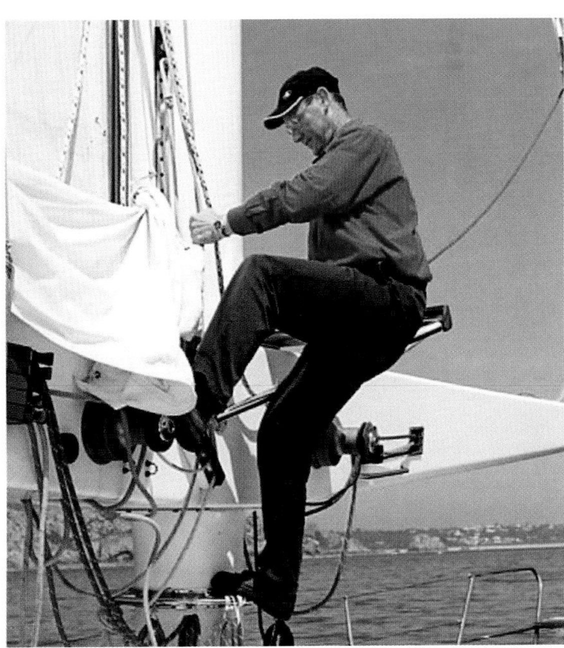

Seamanship is just as important today as it was in ancient times. This modern skipper with his high-tech Aerorig is drawing on skills that have evolved over many centuries.

Hull Forms

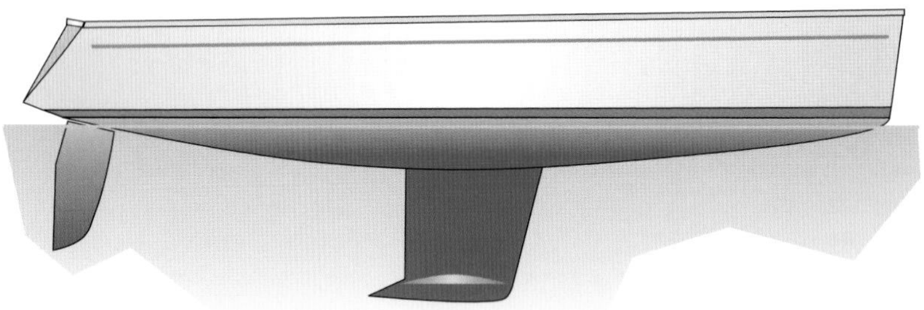

Sailing craft

Some boats handle beautifully in harbour even in strong winds. Others are blown around like leaves in autumn. Many are quite content to steer reliably astern, while a sizeable minority appear to have minds of their own. A storm survival tactic that is safe for one group may be suicidal for another, yet the second type may be able to make up the shortfall by strength in a different area. No matter what boat you operate, sail or power, her behaviour at sea and in harbour will be based on hull form. Rig or superstructure disposition may modify this, but the hull remains the bedrock. The main factors include where her rudder or rudders are sited in relation to her propellers, how long her keel is, how beamy she may be, how heavy her displacement, whether her forefoot is deep or cut away, and how much windage her topsides generate in relation to her underwater lateral area. Depending on these elements, performance is largely predictable. Set out below are some of the main categories.

Long or short keel

The most important sub-division in monohulled sailing yachts is whether a boat has a short or a long keel. Both types may vary greatly in specification, but the essential difference is that in a long-keeled hull, the rudder is hung from the aft end of the keel itself. In a short-keeler, the rudder is a separate unit suspended as far aft as practicable.

As a general principle, a boat with a long keel will be of heavier displacement and steady in her character at sea, resisting tendencies to eccentric behaviour in gusty weather. She will not be notably close-winded, however, and may prove difficult to steer when motoring astern. The fin-keeler has a better potential to point high to windward, often handles more quickly on the helm and in many cases steers well astern. The long-keeled boat may find she has more options in heavy weather survival situations where sea room is not an issue, while the fin-and-rudder configuration usually tacks more reliably and exhibits more dinghy-like handling characteristics.

Long-keeled variants

Long-keeled sailing yachts fall into three essential types with infinite variation between them. The traditional work-boat form, the yachts which evolved from it, and the fully developed modern long keel.

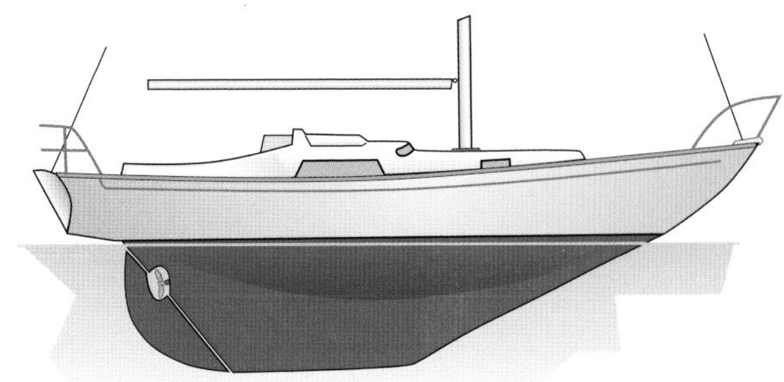

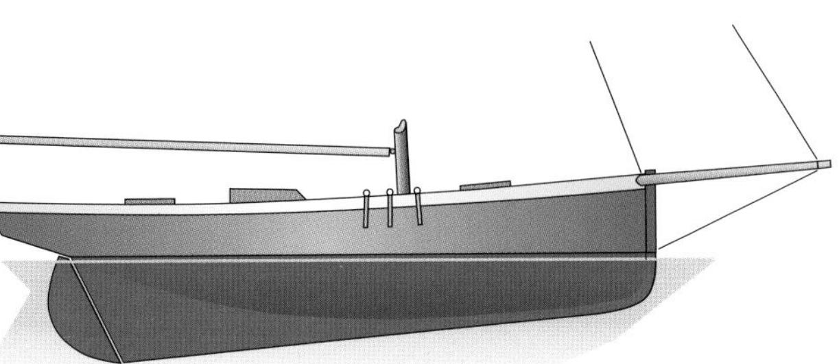

The classic long-keeled yacht

During the middle years of the twentieth century, the forefoot of the work-boat 'originals' was cut back by yacht designers to reduce the wetted area. Often, the stern post was angled forward for the same reason. Like workboats, these hulls may have a counter or a transom stern. Also like them, the form selected will not greatly affect handling. Such long-keeled classics are generally easily driven for their displacement. They are certain on the helm when manoeuvring ahead under power or sail, and are steady at sea, but they do not heave to as well as workboats.

The traditional straight-stemmed workboat

This is typified by healthy draught, heavy displacement, moderate beam, a plumb stem and a deep forefoot. It may have a transom stern (planked across, with the rudder hung from it) or a counter with the rudder post coming up through the deck. Boats with this sort of hull often feature a bowsprit to balance the rig and carry the sail area needed to drive so substantial a weight. The shape was developed because a long, straight keel was a vital structural element for wooden boat builders working in simple circumstances, but it paid dividends at sea by steadiness on the helm. Good examples are well balanced so that the tiller can be left lashed for long periods. The deep forefoot gives a solid grip, invaluable when heaving to in hard weather (see page 106). Like all long-keelers, such craft are unwilling to handle astern under power. Many are now built as 'retro' and character cruisers.

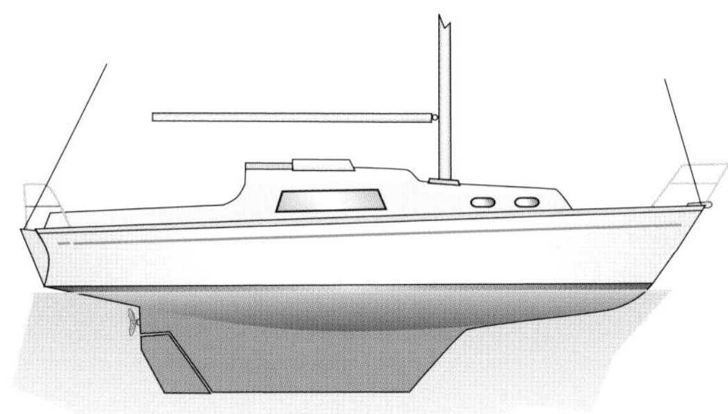

The modern long-keeler

Towards the end of the 20th century, the forefoot was cut away even more. This creates boats which steer well when running downwind, but at the cost of lost grip on the water up forward. Such craft make first-class downwind passage makers and many are successful world cruisers, but often their handling under sail in close quarters is not so positive as either of the other types of long keeler. Like the classic yacht, their capacity to hold their heads up to the wind when hove to in a big sea is not nearly so good as that of the workboat. Indeed, some end up undesirably beam-on to the weather.

Short-keeled variants

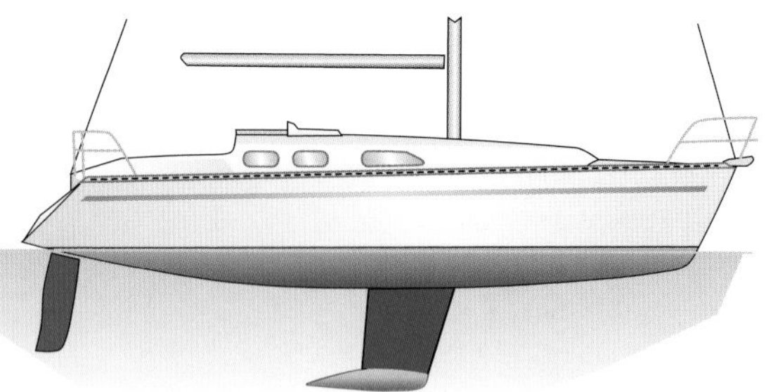

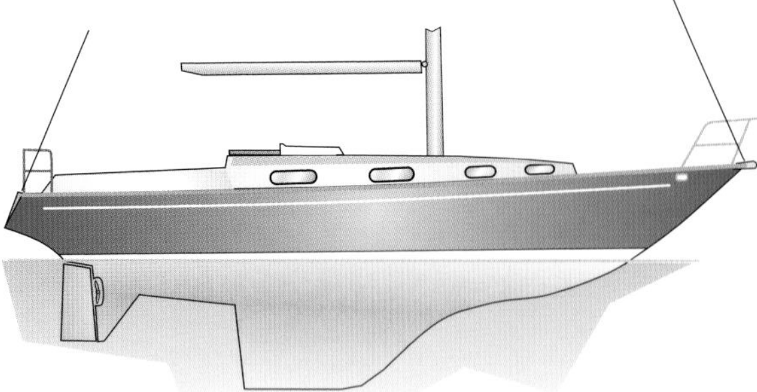

Fin and skeg

These boats began to appear when the continual shortening of the classic yacht keel had moved the rudder too close to the centre of lateral resistance for it to work properly. The logical answer was to separate the rudder from the keel and hang it right aft for maximum leverage. The original 'short' keels are long by modern standards; they also remain moulded into the hull rather than being bolted on, conferring handling characteristics more like a classic yacht than later short-keeled variants. The rudder is securely hung from a skeg which, like the keel, is moulded into the hull, while the forefoot shows signs of the classics from whence it came. Such yachts often deliver a wholesome compromise between precise steering at sea, comfort, and athletic turning in harbour. Their general stability ratings can be very promising, but, like most of the more recent hull forms, they tend to lie beam-on to the wind if left to their own devices.

Fin and spade

The logical development from the fin-and-skeg form was to make the hull into a lighter displacement 'canoe body' type with a bolt-on keel. The keel could now be shorter and thus potentially more efficient to windward, especially when complemented by a deep, hydrodynamic 'spade' rudder. A spade rudder is unsupported except for the stock with its through-hull bearings. Although these rudders have long since overcome their structural teething problems, they remain more vulnerable than rudders which carry bearings nearer to or at their lower ends. Fin-and-spade craft are typically beamier than their predecessors, with high internal volume. They should perform well in terms of speed and pointing, but often prove less comfortable in a seaway when the virtually non-existent forefoot pounds upwind. Many – but not all – such cruisers exhibit difficult steering characteristics in gusty weather, leading to a serious imbalance at high angles of heel if wide beam is carried a long way aft to create the space demanded by stern cabins. The salient keel and rudder, as well as the propeller which must inevitably be hung on a bracket, are all vulnerable to picking up ropes and other obstructions that would slide off a long-keeled hull with a stern-hung rudder and propeller aperture. The pay-off is a roomy craft which can be a delight to steer astern.

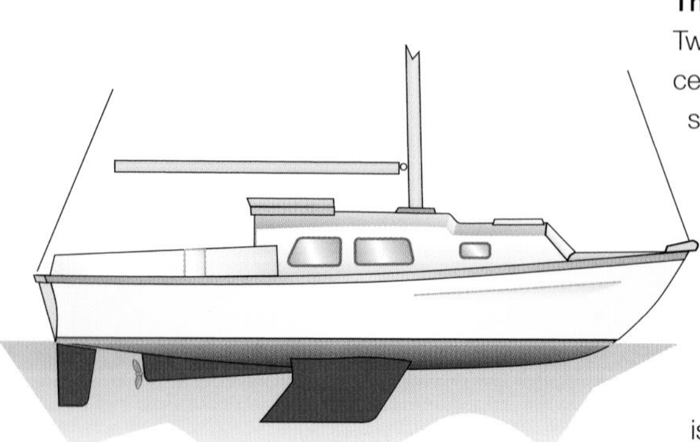

The bilge keeler

Twin bilge keels as an alternative to a single fin or the rarer centreboard were developed in the mid-20th century in a successful attempt to reduce draught while retaining reasonable sailing ability and seaworthiness. The bilge-keeler has the advantage of being able to sit upright on the bottom. This means she can dry out unsupported on the tide. The price for this huge benefit is some cost in pointing ability and, in some cases, ultimate stability, but since most bilge-keelers are not used for deep-ocean voyaging, storm survival is an unlikely issue. At sea, their generally moderate characteristics mean that most steer without problems. Rudders are well aft and usually protected by a skeg.

Power boats

Power boat hulls are many and various in type, but two essential groups are distinct.

Displacement hulls

These are of deep draught and comparatively heavy. Their potential speed is limited by the waterline length rules (see page 12), and they steer with rudders which work in their own right. That is to say, if the engine is out of gear and the vessel has sufficient way on, she will steer perfectly well. The rudder does more than merely divert the stream of water flowing off the propeller or propellers. Such craft often manoeuvre in a similar way to traditional sailing boat types, which is not surprising as many are directly developed from them. The classic Motor Fishing Vessel (MFV) is a case in point.

Planing and semi-displacement hulls

The pure planing hull is shallow in draught and light of displacement so that she can readily lift out of the water and travel at high speed. She may well carry her propellers on out-drive units, in which case she will have no rudders at all, steering by turning the legs of her drives. If the engines are pure inboard units, the propellers will stand proud under the hull and are thus vulnerable in groundings. The rudders are small and sited immediately abaft the screws, steering by diverting the propeller wash rather than by having an effect in their own right.

A semi-displacement hull

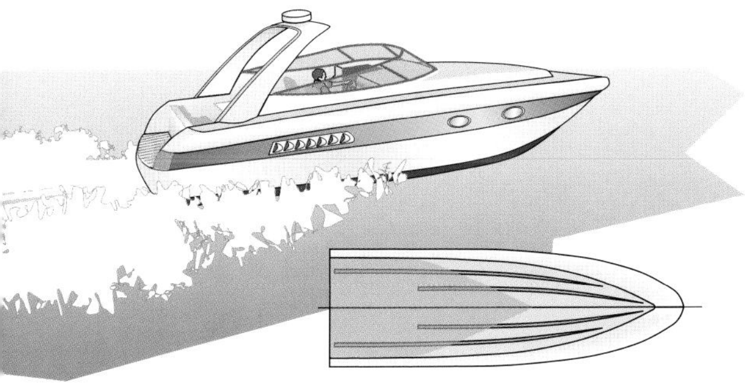

A planing hull

Semi-displacement hulls are somewhat heavier and may be deeper, but they exhibit similar characteristics.

Many of these craft have twin engines and manoeuvre extremely well in harbour. They also double their chances of at least one unit remaining in action in the event of mechanical failure.

Most sea-going boats today with any potential for planing are of the seaworthy and relatively comfortable 'deep-vee' form. This confers the ability to cut through waves as well as being directionally stable at high speed.

Speed in theory and practice

Hull Speed

The theoretical maximum speed of all hulls is governed by one essential rule, irrespective of whether the vessel is driven by power, sail or is being dragged along a canal by a shire horse. These limits can be circumvented in a number of ways, but understanding and applying the theory remains central to the intelligent operation of any boat.

As a vessel moves through water, a small wave appears at either side of the bow *(a)*. When speed increases, another pair makes itself known further aft *(b)*. More speed enlarges both sets. At the same time, the distance between them increases until the boat is apparently hanging between the bow wave and its counterpart under the quarter *(c)*. This velocity is the maximum rate of knots that the hull can reach without riding up onto its own bow wave and planing. It is generally known as 'hull speed'. Unless the boat can be persuaded to plane, piling on either power or sail has little further effect, other than to amplify the size of the waves.

Calculating hull speed

Hull speed in knots can be calculated readily by multiplying the square root of a boat's waterline length in feet by some constant. For most boats, this constant is about $1\frac{1}{3}$, or 1.34.

Eg:

a 13.1m sailing yacht might have a waterline length of 11m. This converts readily to around 36ft.

$\sqrt{36} = 6$

$6 \times 1\frac{1}{3} = 8$ knots. Thus, 'give-or-take' a few percentage points, the yacht will struggle to exceed 8 knots.

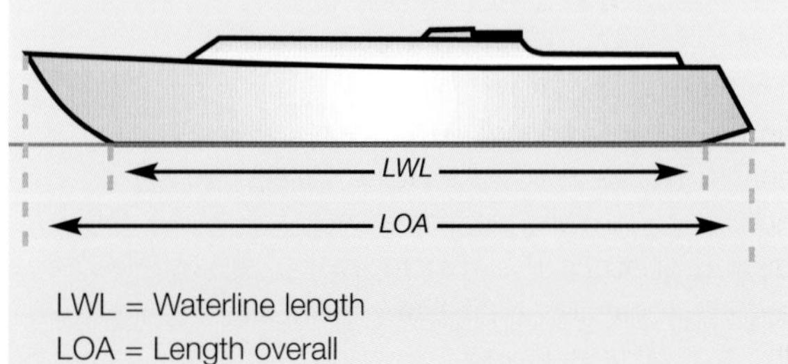

LWL = Waterline length
LOA = Length overall

Water speed / ground speed

Unless modified by a linked function, satellite navigation systems read out speed over the ground (SOG), which is the resultant of speed through the water modified by the effects of tide or current. Water speed, or 'boat speed' is the basic building block on which all performance calculations should be based. It is measured by the log which, if not correctly calibrated, will render much of this chapter superfluous.

Modifying factors to hull speed – Sail

Multihulls and modern race boats

Very narrow hulls of light displacement and shallow body draught, such as fast, racing multihulls, increase the value of the multiplying constant (normally around 1.3) by virtue of being exceptionally easily driven. Other fast sailing designs do the same with wide, light, shallow hulls operating on the edge of the displacement mode for much of the time.

Many sailing craft have an 'overhang' aft which lies above the waterline at rest, but which is immersed as the stern wave builds with increasing velocity. This hidden extra length is factored into a boat's true hull speed, which accounts for some boats being faster than might at first sight seem likely. Similar effects are achieved by long overhangs at bow and stern when a boat heels to the wind.

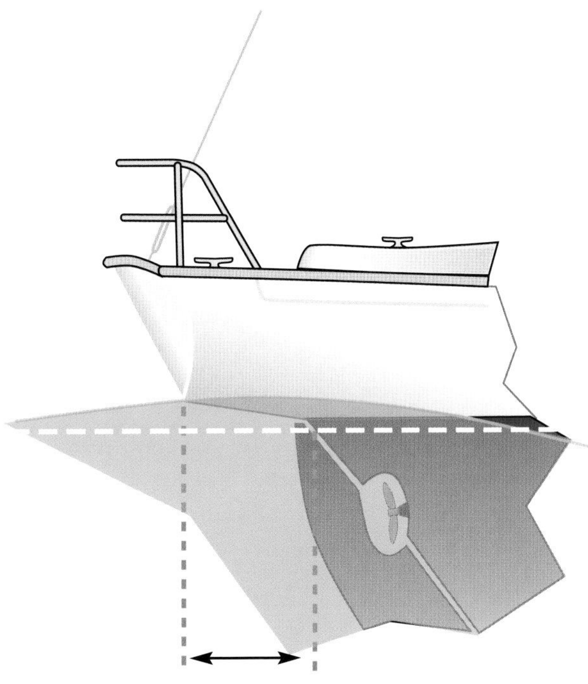

Extra length gained by stern wave

Planing

Racing dinghies are able to exceed their hull speeds by rising up onto their own bow waves and planing. Once this state has been achieved, speed is limited only by sail area, stability and the skill of the jockey.

Surfing

The highest speeds experienced by most displacement sailing yachts come when travelling downwind in waves. If pushed sufficiently hard a wave picks up the stern and the boat careers down the face of the wave like a surfboard. She then ceases to be a true displacement hull and can exceed the theoretical maximum. Light displacement yachts surf more readily than heavy, but any vessel can achieve it if driven hard enough under the right circumstances.

A planing dinghy

Easy progress

Hard driving

Practical results of limitations of boat speed - Sail

Closehauled sailing

When a yacht is closehauled, so little of the residual effort of her rig is transferred into forward drive that in all but the most extreme performance craft, hull speed is never attained. A typical cruiser sailing in moderately advantageous conditions will manage little better than the unmodified square root of her waterline length. Thus, a boat of LWL 25ft can expect 5 knots hard on the wind. She may do better, but a skipper who expects no more will rarely be disappointed.

Hard driving

The energy to drive a yacht does not increase in direct proportion to velocity. A reaching sailing craft moves very easily up to what would be her best speed to windward. The final quarter of her theoretical maximum is achieved by applying a rapidly rising amount of sail power. A boat capable of 8 knots will get up to six with little effort. Given the right wind, seven can be sustained by a crew with sufficient enthusiasm, but to drive her at her full 8 knots for more than short bursts will be a dramatic business, and very demanding on both gear and crew.

Net effects of hull-speed factors on sailing boats

Life aboard a boat sailing free in a strong or even moderate breeze is generally easier if her rate of knots is ten or fifteen per cent below the theoretical maximum. On the other hand, driving her at near-displacement speeds can be a race-winner, and most cruisers love a fast passage time. The same paradox must be addressed at lower boat speeds when sailing closehauled. The last half-knot may involve a substantial trade-off in comfort and load on the yacht's gear, but once the sea gets up nothing from a dinghy to a square-rigger will sail properly to windward unless driven reasonably hard. This is the dilemma. The seamanlike answer is to understand the issues, then make a sensible decision appropriate to the circumstances.

Sailing craft under auxiliary power

We have seen that a sailing hull will readily work up to a velocity equivalent to the simple square root of her waterline length. She is then well short of her full capacity for making waves and is pulling dramatically less wash than she would at full displacement speed. She is thus burning far less fuel. Many of today's cruisers have engines which can push them up to hull speed, and it can be illuminating to compare engine revolutions and fuel flow at the 'root waterline length' speed with the flat-out equivalent. Similarly enlightening is the wash, with a powerful engine, one glance astern will tell more than a book full of words. Large auxiliaries come into their own when the yacht must smash her way into a head sea under power in a strong wind.

Modifying factors on displacement speed – Power

Length - Beam ratio

As in a sailing boat, the most fuel-efficient way of beating the barrier of the standard waterline length constant is to create a long narrow hull. The Irens-designed Adventurer, a slender monohull with two sponsons for stability, set a circumnavigation record by applying the same principles as the racing multihull sailboat. At the time of writing, this concept has yet to be adopted commercially.

Planing

Like a sailing dinghy, a power boat of the right configuration can lift onto her own bow wave and move beyond the displacement mode. Once planing, her speed can increase dramatically. Suitable hulls may be of various shapes, including flat floored and deep-vee. Most will feature so-called 'lifting chines'.

Semi-displacement

The requirement for internal volume and comfort leads to a compromise for many large and medium-sized cruisers. Technically 'semi-displacement' hulls, these craft have sufficient power and lift to exceed their displacement speed without the full freedom of a totally planing hull.

Fuel economy and displacement

For a vessel operating in the displacement (non-planing) mode, wave-making and fuel consumption are inextricably linked. As wake builds up with approaching hull speed, a diminishing return is reaped by opening the throttle, although with a powerful engine the effects are not always instantly obvious. Anyone in doubt about this should watch a slab-sterned fishing boat hurrying home to market. The wave running down her sides indicates that she is travelling at displacement speed. Virtually nothing she can do will increase this, yet she is pulling a wake almost as high as her hull. To extract an extra fraction of a knot she is deploying the power reserves normally employed in dragging her trawl, and the reality is that most of the large amount of extra fuel is being burned by the wave. If her skipper settled for one knot less than the maximum, the diesel bill would dramatically diminish. The same, of course, goes for leisure craft.

Depending on engine size, the most economical rate of progress falls around the root waterline (6 knots for a 36-footer). A good compromise is often found around halfway between this and hull speed.

Watch your wake!

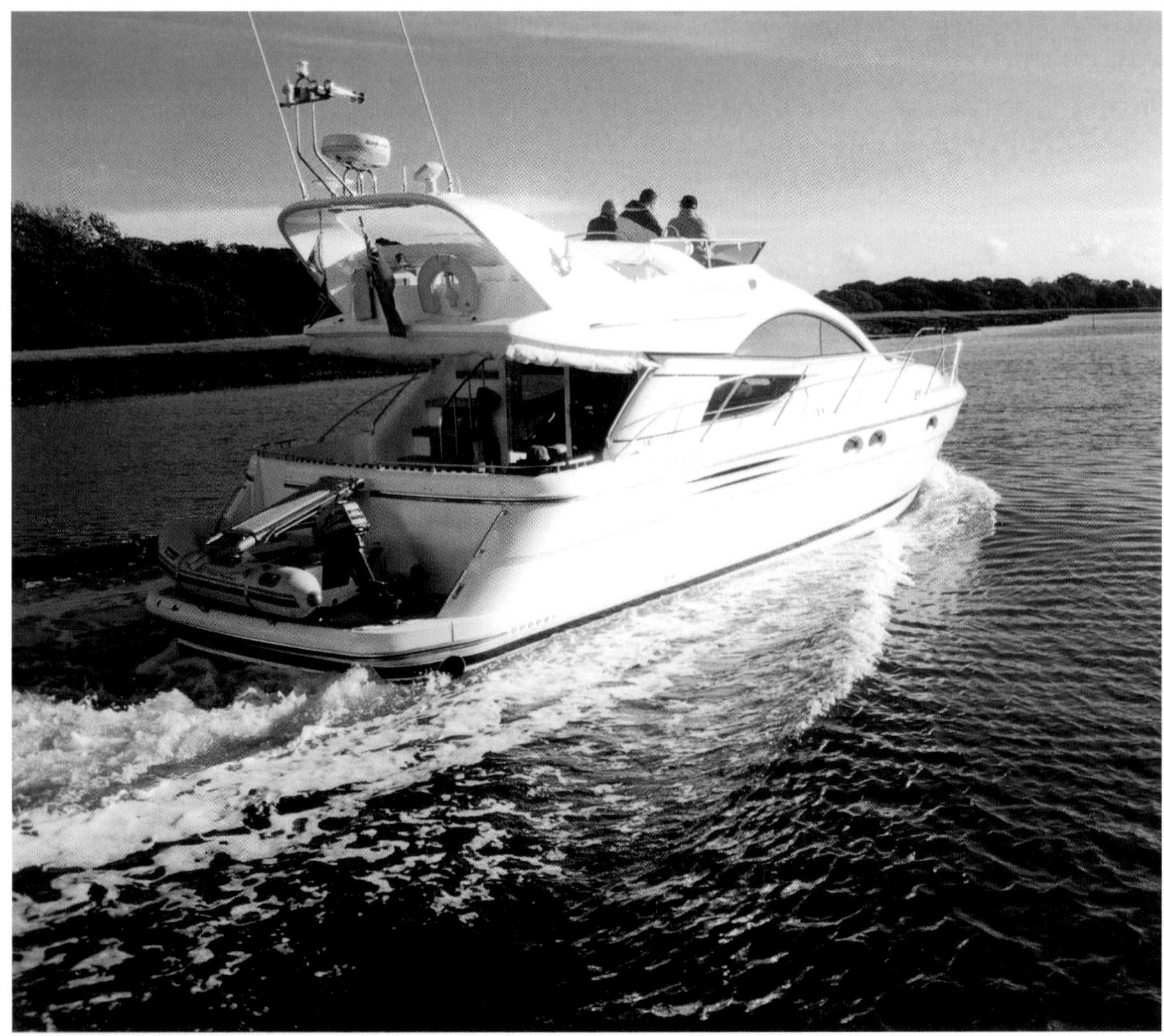

Wave generation in non-displacement hulls

The same criteria on fuel consumption and wave-creation for displacement craft apply to planing or semi-displacement vessels operating at sub-planing speeds. Such boats often leave a clean wake while planing but are inefficient in 'displacement' mode, pulling a huge wash as hull speed is approached. This places their operators in an invidious position in confined waters where traffic and speed limits abound. A semi-inflatable RIB, for example, will certainly make less wash travelling at 25 knots than at six, yet her skipper is constrained for reasons of safety from doing so. Very often, easing back from 6 knots to five can produce a dramatic result. Large, semi-displacement cruisers are especially prone to this phenomenon. The mathematics of what is going on is too complicated to allow general predictions. The only answer is to look astern and watch the wake.

Clean Bottom

Even a modest growth of nothing more than slime can knock a sailing boat's windward performance back by 10% or more. Weed and barnacles will rapidly worsen the situation until it finally begins to affect the boat's ability to handle properly. Such effects are less obvious in motor craft, as there is usually more reserve power to take up the slack. Fuel economy suffers, however, and if propellers themselves are allowed to foul up, loss of speed will soon follow. Whether under power or sail, all efforts to maximise a boat's performance are a waste of time without a clean bottom.

Fuel factors in planing craft

In general, a well-designed planing hull covers more miles for a given amount of fuel at medium planing speeds than at the upper end of her displacement mode. Wave production attests to the truth of this, but the only sure ways to acquire empirical data are to consult a designer's specification or set up a series of trials. One or other should be addressed before taking such a vessel seriously to sea.

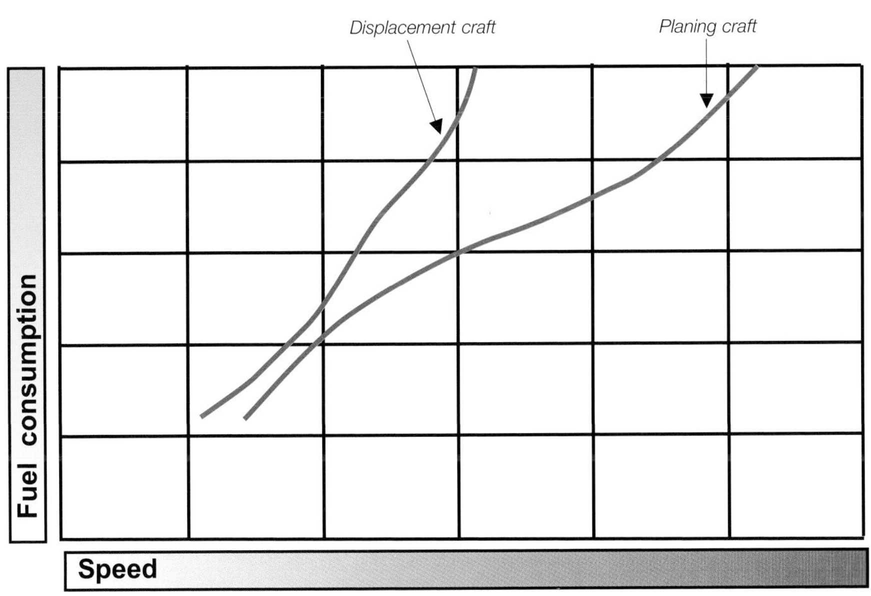

Although fuel consumption is about the same for both displacement and planing craft at low speeds, planing craft will go much faster for the same consumption as speed mounts.

Motive Force – Sail

Common sailing rigs

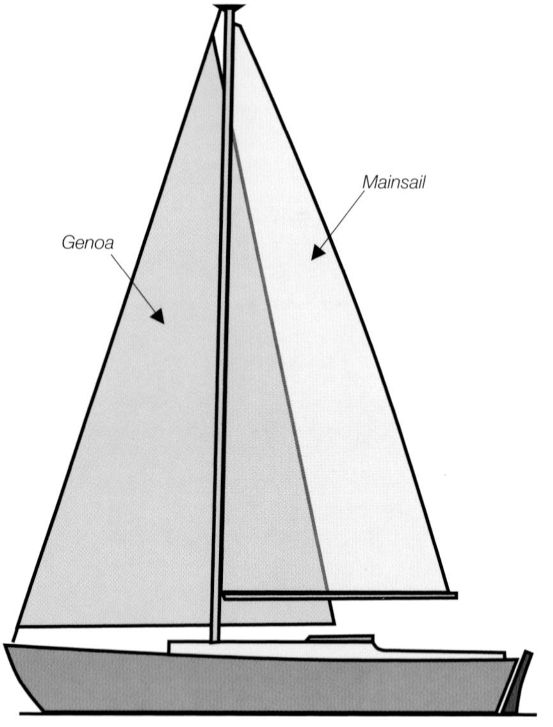

Sloop
The simplest, most common yacht rig. It has one mast. The forestay originates either at the masthead in a masthead sloop, or lower down if it is a fractional rig.

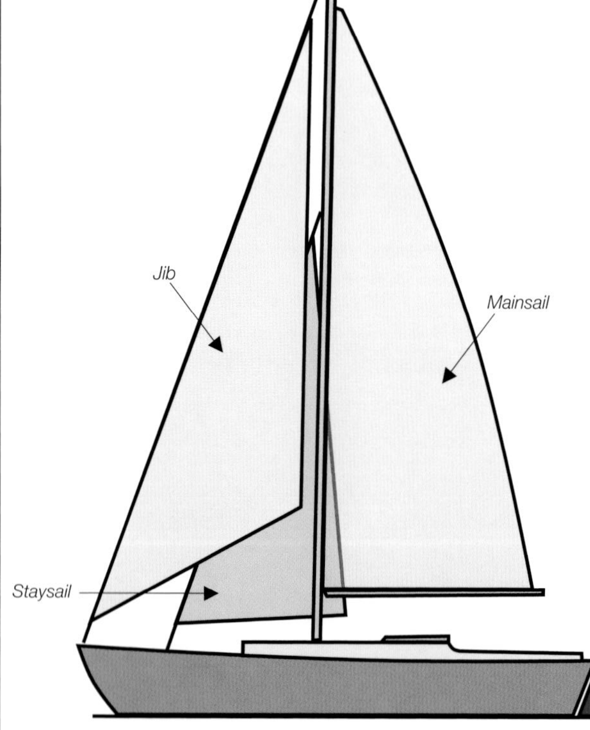

Cutter
One mast, two forestays. Modern yachts generally take one of these to the masthead and the second well below it. Cutters may rig short bowsprits. Not to be confused with sloops that opt to carry a choice of roller headsails on two adjacent forestays.

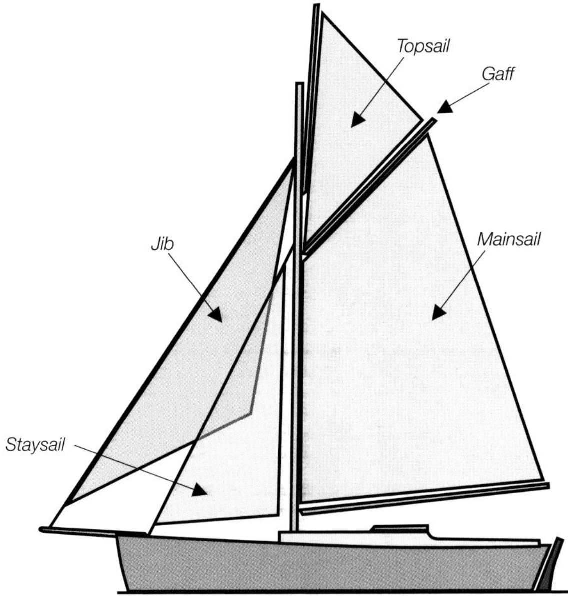

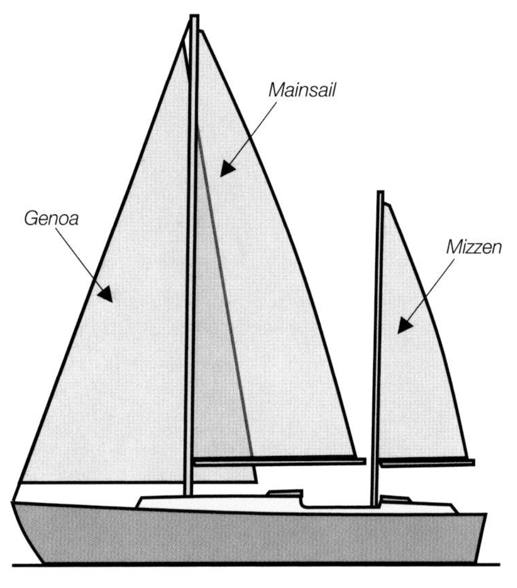

Gaff rig

The most common traditional rig, named after the upper spar spreading the head of the mainsail (the 'gaff'). 'Gaffers' can appear as sloops, ketches, schooners etc.

Ketch

Two masts break up the sail plan into more manageable areas. The trade-off is some loss in performance upwind and directly downwind. A ketch's mizzen mast is stepped forward of the rudder post.

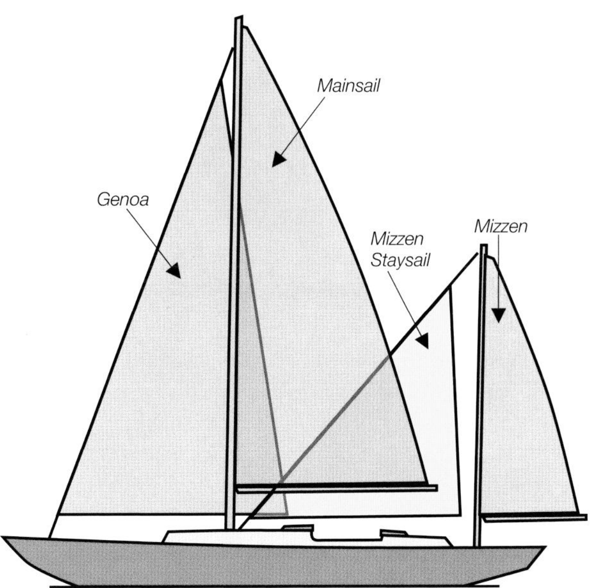

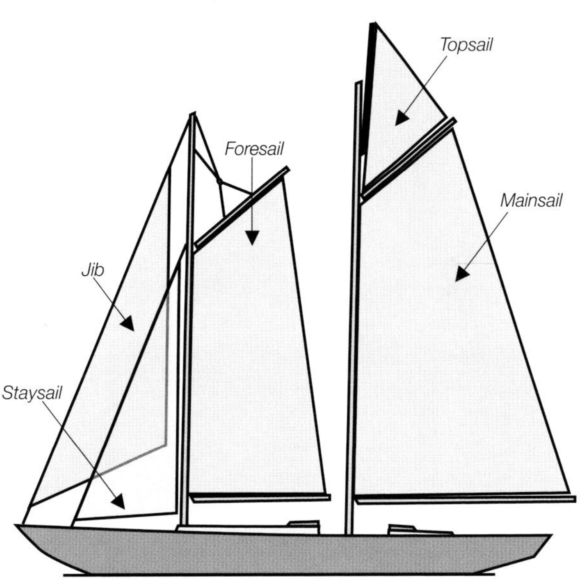

Yawl

Really a sloop or cutter with an extra mast aft to assist manoeuvring and balance. Like a ketch, a yawl's mizzen mast can set a mizzen staysail (as shown) when reaching. The yawl's mizzen is stepped abaft the rudder post.

Schooner

A two-masted vessel (gaff or Bermudan) having the mainmast aft. The foremast is traditionally shorter than the main, but it may be of equal height. A schooner can have three or more masts, in which case she is designated a 'three-masted schooner', and so on, but she can never be a 'two-masted schooner', which is tautology. Only a schooner setting square topsails (not gaff topsails) on the foremast is called a topsail schooner.

Standing Rigging

Standing rigging is the generic name given to the system of wires, spreaders and tensioning devices which maintain a mast in position under sailing loads. As yachts grow larger and more sophisticated, the potential for complexity is substantial, but the principles remain the same. A simple masthead sloop rig such as might be found on a yacht up to 40ft is supported by a forestay, a backstay and a pair of cap shrouds. These pass over spreaders mounted at the 'hounds' halfway down the mast to improve their angle. One or two pairs of lower shrouds run between deck and hounds to stiffen the central part of the spar.

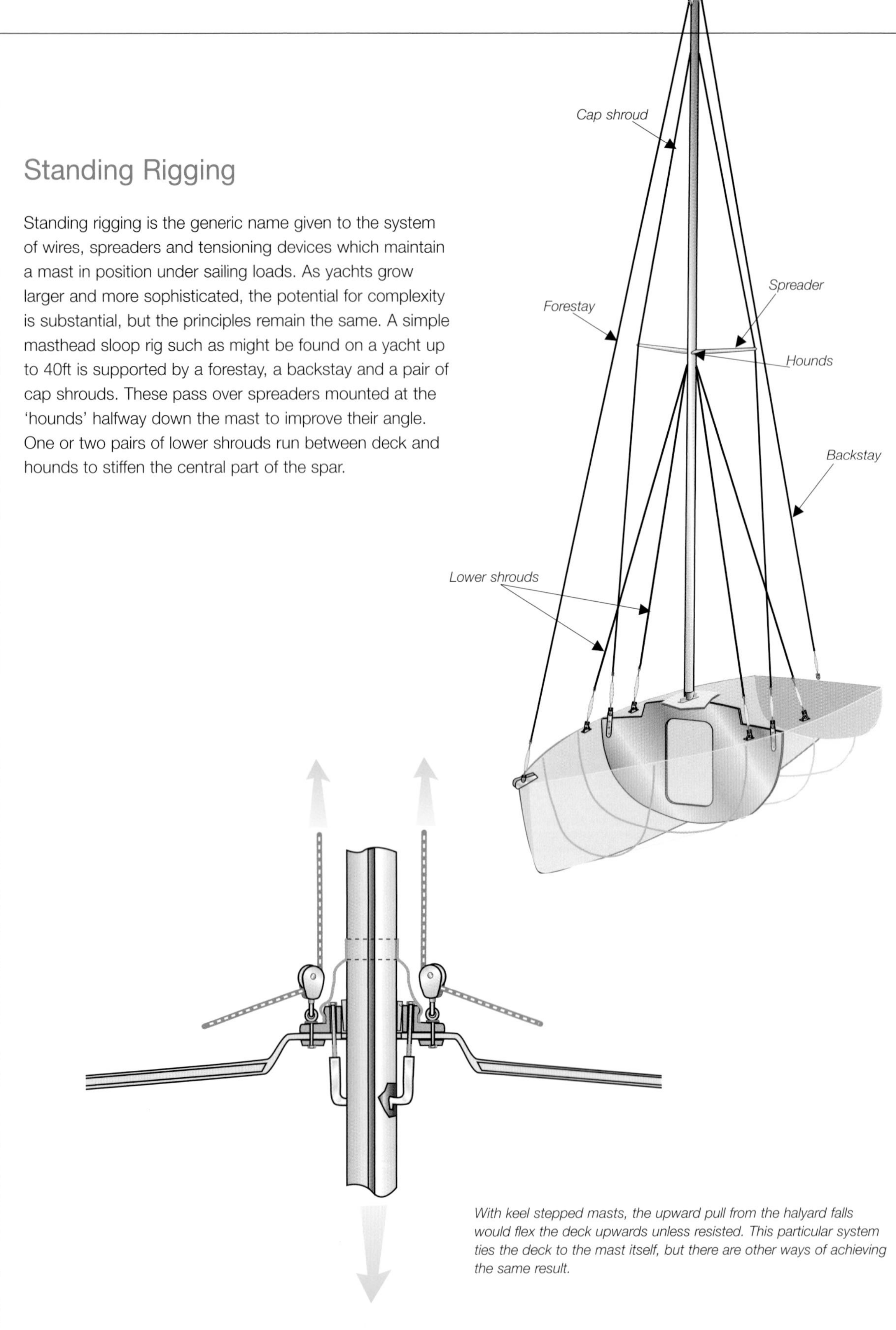

With keel stepped masts, the upward pull from the halyard falls would flex the deck upwards unless resisted. This particular system ties the deck to the mast itself, but there are other ways of achieving the same result.

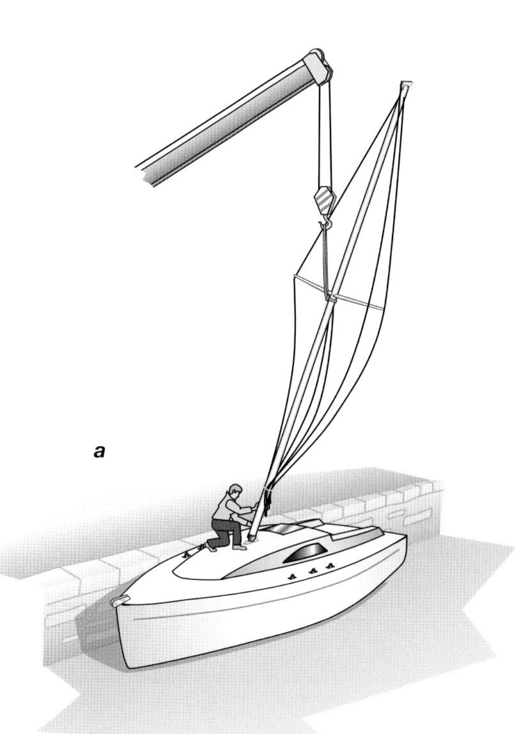

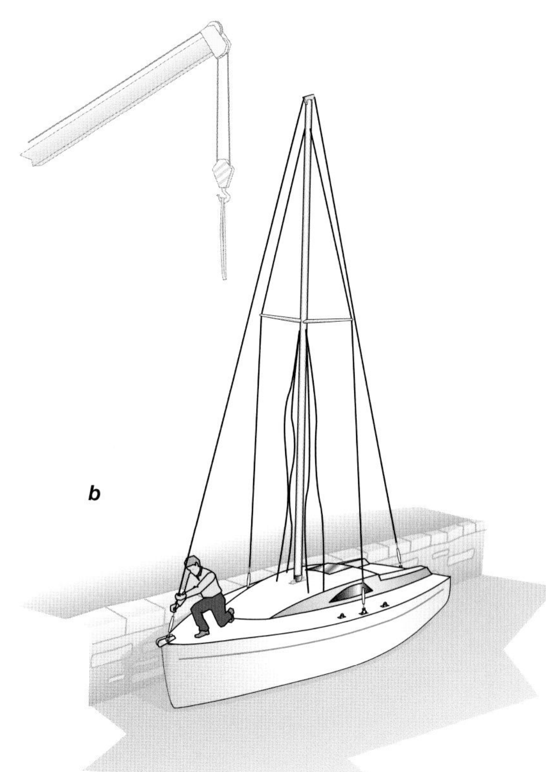

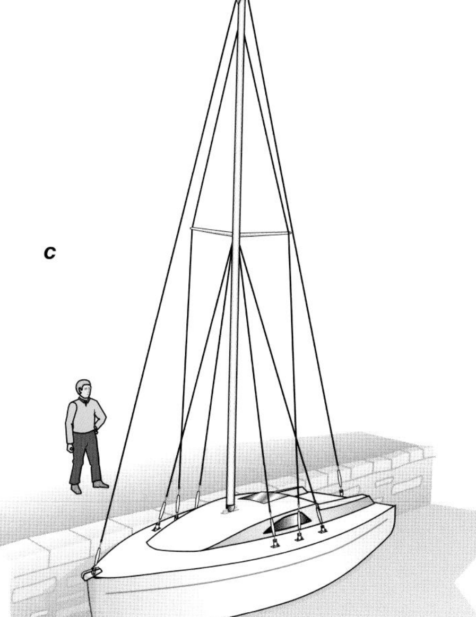

Setting up a masthead sloop rig

a The mast is stepped by crane, either onto a deck step or through the deck onto a step mounted above the keel. The crane stays in place.

b The forestay, backstay and cap shrouds are tensioned just enough to support the mast.

c The crane is removed. No wedges are yet inserted into the mast partners of a keel-stepped spar.

(Continued overleaf)

A bottle screw or turnbuckle is extremely powerful and care must be taken not to overtighten. As a guide, no lever of greater length than an 8in screwdriver should be used to wind them up in any but the largest yachts.

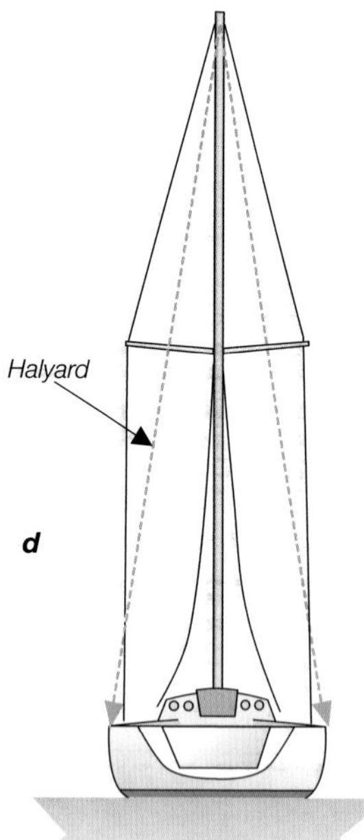

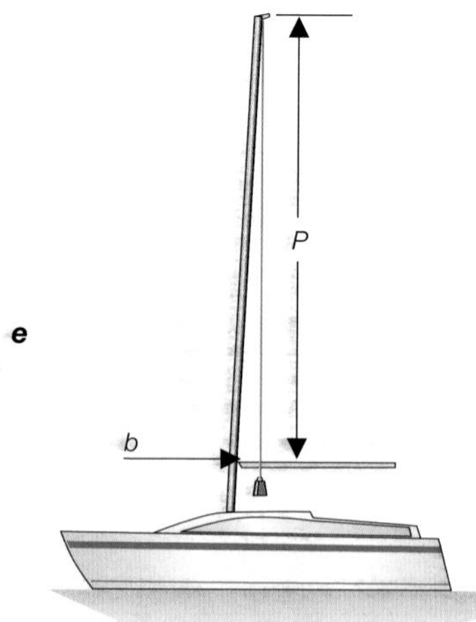

d Using a halyard led from the masthead to each toerail successively, check that the mast is upright athwartships. The cap shrouds are progressively equally tensioned by their bottle screws (turnbuckles). Keep re-checking the upright state.

e Next, fore-and-aft rake is set. Typically, this will be between 1° and 3° aft, which looks good and helps upwind performance. To determine rake, suspend a weight from the masthead by sending up a light line on the main halyard, then tighten the forestay and backstay accordingly.

- To measure rake, use the dimensions 'P' and 'b'. For 1° of rake, 'b' equals about 1.75cm for every metre of 'P'. This means that for a mast whose 'P' measurement is 10m, 'b' will equal 17.5cm (10 x 1.75) with the mast raked at 1°. At 2° rake 'b' increases to 35cm (2 x 10 x 1.75) and at 3° it becomes 52.5cm. Masthead rigs tend to have less rake than fraction rigs – 1° to 2° being typical for the former and 2° to 3° for the latter.

Insert wedges at the deck for keel-stepped masts. Set the aft one first.

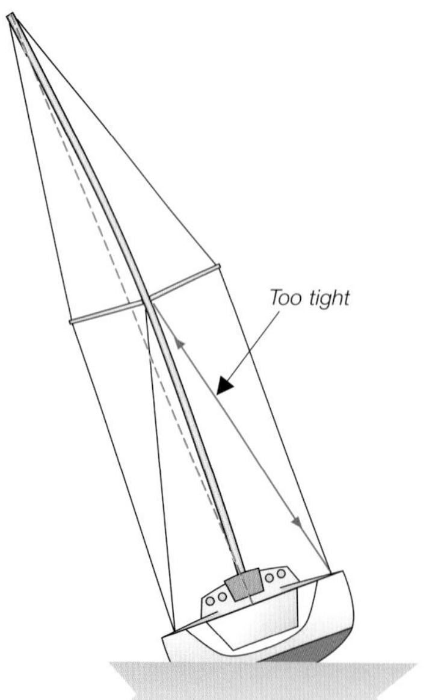

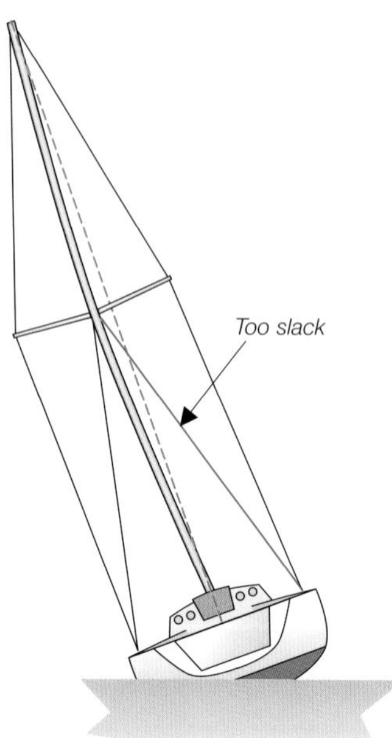

f Tension the lower shrouds. These are finally adjusted when sailing so as to keep the mast straight. If two pairs of lowers are present, the forward ones should be the tightest to induce a touch of forward curvature known as 'pre-bend'.

Care of standing rigging

Toggles
All standing rigging terminals at deck level should be equipped with toggles to allow universal movement. Failure to do this can lead to metal fatigue and early failure.

Split pins (Cotter pins)
It is tempting to open these right up and even bend them back against themselves to tidy things up and ensure security. A split pin bent open by 15° is just as safe and can be removed far more easily when the time comes. If new pins are in short supply, it can sometimes be safely refitted. Unless there is an overwhelming reason to bend the ends back, don't. Any tendency for a split pin to snag can be mitigated by either taping it up or giving it a squirt of silicone, which will also protect it and stop it turning.

Watch the salt
Salt is an insidious enemy of stainless steel and older-style galvanised rigging. Rinsing off the lower parts of the standing rig when the deck is swabbed with fresh water will extend its life.

Keep surveying
Watch out for any broken strands and condemn the wire immediately. Crevice corrosion may be going on unseen in other places. Survey all fittings meticulously on a regular basis, both on deck and aloft. Look for any signs of fatigue cracks, and replace immediately.

Sight up the mast
The mast should be regularly checked for alignment while at sea. When sailing closehauled, sight up the mainsail track and make any adjustments needed to keep the spar in column. Sight up the forestay to check for excessive sag, some is inevitable, but too much destroys windward performance. If in doubt, increase backstay tension.

Age-induced failure
Stainless steel standing rigging has a finite lifespan depending on salt ingress, quality, mileage and age. If rigging is 7-10 years old, consider replacing it as a matter of course.

Rigging toggle

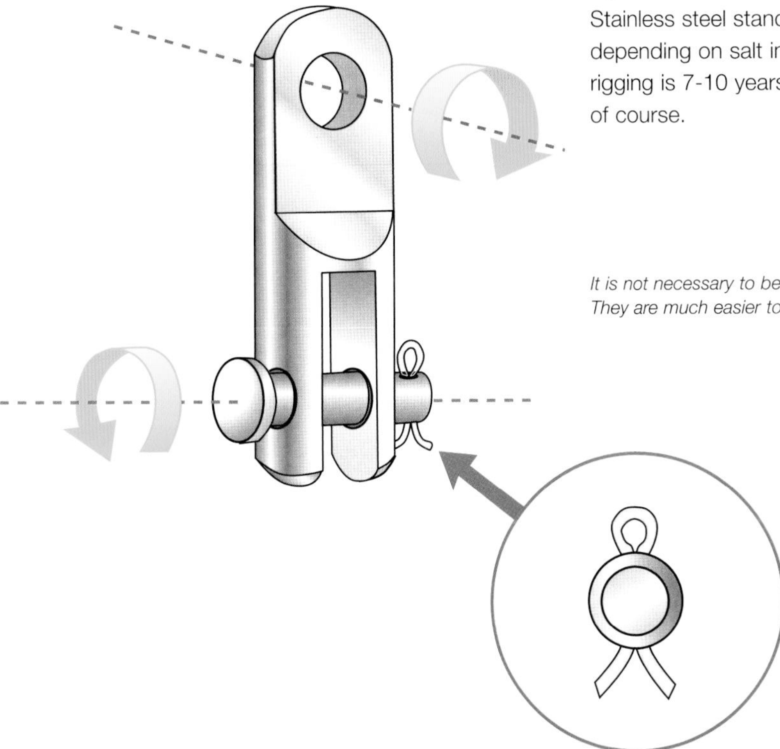

It is not necessary to bend the ends right back to secure a split pin. They are much easier to remove if opened just a few degrees.

Sail systems

Headsails

The hanked-on headsail

Rarely seen today, each hanked-on headsail is specific to one particular wind condition, so a minimum of three should be carried. For short-handed work, the system is superior to the racing headfoil arrangement in that the sail is more readily controlled while hoisting or lowering. Its advantage over the more usual roller headsail is that smaller, dedicated sails set better for stronger conditions than part-rolled genoas.

Changing a headsail at sea

The foredeck can be an ugly place for a person struggling with a sail, so it is important for crew to be protected, particularly when changing down headsails in a rising wind. Matters can be eased greatly by heaving to if searoom is limited (see page 106), or running off the wind and 'hiding' the headsail in the lee of the mainsail, when space and time permit. The same techniques can be deployed for any emergency on the foredeck.

Roller genoa and parts of a sail

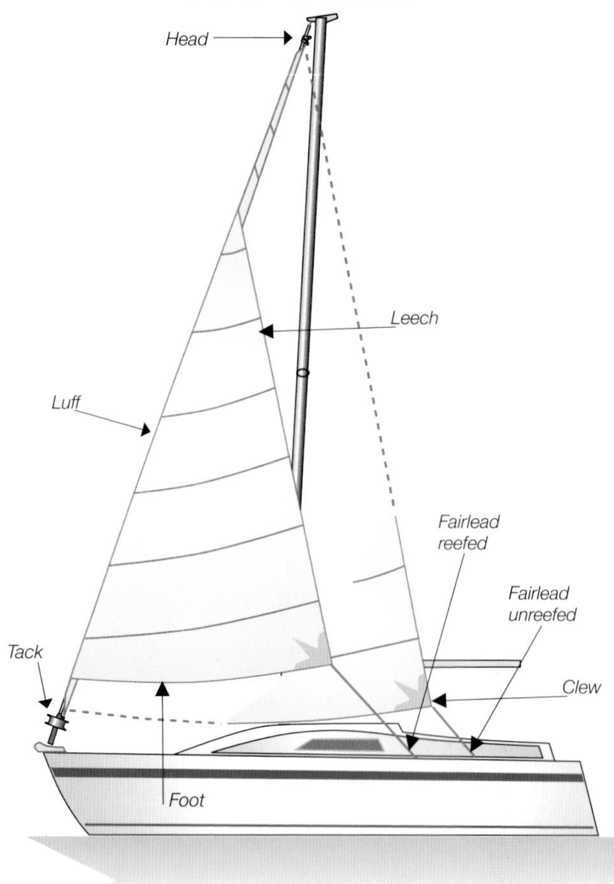

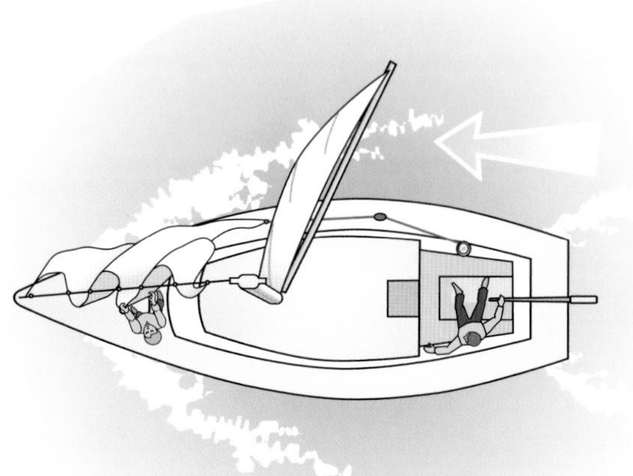

The roller genoa

Roller-reefing genoas have the huge advantage that a boat can carry the right area of canvas at all times with comparatively little trouble. This to some extent offsets the fact that even the finest examples do not set so well as a hanked-on sail when reefed. To optimise the shape of a progressively reefed sail, first make sure there is plenty of halyard and backstay tension, then address the position of the sheet fairlead, which should usually change as the sail is shortened. Most boats have a 'car' system for this. Ideally, this is adjusted by leading the tail of a tackle securing the fairlead to the cockpit. As the sail is shortened, the car should be moved forward so that neither the foot of the sail nor the leech becomes too full. To be sure the position is right, close-haul the sail, then steer progressively up to windward and note whether the luff begins to 'break' all the way up simultaneously. If the lower part backwinds first, move the car aft; if the upper, move it forward. Make a note of the correct car position for the number of rolls in the sail, and setting up will be easy next time.

Mainsails

The Bermudan mainsail is not a difficult sail to handle left to its own devices, but over the years a number of systems have developed for making the job even easier.

Lazy Jacks

A system of permanently rigged light lines between mast and boom which can be adjusted for tension and make an excellent way of controlling a mainsail as it is lowered. The lines are called 'lazy jacks', presumably because they allow Jolly Jack the sailorman to sit back and watch them doing all the work. A simple arrangement like *(a)* is cheap to rig, but the sail tends to bunch up forward unless the boat is brought head to wind when lowering. Also, although the sail is basically controlled, gaskets (sail ties) will usually be required to tidy things up. The answer is to heave the leech aft as the sail comes down. Not an ideal answer, but the arrangement is inexpensive and easy to rig with an existing sail.

A fully battened mainsail *(b)* has at least some battens running right across from luff to leech. This stiffens the sail, holding the leech aft as it stows, greatly assisting the lazy jacks. Such a sail will sometimes hang in the lazy jacks sufficiently neatly requiring no gaskets in the short term. A superior arrangement is to have a permanently rigged sail cover integrated with the lazy jacks to form a StackPack® *(c)*. The fully battened sail drops into this cleanly and the cover is generally closed away with a zip, leaving the sail storm-proof. The downside of the arrangement is that the battens can easily become snagged by the lazy jacks if the boat is not head to wind for sail hoisting. Vigilance and teamwork between helm and halyard hand are important, but the inconvenience is worth the trouble.

All lazy jack systems should be rigged so that the lines when required can be slacked away clear of the set sail, especially on long passages. Otherwise, chafe may result.

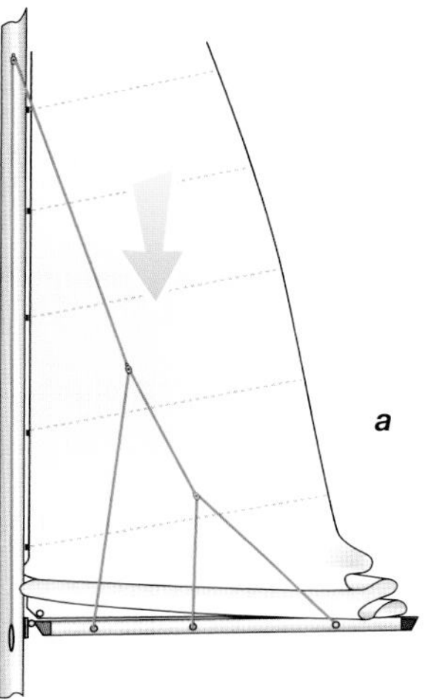

Lazy jacks can be a simple arrangement of ropes...

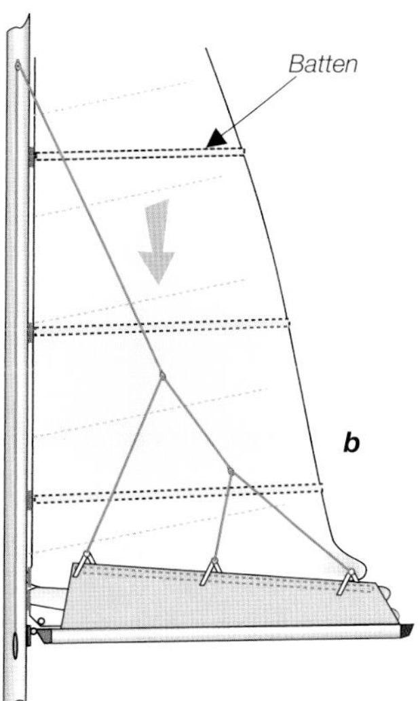

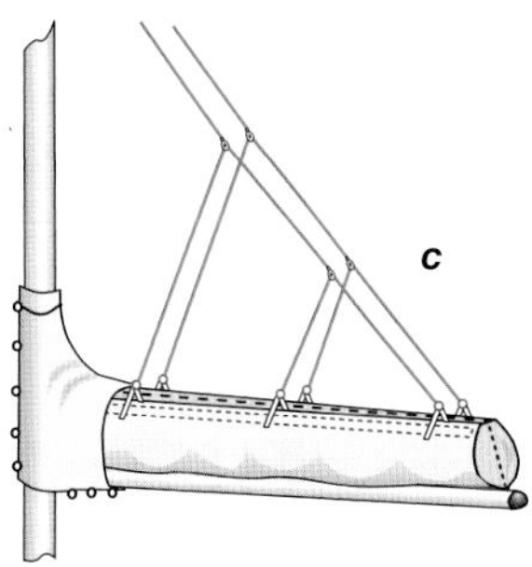

...whereas the StackPack® type systems incorporate a canvas 'hammock' which doubles as a sail cover when zipped up.

In-mast stowing and reefing

Many larger yachts stow and reef their mainsails by rolling them into the mast. Although thoroughly effective in removing all traces of the sail and making reefing simple and easy, these often demand that the boat be head-to-wind for the sail to be rolled, which may not be convenient if manoeuvring adventurously. Another drawback is that the sail cannot use conventional fore-and-aft battens to maintain a leech roach. Lack of roach de-powers it and, to the informed eye, does not look right, although some creative sailmakers have addressed the question by experimenting with vertical battens. It is not unknown for an in-mast mainsail to fold its leech over as it is drawn into the mast in heavy weather. The double thickness of canvas then catches in the groove through which the sail is furled, jamming with the sail half-rolled. A further disadvantage is that the full weight of the sail and all its gear is permanently aloft, even when stowed to some extent adversely affecting stability. In cases where this may be important because of the nature of the vessel's work, it is vital that enquiries are made with the designer before fitting such a system or at least before proceeding to sea in potentially testing conditions. Despite all the negative factors, the sheer saving of manpower has found these systems an appropriate place among very large yachts and in smaller craft whose crews do not wish to go on deck to handle sails.

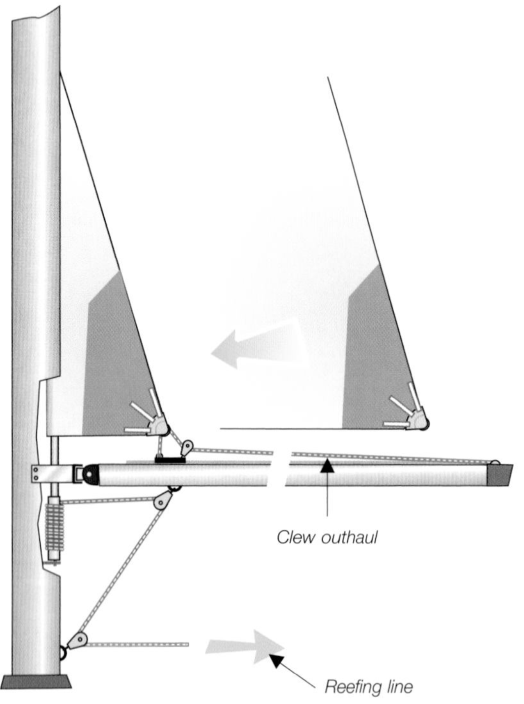

In-boom stowing and reefing

In-boom stowing and reefing rolls the mainsail into the boom itself. It presents a number of technical difficulties, often surrounding the kicker which must be fixed, but if it works well it has several advantages over in-mast systems.

- The moving parts are essentially the same as in-mast systems except that they are in the boom, so they can be reached more readily if anything should fail.
- If the system melts down completely, you can always ease away on the halyard and dump the sail on deck.
- There is nothing to stop the sail from being cut with a full roach for power and appearance.
- Weight is kept low, so there are no stability issues.

Asymmetric downwind sails

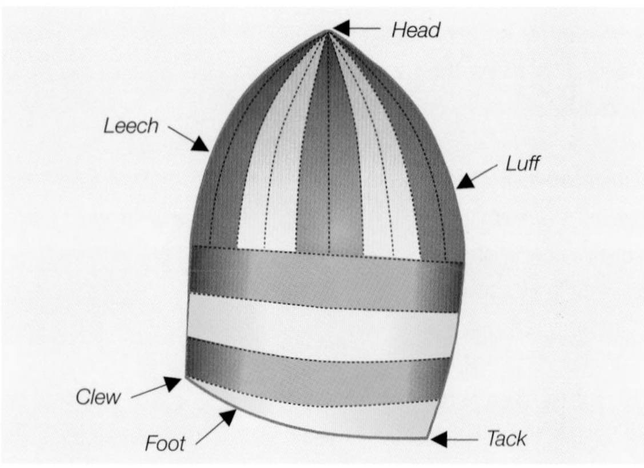

The problem of lack of apparent wind when sailing to leeward has long been addressed by large, light-weight sails. In the 1990s, these developed away from the balloon spinnaker with its complicated poles and potentially dramatic handling characteristics and moved towards the so-called 'asymmetric' downwind sails. These can be very large - sometimes called a 'gennaker' - but smaller versions known as cruising chutes are more common. These sails can be set from a short carbon fibre bowsprit, but most cruising yachts tack them down as far forward as possible on the foredeck itself. Although an asymmetric can be set flying, various systems exist to control them, the most popular is the 'snuffer'.

Rigging a chute with a snuffer

A chute controlled by a snuffer comes out of the bag like a long sausage whose skin is the snuffer itself. In addition to the lanyards that peel up or haul down on the snuffer, the sail has three lines to rig:

- The tack line, running from the tack of the sail via a block as far forward in the bows as can be arranged, thence to a cleat or, on a larger boat, a tackle or a spare winch. Chafe issues sometimes arise with the tack line, and compromises may have to be accepted.
- The sheet, attached to the clew of the sail and led outboard of everything via a quarter block to a cockpit winch.
- The halyard, which should ideally be at the masthead on a swivel block above the forestay attachment point.

Setting a chute

- Roll up or drop the working headsail, then rig the chute as described in the previous paragraph.

a With tack and clew attached but not set up tight, hoist the snuffed sail to the masthead.

b Once the sail is fully hoisted, bear away onto a broad reach and haul the snuffer aloft.

c Haul down on the tack line and sheet in until the sail fills.

Trimming the chute

This is a dynamic process. It is always possible to oversheet the sail and take the rest of the afternoon off, but to do so is an unseamanlike way of handling this useful area of canvas.

Trimming on a reach

- Experiment with hauling the tack line well down to keep the luff comparatively straight.
- With the sail filling, ease the sheet as far as possible. This allows the clew to rise which opens the leech and generates maximum forward drive with minimum tendency to interfere with steering.
- When the luff curls in, heave the sheet just far enough to settle it, then begin easing again until the ideal is achieved.

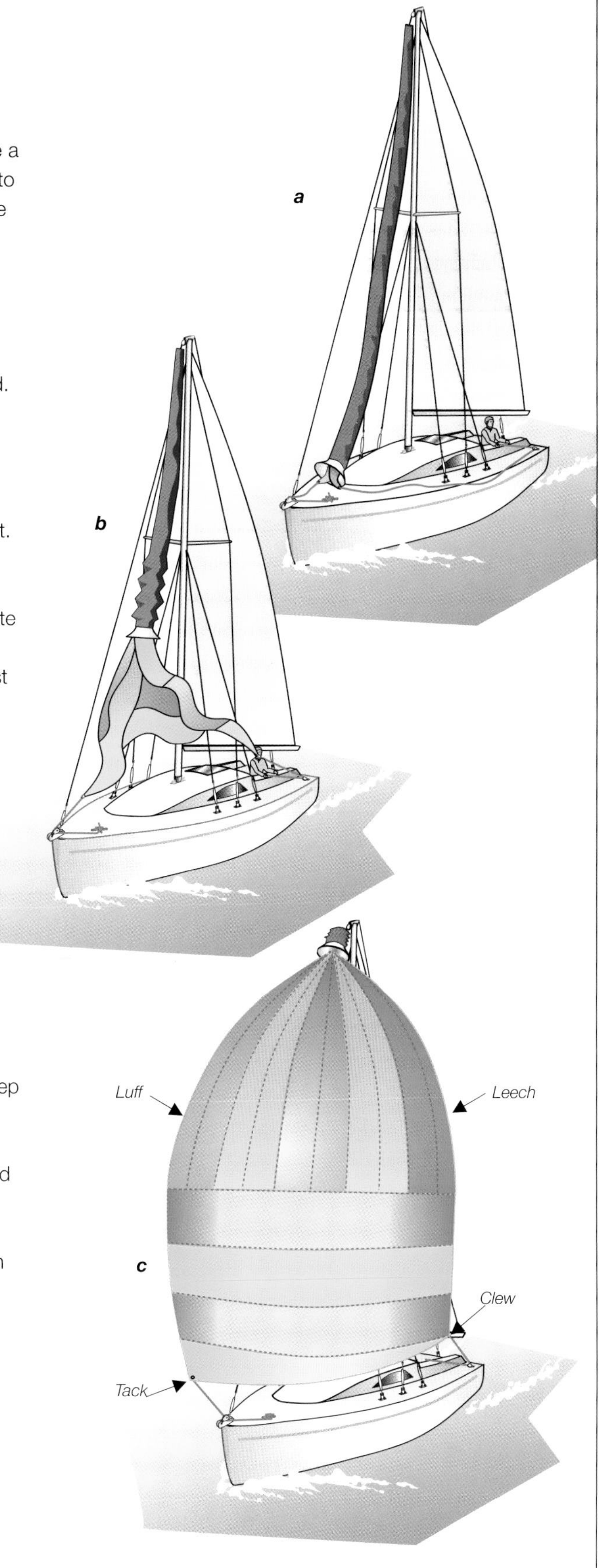

Trimming on a near-run

- Ease the tack line off to encourage the tack to drift up and out to windward a little. This allows air to enter the luff from the 'weather' side of the mast.
- Trim the sheet just as you would when reaching.
- If the boat falls away onto a dead run the sail may collapse in the lee of the mainsail. The helm should avoid this, while the trimmer must be ready to note what is happening. The two work together at all times.

Dropping a chute

- Run the boat off the wind to de-power the chute in the lee of the mainsail.
- Ease the sheet away and crack the tack line a foot or two.
- Haul down on the snuffer until the sail is completely captured.
- Lower the sail and stow it.

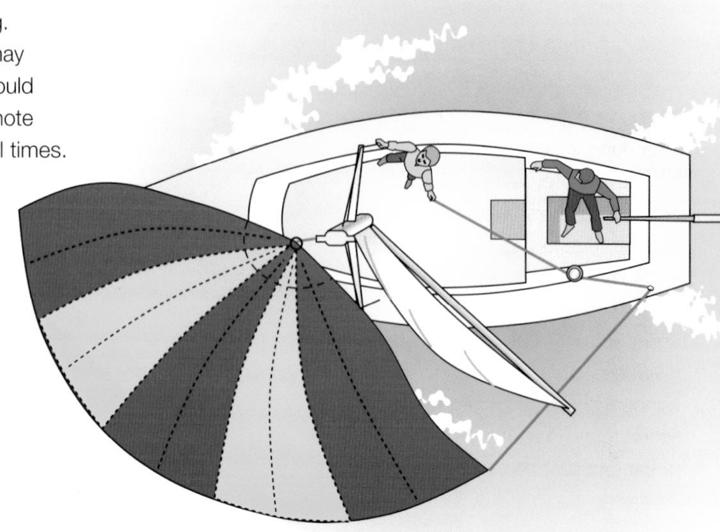

Trimming a spinnaker is a continuous process. The trimmer should locate himself where he can clearly see the sail's luff.

Emergency drops

If the snuffer is fouled in some way or the sail has been set without a snuffer, it can be dropped safely as follows:

- Run square off the wind to collapse the chute in the lee of the mainsail.
- Ease the tack line well away.
- Catch hold of the bight of the sheet and ease away on the halyard.
- Drag the sail down the companionway as the halyard is further eased.
- When the halyard shackle is in hand, let go the tack, bag and the sail and stow the gear.

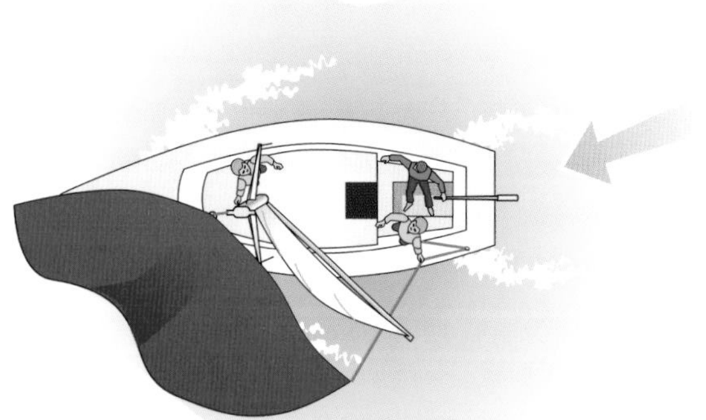

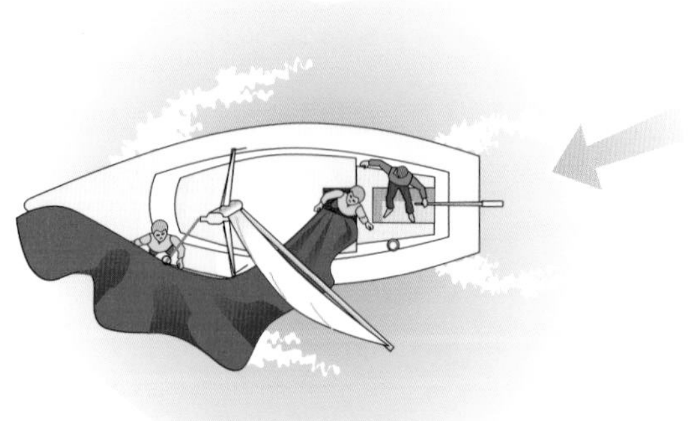

Power units

All those in charge of small craft at sea must have at least a working knowledge of a typical power unit. Whether the boat is a motor vessel or an auxiliary sailing yacht, this essential understanding makes the difference between a mishap rectified from within the boat's own resources and a lifeboat call-out. A 'can-do' attitude to fixing engines is as important to the twenty-first century seaman as the ability to turn in an eye splice was to his historical predecessors. Since this manual is a general one, it will concentrate on the commonly used inboard diesel engine. Petrol (gasoline) engines, excepting outboards, are now rarely found at sea.

The inboard engine drive chain

An inboard diesel can be thought of as a device for converting the contents of a fuel tank into propulsive force. The interdependent chain of systems involves a number of universal elements which must be understood if typical operational faults are to be rectified:

Fuel and tanks

The first essential is a plentiful supply of pure, water-free diesel. Tanks must be cleaned internally whenever the opportunity arises, and kept well topped up in operation. If a tank is run near-empty in a seaway, there is a chance that the lift pump may suck air as the fuel surges, even though this tendency should be reduced by internal baffles. Furthermore, any sludge collecting at the bottom of a tank will concentrate as the fuel level declines.

Tap

All tanks should have a tap which can be turned off remotely from the engine in the event of fire. Find out where this is and make sure it works.

Primary (or Pre-)filter

Most installations feature a filter between the tank and the engine that takes dirt and water out of the fuel. This needs to be maintained in a clean condition and checked regularly for water. Spare elements should be carried.

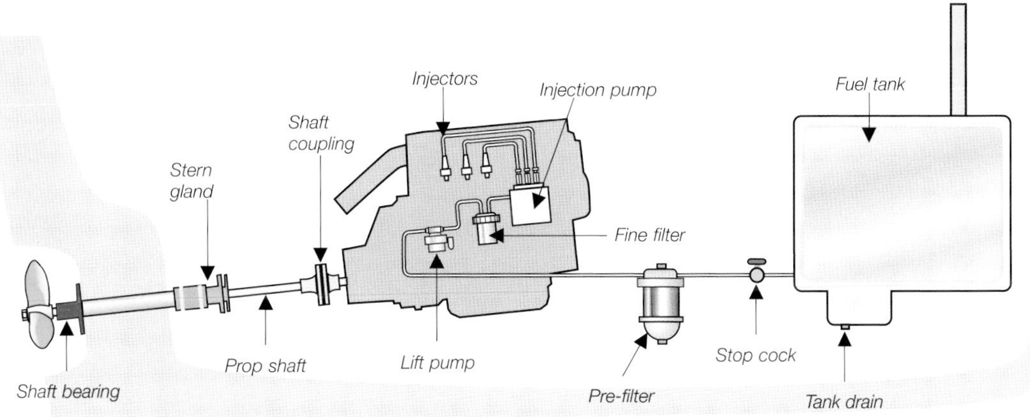

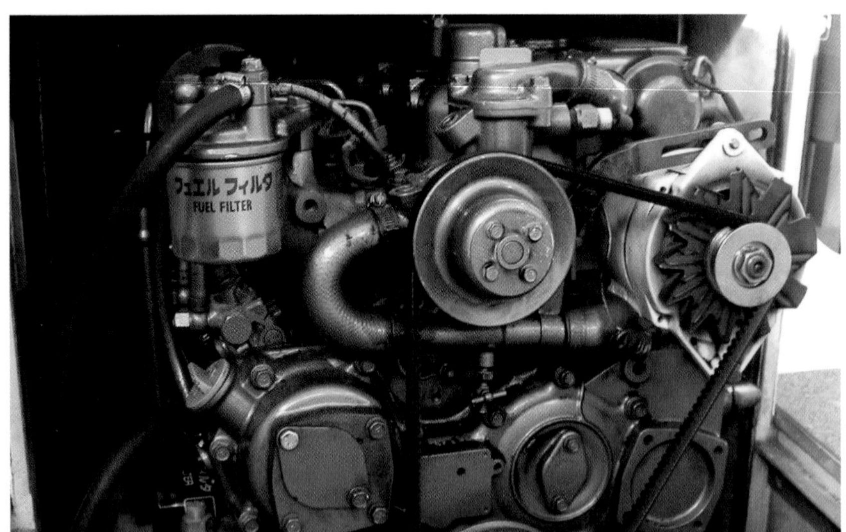

Modern marine engines are smaller, lighter and more powerful than older engines.

Lift pump

This comparatively small unit lifts fuel to the engine filter and hence to the injector pump itself. It is integral in most engines and usually mounted on the block low down near the back. If you can't find it, follow the fuel line towards the engine from the primary filter. It's the next thing you come to.

Engine fuel filter

So long as the primary filter is regularly maintained, this final back-stop against dirty fuel is unlikely to require attention at sea unless the tanks are thoroughly contaminated. However, it may well be a critical part of the bleed process (see below).

Injector pump and injectors

Unlike a petrol engine where an explosive mixture of fuel and air is physically ignited by a sparking plug, the fuel mix in a diesel unit fires spontaneously by the heat generated as it is compressed by the pistons inside the cylinders. Diesel is sprayed by the injector pump into the cylinder head at high pressure via the injectors. Short of replacing an injector with a spare which is not often carried, there is little the non-specialist can do at sea if these units fail. Fortunately, if all else is well looked after they are very reliable, although, like filters, they may require bleeding from time to time.

Gearbox, coupling and shaft

The marine diesel engine delivers power to the propeller via a simple ahead/astern/neutral gearbox. The output shaft is connected to the propeller shaft with a coupling device. These connections are normally secure in service, but involuntary disconnection sometimes occurs. It is therefore important to know where the coupling is, to be familiar with its makeup and to ensure that any tools it may require are carried on board.

Stern tube

This is the gland that allows the shaft to turn freely while keeping the water out of the boat.

Propeller

The propeller is fitted to the tapered, threaded end of the propeller shaft. The nut which secures it is prevented from vibrating loose either by a split pin, in which case the nut will be castellated to accommodate the pin, or by a tab washer which must be bent over one of the flats of the nut. Failure to attend to these precautions will probably lead to the propeller falling off.

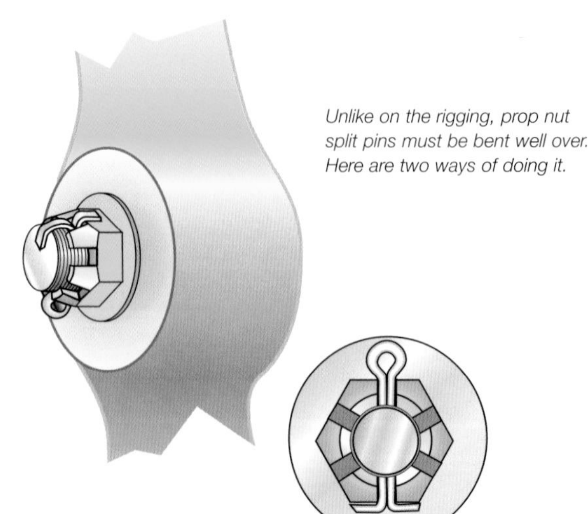

Unlike on the rigging, prop nut split pins must be bent well over. Here are two ways of doing it.

Drive chain troubleshooting

Engine

All the trouble-shooting methods described below assume that catastrophic mechanical failure has not taken place. In most cases this is a reasonable assumption, since the marine diesel engine is extremely robust. If the engine stops in service it will almost certainly be because it has suffered some form of fuel problem or has overheated. The moment the temperature gauge or audible alarm indicates overheating, the engine should be shut down as soon as safely possible. Running in an overheated state may severely damage the unit or even cause it to seize up and stop altogether.

Overheating

Most marine engines are cooled by a liquid circulated by a pump, as are engines in motorcars. Unlike automotive applications, which use radiators to control the temperature of the coolant, the marine unit favours a heat exchanger which is itself cooled by sea water. This 'raw water' is drawn into the boat via a seacock, passed through a filter and then round the heat exchanger which is typically bolted to the engine. From there, the warm water is expelled over the side, usually by way of the engine exhaust outlet where it cools and silences the gases. Most overheating problems arise from the seawater system. If seawater stops flowing, the engine will overheat. The procedure is then as follows:

a Check that sea water circulation has failed by observing the exhaust. If it is gushing out (pulsing strongly is OK), the problem is in the inner coolant circuit and may be difficult to solve. If, as is more likely, water flow from the exhaust has stopped or has reduced to a trickle, check first that the sea water filter (sometimes called the 'strainer') is clear. Turn off the inlet seacock, then follow the pipe to the filter (this may be incorporated in the cock unit or may be remote), open the filter and clear the mesh. Reassemble, open the seacock, and go.

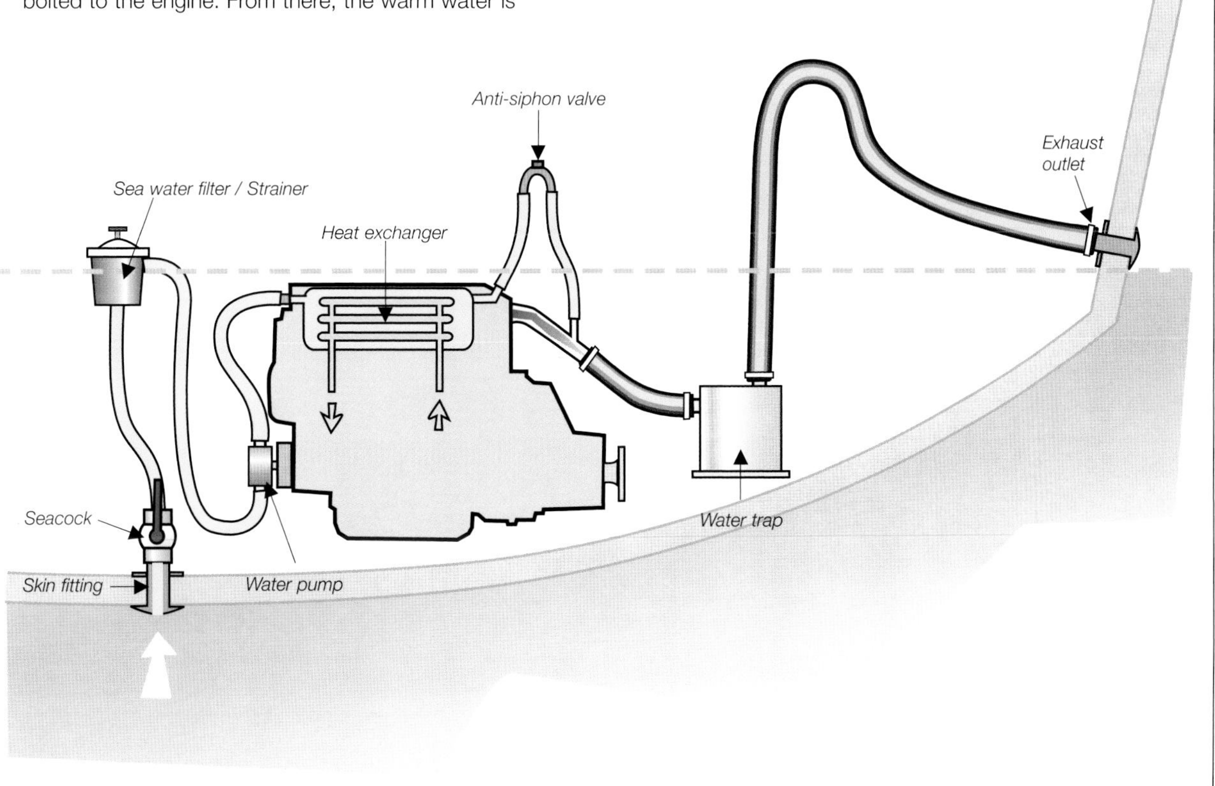

b If the filter is clear and water still fails to circulate, check the sea water pump impeller. Find the pump by following the pipe up from the filter. It will probably be mounted on the engine and will look like the one illustrated below. On most units, the impeller is accessed by removing the end plate. It can be withdrawn by levering it out with two screwdriver blades, one either side. Replace it if there is any sign of damage. If the ship's spare impeller comes as part of a kit from the manufacturer, this will have a spare gasket for the end plate. If not, try to save the original or, failing that, use instant gasket from a tube - all vessels should carry this.

c If the filter is clear and the pump in good condition, check for an air lock. These can occur without warning, especially on sailing craft after an energetic spell under canvas. Find a joint in the sea water system near its highest point and break the union with a spanner (wrench) or unfasten the hose clamp. Start the engine. If an air lock is present, the pipe will sputter for a while, then sea water will begin flowing. Remake the joint while the engine is running and that will temporarily solve the issue. This is a last-ditch and messy solution. Try to divert any escaping water from the engine's electrics, and be extremely careful not to get clothing caught in belts or other moving parts.

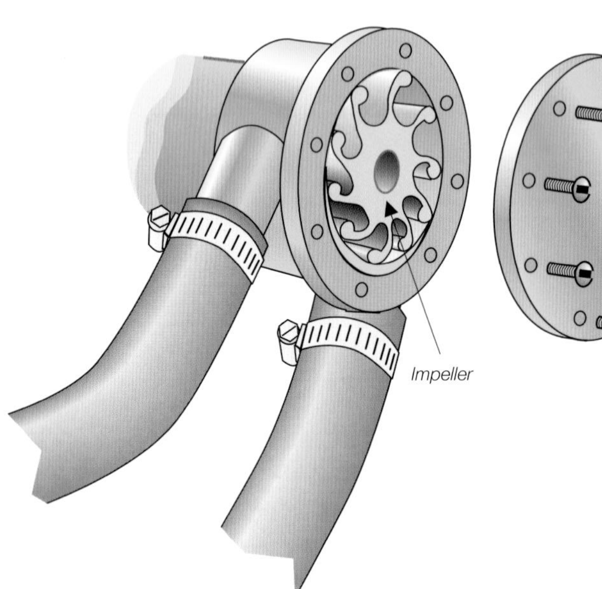

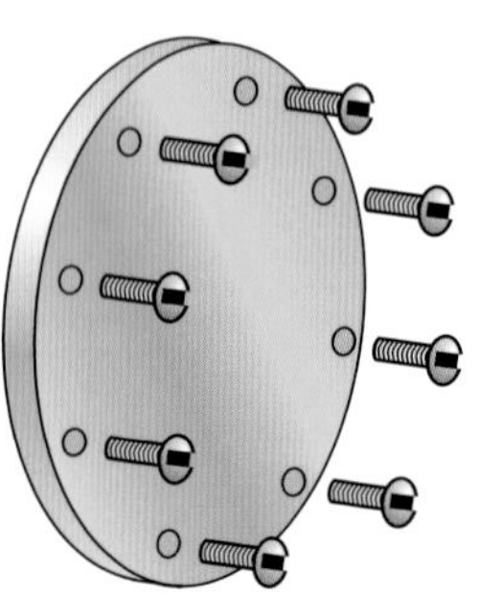

A typical seawater pump

A typical sea water strainer

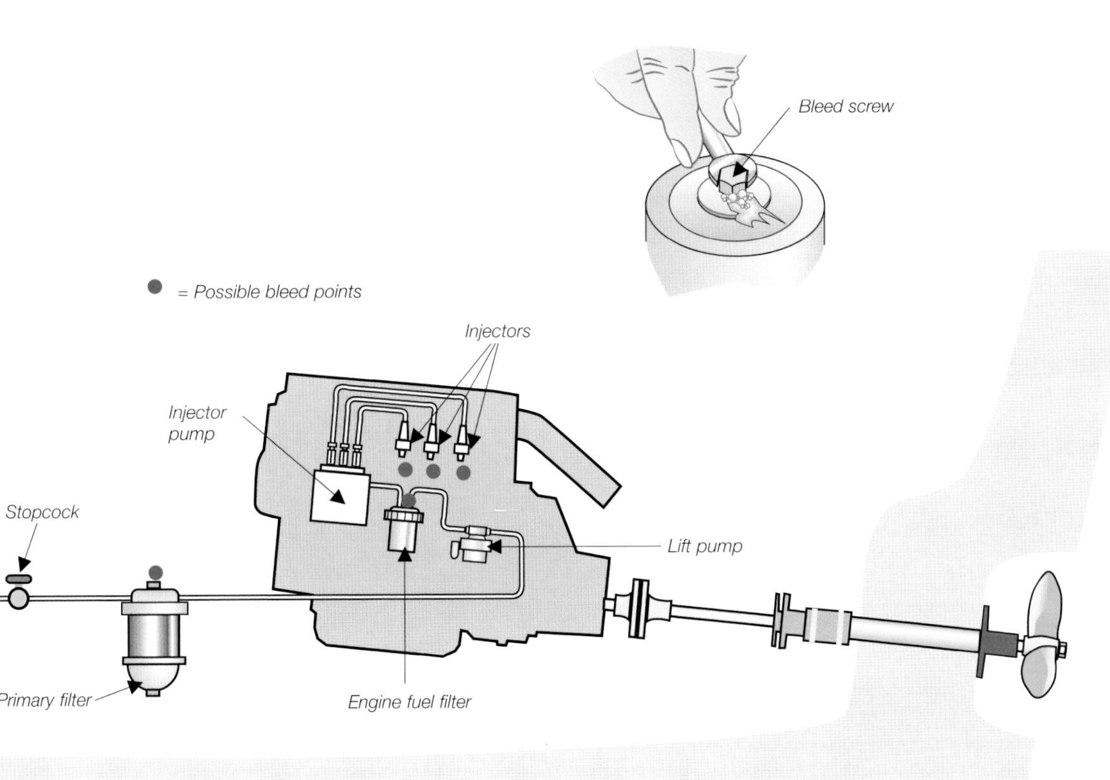

Fuel problems

When a diesel slows down and stops in service, first make sure that the propeller has not fouled. If the prop is clear and the engine has not overheated, it almost certainly has a fuel problem. This must be tackled systematically.

- Make sure there is fuel in the tank and that the cock is turned on.
- If fuel is in good supply, it is likely that either water has entered the fuel or a filter is blocked. Start at the primary filter.
- Depending on the type of filter, there may be a sight glass to check for water and a tap to drain any off. Deal with this first. Next, close the tank fuel cock, open the filter and remove the element. Clean it in fresh diesel, or – more likely – replace it if it is a throwaway cartridge type. It is imperative that spares are carried at all times.
- Re-assemble the filter, re-open the tank cock and, if the tank is above the filter, allow it to fill by gravity. In order for this to happen, you must open the bleed screw on the top to allow air to be displaced. The bleed point may be a hexagonal bolt head requiring a spanner, and it should not be necessary to open it more than a turn or two. It is critical that no air is present in diesel fuel, so wait until the fuel is running clear out of the top (no air bubbles left) before closing the bleed screw.
- Because air may well have been dragged in further up the line when fuel stopped flowing, the engine filter should next be bled. In extreme cases it may also be necessary to change this element as well and at least one spare should be in the boat's kit. Bleeding requires the fuel lift pump to be operated manually to supply the necessary pressure. Find the pump on the engine block by following the fuel pipe from the primary filter towards the engine filter. Next, feel for a small lever which is operated by moving it up and down. Fuel will now flow to the engine filter, which is bled like its predecessor.
- Many engines will now start without further bleeding, but some may require the injector pump also to be bled. In this case, look for a bleed screw on its body, perhaps on the side or top and bleed it using the lift pump as before. If it still won't run, try bleeding the injectors themselves by carefully 'cracking' the union nuts of the fuel pipes.
- Give the engine a prolonged crank and it should now start. If not, check for air as described and try again.

Today's boats have all manner of arrangements for delivering power to propellers. 'Out-drives' on power craft and 'sail-drives' on yachts are but two of these. Such systems do not normally involve a turning shaft passing directly through the hull, with the inevitable potential for leaking. Many craft still use stern tubes, however, and it requires the sailor to understand them and be able to deal with the commoner faults they develop. There are two essential systems:

The stern gland

The traditional stern gland works by passing the shaft through a 'stuffing box' (see opposite), but various alternative forms of rubber seal are available. There are many of these, but for reasons of space we shall consider one of the more common varieties. The aft end of most shafts is supported by a water-lubricated rubber 'cutless bearing' either set into the stern tube or carried externally in a bracket. The cutless bearing's job is not to keep the water out, but to stop the shaft from sagging and whipping around.

The 'face seal'

This type of seal works by having a carbon collar close fitting around the turning shaft, secured to the forward end of a flexible rubber bellows with a pair of hose clamps. The carbon collar butts up 'face-to-face' against a stainless steel equivalent which turns with the shaft. The carbon/stainless interface is virtually friction free and water pressure acting on the carbon ring keeps it watertight. These seals require no maintenance, but since a bad failure is difficult to deal with in the water, it is essential to keep a close eye on the condition of the bellows and the carbon ring.

The most likely cause of failure in this type of seal is the bellows splitting. Should this occur, try a temporary patch-up with duct tape. If the failure is serious and the bellows are beyond repair, the only answer is to rip them away altogether and do what you can to caulk up between the shaft and the stern tube using rags stuffed in with screwdrivers or anything similar which comes to hand.

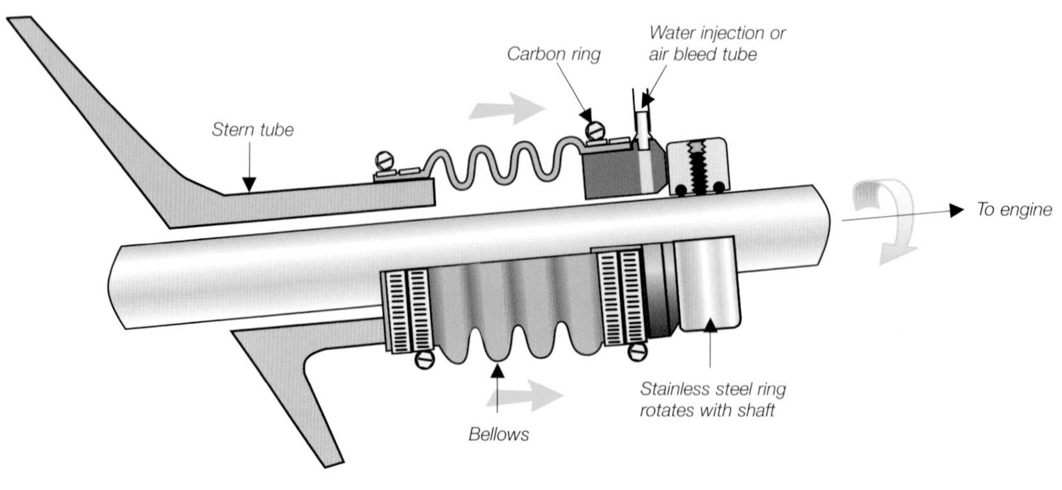

Face-seal stern gland

Stuffing-box stern gland

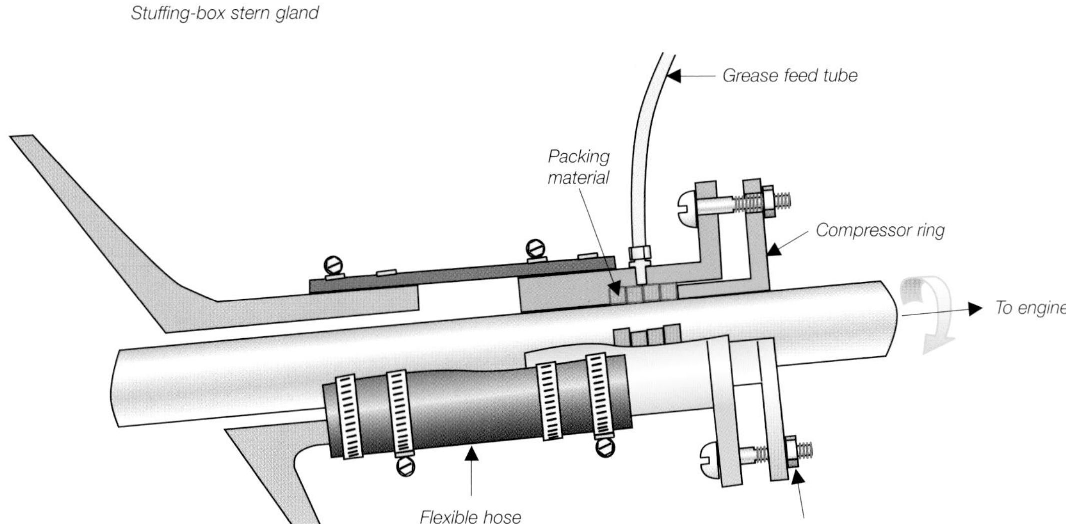

The traditional stuffing box

Here, the seal is supplied by specially made waxed rope packing. This is cut into lengths equal to the shaft's circumference, wrapped around it in the form of rings, slipped into the tube and bedded down by a compression nut which encompasses the whole shaft. This is secured by an equally large locking nut. Instead of a single packing nut, larger craft may have an oval flange tightened down by a pair of smaller nuts onto a similar flange fixed on the stuffing-box body. In either case, the packing is often greased by means of a remotely mounted grease gun.

Such an arrangement will, if properly adjusted, drip occasionally while in use. If the dripping becomes too persistent, the first action is to pump a shot or two of grease into the packing. If this fails, the next stage is to slacken away the lock nut and carefully tighten the packing nut. Too much enthusiasm here can leave the shaft tight, overheated and ultimately suffering damage. Tighten it down gently, ideally feeling to see if the shaft can still be turned by hand with the gears in neutral.

If tightening the packing does not stop the leak, cut a couple of fresh packing rings from the ship's supply. Each turn must be a separate ring. Now back off the nut and slip in the extra packing. Tighten down the nut again and give it some grease. Unless the original packing has totally disintegrated this can be achieved without fear of an inundation, but it makes sense to cut the rings first.

Should the stuffing box fail altogether, you must try to caulk the gap as best you may. This can generally be managed within the capacity of a well-found boat's pumps until harbour is reached and the vessel hauled.

It should be clear from the above that every skipper must be familiar with the stern tube arrangements on his or her boat. If the stern gland is of the stuffing box variety, spare packing must be carried, and it is essential that any tools required are readily to hand. This is especially true in the case of the stuffing-box nut, because these are often by far the biggest on board. A hefty adjustable spanner may well be the answer or, in an emergency, a 'stilson' or pipe wrench, but bear in mind that the nut must be held while the lock nut is tightened, so some means of achieving this must also be contrived. Finally, make sure there is room for your spanner between the nut and the ship's side before you have to find out the hard way.

Engine refuses to start – electrical failure

It is easy to diagnose electrical failure as the reason for a refusal from the engine, because one of four things happens when the key is turned. The first is that the engine whips over with enthusiasm but shows no interest whatever in starting; the second is that absolutely nothing happens at all. The third is the sad sound of a battery without enough life left in it to turn the engine fast enough; the final symptom is an irritating clicking noise.

• Engine turns but does not fire

This may well be a fuel problem, but before considering bleeding the fuel line (see page 33) it is well worth checking that the 'stop' system is not activated. If the engine is stopped by pulling a toggle, make sure that this has been returned to the 'run' position, i.e. shoved back in. This toggle works by shutting down the injector pump and, if manually operated, is not really an electrical issue. However, on many modern diesels the same job is done via an electrical solenoid activated by turning the ignition key. If the engine won't start, make sure this arrangement has not been compromised. To understand how it works, watch the various tiny levers and connections in the vicinity of the injector pump when the 'stop' is being activated. You may well see what happens. If the electrics fail to activate the stop switch, it may 'fail dangerous', leaving the injector pump permanently shut down, a state which you can probably over-ride by pulling out a clevis pin or unfastening a nut. As with much of seamanship, forewarned is fore-armed. There may not be time to experiment when the rocks are looming.

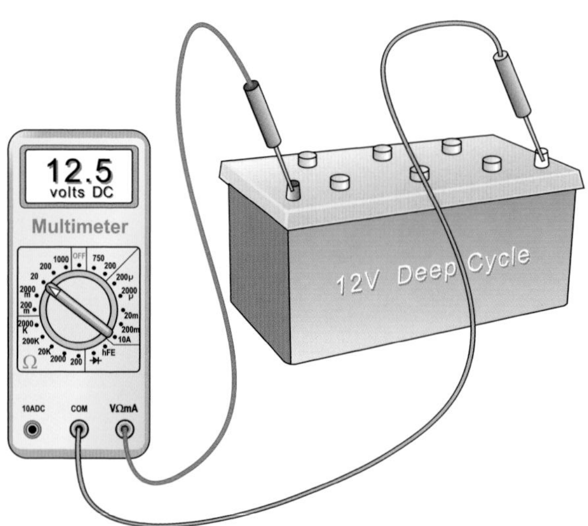

• Nothing happens

Unless the batteries have all taken a serious beating from a short-circuit, it is unlikely that the whole supply will be so flat as to fail to make some sort of show of turning the engine. If total silence meets the start button and the yacht doesn't have a bank of dials reading out the voltage of each battery, it is time to get out the multimeter. Every modern skipper needs to understand the basics of using a multimeter. A workable one should not cost no more than a round of drinks. It measures current (amps), resistance (ohms) and, most importantly in this instance, it will also indicate voltage. Go to the battery box and decide which battery is supposed to be starting the engine. Dial up 'Volts DC' (Direct Current) on the meter, choose 20 volts from the selection, place the red probe on the positive terminal and the black one on the negative and see what the numbers say. A charged, healthy 12-volt battery at rest will usually read about 12.5 volts and 12.0 should start a happy engine. Even if it is down to '11-point-something' it will usually still turn it over and might even do the trick. A 24-volt system works 'pro rata'. When nothing is happening and the battery has enough volts to do the job, then either a bad connection is to blame, or something untoward has happened to the vessel's switching arrangements.

If the engine start battery has its own switch, is it on? If it is, inspect all the connections between the starter motor and the battery. In a case of total failure, the problem is more likely to be in a small wire leading from the switch to a relay or solenoid than one of the big ones delivering the main punch, so examine these as well, even if you don't understand what they all do.

Boats have different wiring systems and varying methods of connecting the battery to the starter motor, so it is impossible to generalise. A trained eye can read the wiring diagram supplied by the engine manufacturer, but for the average skipper this may prove too big a challenge. However, a wire hanging off is a wire hanging off, and it might just be the one you're looking for! The impetus of this section is to encourage a seamanlike, systematic search for such a problem. To remake connections, the ship should carry a good supply of electrical terminals – 'spades' and rings of assorted sizes – as well as insulating tape, spare wire of varying gauges, cutters and some means of crimping a terminal. Ideally this will be a purpose-designed crimper, but a small pair of mole grips (vise grips) will serve. None of these items is expensive.

Terminals cost literally pennies. Yet a supply of them can save the vessel and all aboard.

A less likely scenario is that the relay which sends power to the starter motor or solenoid has given up the ghost. You can't repair these and they aren't easy for an amateur to diagnose, but if you carry a spare and all else fails, they are simple enough to replace.

• Flat battery

When power is switched in to the starter motor, it comes first to an integral solenoid. This is an electrical switch that opens the floodgates to the massive current needed to turn the engine. When the solenoid 'throws', the big power is released to the starter motor itself. The sad, dying grunt of one of these trying to start an engine on a flat battery is unmistakable. So is the final expiring click of a solenoid that isn't powered up enough to activate itself, let alone the main unit. Either of these noises confirms that power is getting to where it's needed, but that there isn't enough of it.

The question as to why the battery is flat is important, but it can wait for now. If you can hand-start the engine, do it. If not, the next thing is to find some volts from somewhere else.

Single-battery boats – Where the boat has only one battery and the multimeter shows the voltage has gone down the plughole, you're a dead duck. You'll have to find either a jump start from another boat, or a source of mains power to plug in your handy battery charger. Even if you have more than one battery, every boat should still carry a set of heavy duty jump leads. You may only use them once in a decade, but when the day finally comes, nothing else will do. Here's the process for jump-starting safely:

- Turn off all electrics, including anything that might be plugged into a charger. Visually check that your battery casing is not cracked. If it is, DO NOT attempt to jump-start it. It may burst, with consequences too awful to contemplate.
- Check the voltage on the donor battery. It should be well above the 12.0-volt margin.
- Connect the positive terminal of the flat battery to the positive terminal on the donor battery using the red jump lead **(1)**.
- Connect one end of the black jump lead to the negative terminal on the donor battery **(2)**. The other end should be clipped onto a hefty bright metal fitting on the block of the engine suffering the flat battery **(3)**. Don't use a painted or oily fitting. A big nut is good. Hooking up the two negative battery terminals works well but it may spark, which in extreme circumstances can be an explosion hazard. Do it only if you can't get a good earth the other way.
- Activate your starter motor. Assuming the engine is healthy and the donor battery is good, it should fire up promptly.
- If it doesn't, check connections (there may be a few small sparks as you do this – no problem) and try again.
- With the engine now running, disconnect as follows:
  Remove the black lead from your engine block, then the other end from the donor battery.
  Take the red cable off the donor battery then from your own.
- Keep your engine running for at least half an hour to charge your battery. The longer the better.

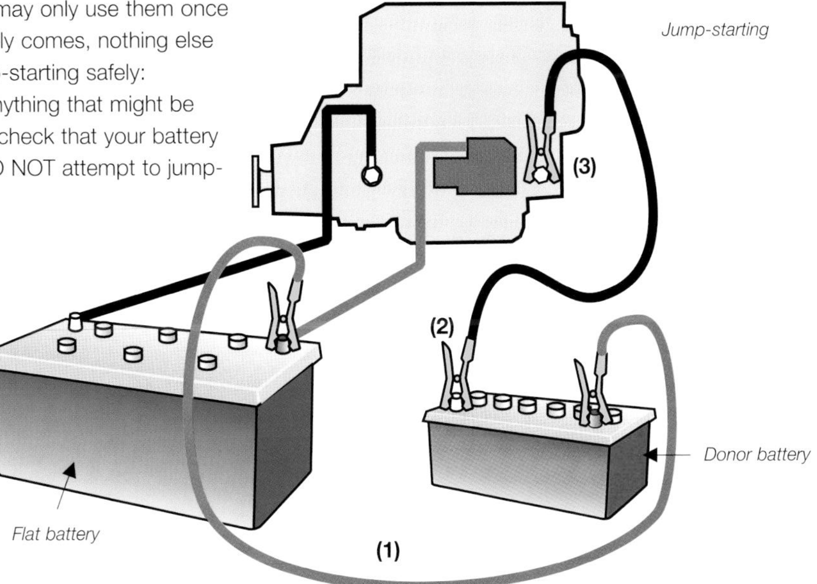

Jump-starting

Boats with more than one battery – Various systems exist for ensuring that an engine start battery is never flattened, but most follow one of two arrangements. Either the engine battery is a dedicated unit that is never used for anything other than starting the engine, with domestic ('house') batteries fulfilling all other functions, or the boat has two battery sources which can be interchanged at will.

- Dedicated engine batteries are often smaller than the ship's domestic supplies. They are typically switched on and off independently. If they're off, the engine won't start. With most dedicated systems, the charging relays or diodes are arranged so that as soon as the engine fires up, the alternator charges the start battery first. This ensures that it is always ready for next time. As it approaches peak capacity, charge is progressively spilled over into the domestic batteries. With such a system, you don't have any thinking to do. Just make sure that all batteries are 'on' and fire up the engine. So long as the charging system is working, you're in business. Dedicated batteries should be wired up so that in the unlikely event of the engine unit going flat, the domestic banks can be switched in to start her up. Such switches are rarely tested and have been known to fail. Hence the jump leads…

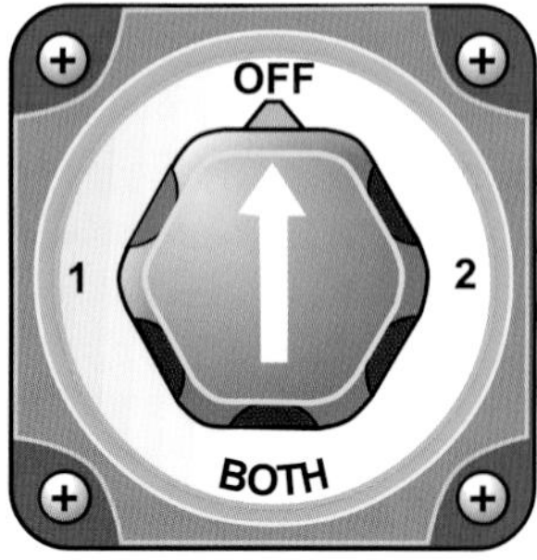

Combined isolator and selector switch

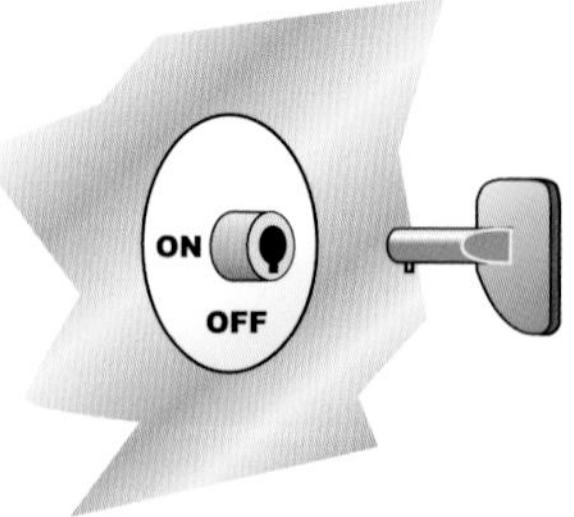

Key type isolator switch

- Interchangeable batteries are often of equal capacities and controlled by a 4-way switch offering 'Battery 1', 'Battery 2', 'Both' or 'Off'. What you elect to do with these options is a matter of personal choice, but you must decide whether to use one battery as 'engine start' and stick to it, or whether to change them over from time to time to share the hammering dished out by domestic demands. In either case, make sure that 'Both' is selected while the engine is actually running, so as to charge everything. If one battery is too flat to start the engine, it's generally better to use the other on its own rather than opt for 'Both', because the dead one may compromise its opposite number.

Power consumption

The basic principles of electrical power storage and consumption are an integral part of managing a yacht or motor cruiser. The simplest way to think of this is to imagine a battery as a storage dump containing units called 'amp hours'. An electrical consumer such as a light bulb, a fridge or a GPS receiver uses flowing current, which is measured in amps. If it pulls five amps, then in one hour it will use five amp hours. Its demand, or capacity, is expressed in 'watts', and the power to shove the amps down the wires to feed it is given in volts. The essence of power management lies in understanding the relationship between these three elements. Fortunately, the arithmetic is as simple as it gets. Here it is:
Watts = Volts x Amps
It follows that Amps = Watts ÷ Volts.
This means that a 25-watt bulb such as is used for a masthead tricolour lamp in a 12-volt system draws 25÷12 Amps — more or less 2 amps.
In one hour, it consumes 2 amp hours.
No battery can really deliver as much as imanufacturers' claim, and a 110 amp-hour battery's capacity may be as limited as 65 amps in typical use on a sailing craft. This means that the tricolour will flatten it in just over 30 hours. Now add up everything else that is drawing power in the same way, and you can work out what's required.

A boat fridge can be a thirsty guzzler of battery power, demanding heavy work from the alternator.

Battery charging

In the absence of additional charging systems, yacht batteries are topped up by an alternator driven by a belt from the main engine. The potential output is measured in amps, so that a 50-amp alternator running for an hour can in theory put 50 amp hours into a battery. In practice, the fuller a battery becomes, the harder it is to charge and the older it grows, the more resistant to a charge it becomes, so such high ideals are rarely reached. Charging a 12volt 110 amp-hour battery up to 100 amp hours from 50 could easily take three hours. The whole issue of how much charge can be pushed into a battery is complex and beyond the scope of this manual, but the figures mentioned should form a practical starting point.

Volt meters – Many sailing yachts and power cruisers are equipped with meters indicating the present voltage of the batteries. As we have seen in the paragraphs on multimeters, knowing this is the most convenient way of determining the condition of a battery. So long as the meter reads well above 12 volts (or 24 if that is the system), it can do its work. If it falls much below that mark, it is high time for a boost. On charge, the voltage may rise to over 14 volts. This is fine, but don't expect it to stay there long once charging has ceased.

Electrical tool kit and spares:

Multimeter – preferably digital type

Wire strippers and crimpers

Test light – often with a small screwdriver as a probe

Spare of every bulb you have on board

Spare batteries for every item of equipment

Fuses

De-ionised water for battery top up

Spare crimp type connectors in a variety of sizes

Insulating tape

Heat shrink tape

Petroleum jelly (Vaseline)

Ropes and ropework

Rope Types

Today's manufacturers create synthetic ropes to suit any purpose. The skipper's job is to know which are appropriate for the various jobs on board and ensure that the best choice is on board.

'Traditional synthetics'

Polyester – can be either three-strand traditional rope or braidline. Polyester is an all-purpose cordage offering good strength and stretch resistance. It is reasonably resilient to the degrading effects of sunlight and chafe, retaining flexibility into comparative old age. In its pre-stretched form it has even better resistance to stretch and may sometimes be stronger. Suitable for sheets, halyards and general on-board use, although a more economical material for example polypropylene is often used for docklines.

Nylon Very strong, chafe resistant, and the most stretchy rope you are likely to find. This helps it to absorb shock and makes it perfect for anchor rode.

Polypropylene Often lighter than water, so it floats. Great for heaving lines. Although not as strong as nylon or polyester, it is considerably cheaper, so if you go up a gauge or two in size it makes grand docklines. Polypropylene degrades faster than other types in sunlight, so watch for it beginning to 'powder' and expect a limited lifespan once it does.

'Extra-strength synthetics '

High Modulus polyethylene (HMPE) often seen as 'Spectra®' or 'Dyneema®' is light, incredibly stretch-resistant and phenomenally strong. Used extensively in racing yachts and increasingly on cruising sailboats where these characteristics are desirable, it is not cheap, but with its surprising ability to cope with chafe it lasts a long time. Excellent for halyards, downhauls, reefing pennants and for operating systems such as a single-line reefing that may otherwise be doomed by stretch.

Aramid or Kevlar®, is less resistant to sunlight than other hi-tech ropes. It also loses more strength when knotted, and is heavier than HMPE.

Liquid Crystal Polymers such as Vectran are even better in many respects than the seemingly unbeatable HMPE, but because it is prone to deterioration in sunlight, it is best used inside a braidline sheath.

Marlinespike seamanship

Essential knots

Nomenclature The *standing part* of a rope is the section between the load and the knot. The *working end* is the part between the knot as it is made and the extreme end of the rope. The *bight* is any loop or 'bent' part of the rope within the knot, as well as a larger loop of rope on the deck.

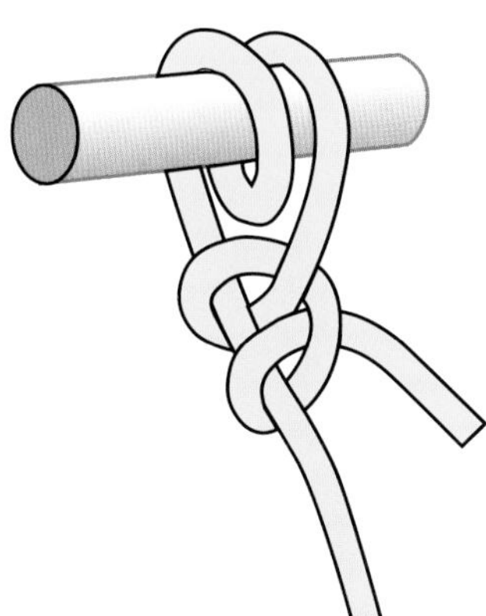

Round turn and two half-hitches A self-explanatory knot to tie, but note that you must make a full turn as shown. This really means it's $1\frac{1}{2}$ turns rather than a half-turn. Also, make sure the half hitches form a clove-hitch shape on the standing part of the line. Used for securing to a fixed point such as a ring, a bollard or post. The preferred knot for a dinghy painter.

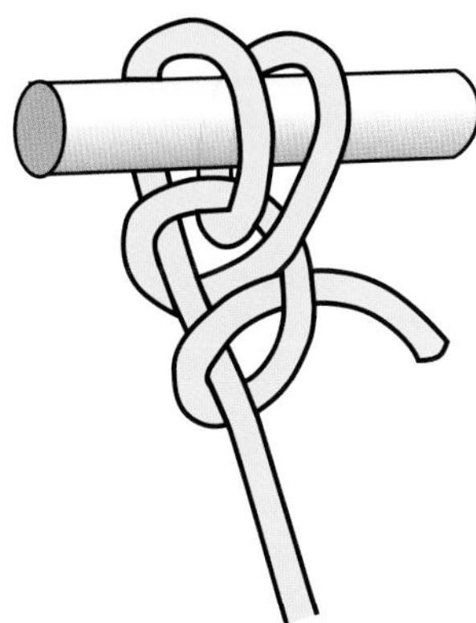

Anchor bend (Fisherman's bend) Pass a turn around the ring, then lead the first half-hitch under the turn itself before pulling the whole thing tight. Add a second half hitch for security, or seize the working end back to the standing part.

A totally secure way of bending a rope to a ring as may be found on an anchor or a dinghy. The harder you pull, the tighter it bites, yet with a little persuasion at the bight of the half-hitch, it will always come undone when asked.

Clove hitch Depending on what you are securing to, there are various ways of making a clove hitch, none of which is at all difficult. The important thing is that it looks like this one. If it doesn't, it's a 'cow hitch' and will not be so reliable.

The clove hitch is fine for securing a rope to the middle of another rope under load, such as a fender lanyard to a guard rail. To make it doubly secure, back it up with a half hitch as well.

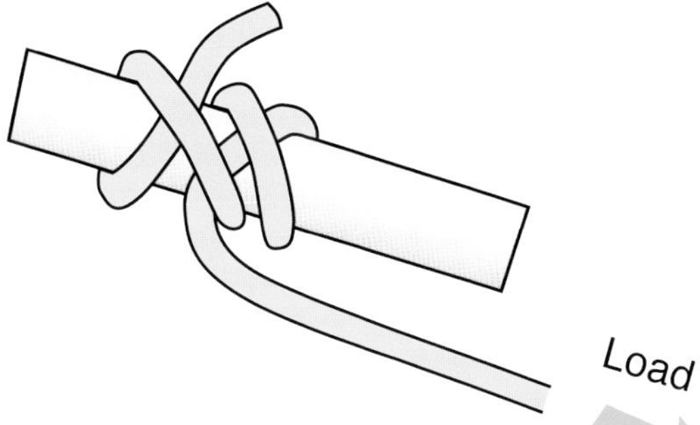

Rolling hitch Just like a clove hitch, except that it is designed to take an oblique pull without slipping. Do an extra turn into the knot at the side where the pull will come, and it won't slide along. Used to take the strain off a rope that you cannot otherwise relieve, such as a loaded jib sheet jammed by a riding turn on the winch.

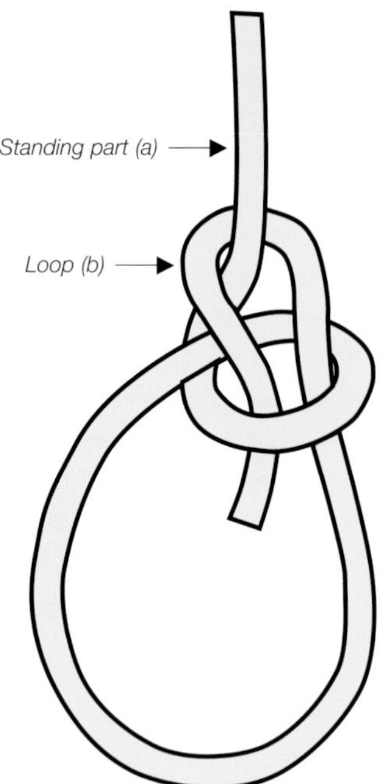

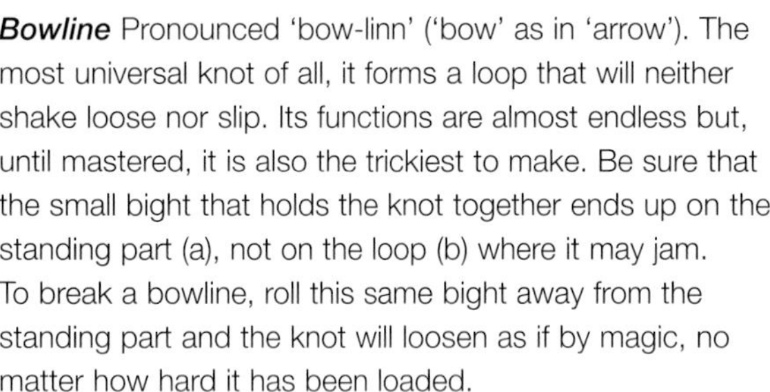

Bowline Pronounced 'bow-linn' ('bow' as in 'arrow'). The most universal knot of all, it forms a loop that will neither shake loose nor slip. Its functions are almost endless but, until mastered, it is also the trickiest to make. Be sure that the small bight that holds the knot together ends up on the standing part (a), not on the loop (b) where it may jam. To break a bowline, roll this same bight away from the standing part and the knot will loosen as if by magic, no matter how hard it has been loaded.

Used for bending sheets to sails, for loops on shorelines, etc. Two tied into one another can even be used for knotting ropes together if you have forgotten your bends.

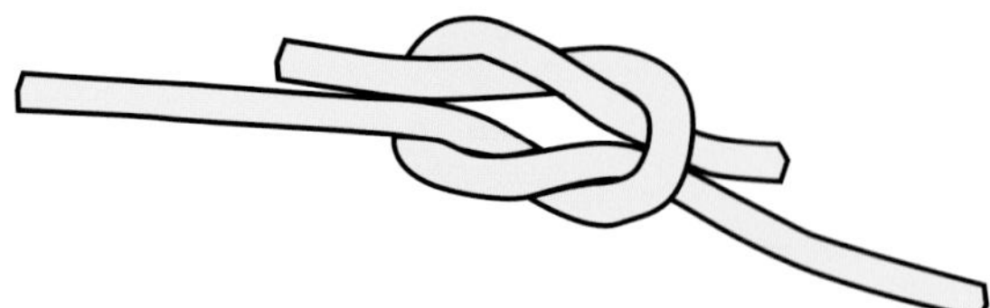

Reef Knot Made exactly as you tie your shoelace. 'Right over left and under, left over right and under.' The only difference is that you don't slip the loops as in the bow, although there is no reason why you shouldn't slip at least one for ease of untying later. The knot should look symmetrical as shown. If it doesn't, you've tied a 'granny'. Inspect the picture and try again.

The only knot for securing reef points or lashings. This is not a bend and is insecure for tying two ropes together.

Single sheet bend First make a bight in one line (the larger if they're not the same size), then pass the other up through it, round the back, then across the front under itself but not down through the bight again. Used for bending two ropes together quickly and reliably, so long as they remain under load.

Double sheet bend Made like the single sheet bend, except that the working end is taken twice around the bight, passing it through itself at the front on each turn as shown. Preferable to the single sheet bend if the load is to come on and off repeatedly, because the single sheet bend can slip if the load is jerked and slackened.

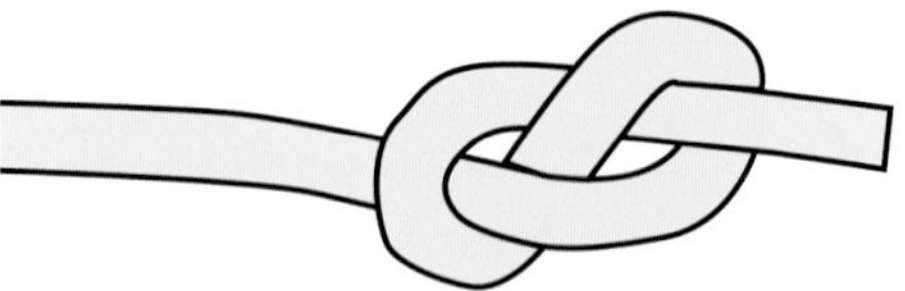

Figure of Eight A 'stopper knot' used to prevent a rope from running out of a hole or fairlead. The classic use is on the aft end of a headsail sheet to stop it from escaping from the cockpit turning blocks.

Splices

The crown knot and back splice – mastering the sequence is the key to all three-strand splicing. Note that if the rope is especially hard, or falls apart when cut, you may find a Swedish fid (see page 161) to be an invaluable assistant for pushing pieces of rope through one another. `

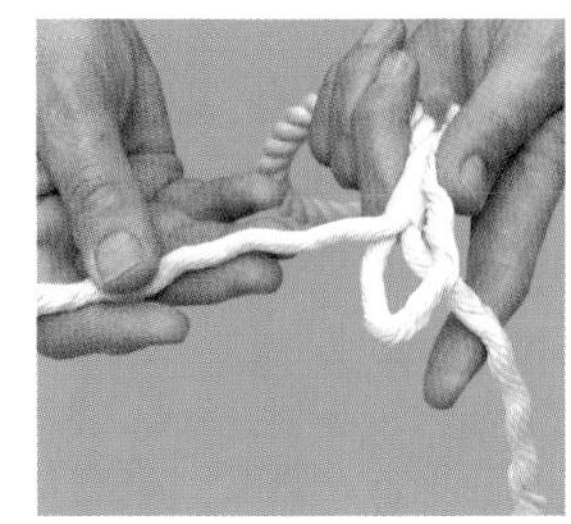

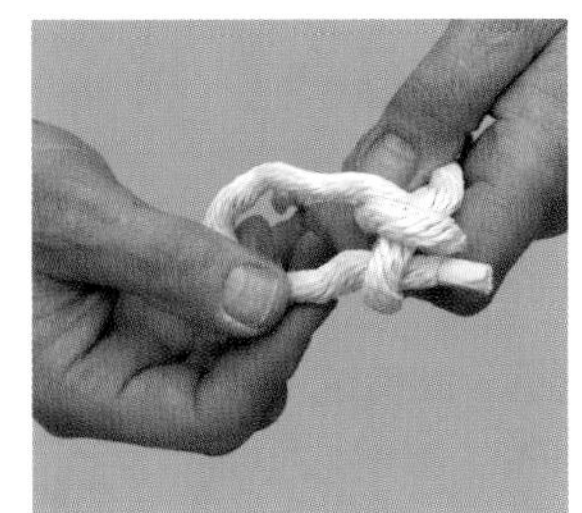

First the crown knot...

Unlay a generous length of line, then seize it to prevent further unlaying. This can be done with a twist of masking tape. It will probably also pay to burn or tape the ends of the strands to stabilise them.

- Arrange the three strands as shown with the middle one away from you.
- Loop this across towards you so that it lands between the others.
- Take the left-hand strand across the front, outside the centre strand and on round the back beneath the right-hand strand, so that it ends up facing the back of the knot.
- Pass the right-hand strand under the left-hand one, and on through the loop in the centre strand.
- Tighten each strand carefully to form a neat knot in the shape of a crown.
- Remove the tape.

...then the splice

- Beginning from the crown knot, take one strand downwards, over the strand immediately below it, then under the next one and out again. Always work against, or across, the lay of the rope.
- Follow suit with the others so that each comes out of its corresponding 'hole' in the lay of the rope. The splice should be symmetrical now. If not, go back and find the strand you have taken through two, or none.
- Make another tuck with each strand. 'Over and under' is the watchword. Roll the splice between your hands to even it up.
- Always make at least three tucks. If in doubt, perhaps because the rope is very soft in its lay up, make a fourth to be sure.
- Tighten up, cut off the ends and burn them carefully to finish the job.
- To make the spice look really good, cut off half of each strand at the final tuck, then tuck the remainder again to create a tapered effect. The real pros do it twice, taking off one third at a time.

The eye splice

For traditional sailors, the eye splice is the staff of life, and it has many uses in more modern craft too. Once you've got it going, it's no harder to turn in than a back splice. The tricky bit is the first tuck. Unlay the rope and tape or burn it as for the back splice.

- Make the eye by laying two strands over and one under the standing part.
- Working against the lay as always, tuck the top two strands over and under successive strands of the standing part.
- Now turn the splice over and tuck the third strand as shown. This action demands a knack, and the best way of deciding which of the other strands to work it under is to let the strand you are tucking find its own way. Don't force it. Just see where it wants to go, and note that it may seem as if you are tucking it backwards.
- The effect of the previous tuck is to leave the first strand behind, as it were. Now tuck this over and under against the lay so that it can catch up. At this stage, you should have a symmetrical splice to begin your next row of tucks.
- Finishing the splice is merely a matter of popping in a further three tucks. The eye formed is 95% as strong as the rope.

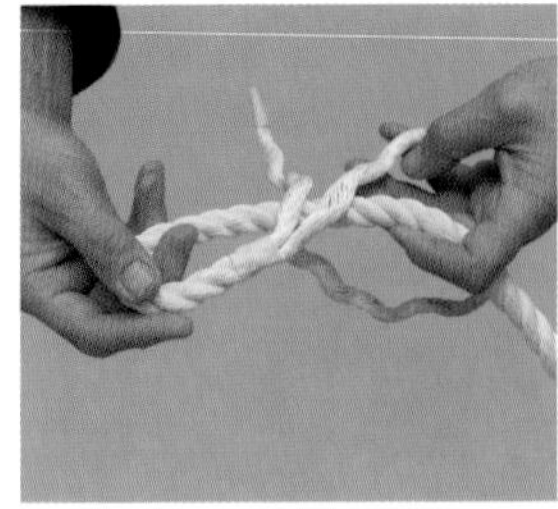

If you intend to work a thimble into the splice to create a hard eye, do it at 'first-tuck' stage by making the splice slightly smaller than the thimble, then heaving up the first couple of tucks hard to tighten it.

Whippings

When you're in a hurry there may be some excuse for taping a rope's end or burning it over to prevent it unlaying. A sailor's boat, however, has its ropes' ends whipped for extra security, good looks, and a bit of honest pride.

The common whipping

This does not have much place at sea where chafe or a rope's end thrashing in the wind can shake it off, but as with the back splice, mastering it is the key to being able to work more sophisticated methods that really work well.

- Start with a good length of whipping twine. For 14mm rope a metre or so is ideal.
- Lay a bight of twine along the rope to be whipped, with the loop standing proud of the end and enough length below where the whipping will be to let you get a good grip on it when its time comes.
- Starting from a point 3cm or so from the end (for 14mm line. Other sizes pro rata), whip the twine firmly around the rope against the lay, working towards the end and enclosing the bight you have already made.
- When you've laid on as many turns as the rope is wide, but not so close to the end that the whipping can easily fall off, tuck the end of your working twine through the bight.
- Pull the bight through from the end left poking out at the bottom, so that the bight drags the working end down into the whipping and disappears.
- Cut off both ends of the whipping twine flush with the outer ends of the whipping.

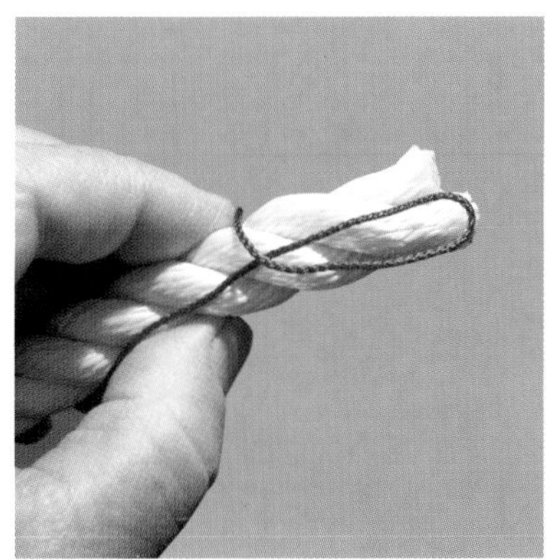

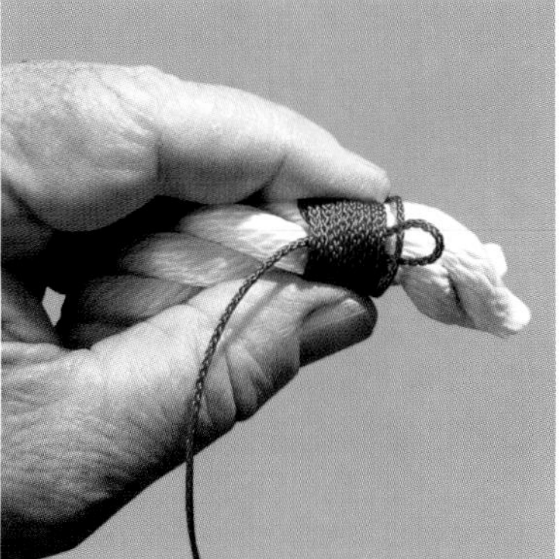

Sail makers' whippings

These whippings will not shake or chafe off the rope's end. They're easier to execute than they look, and they set any yacht's appearance off in a proper manner.

The gaffer's quickie

A swift way of making a well-frapped whipping requiring no tools – for three-strand rope only.

- Begin exactly as for a common whipping, by laying a bight of twine along the rope and binding up towards the end against the lay.
- When you are 1cm from the end of a 14mm rope, pass the twine around the exposed strand next to the bight of the twine that will be used to pull the whipping tight, then pass it down outside the whipping following the natural lay of the rope.
- Now worm it through the lay of the rope and back out again at the next gap.
- Next, pass it back up the score outside the whipping to the top, around the next strand, and back down again.
- Continue through the lay, back up and so on until you have two complete sets of these 'frapping turns'. The working end will now be lying alongside the original bight where it exits the whipping.
- Pass the twine through the bight and pull it tightly into the whipping from the bottom, as in the common whipping.
- Cut the ends off flush.

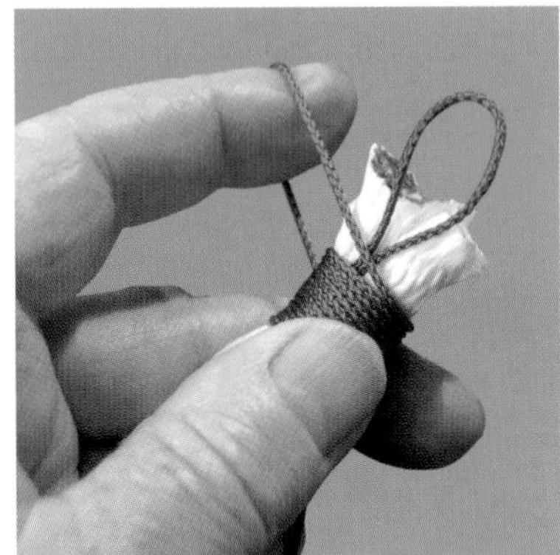

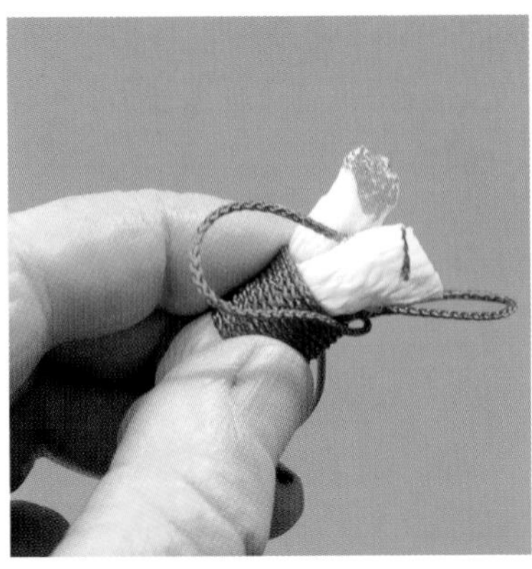

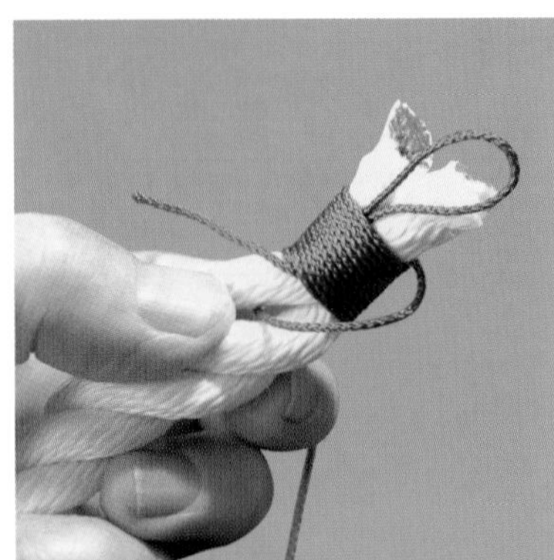

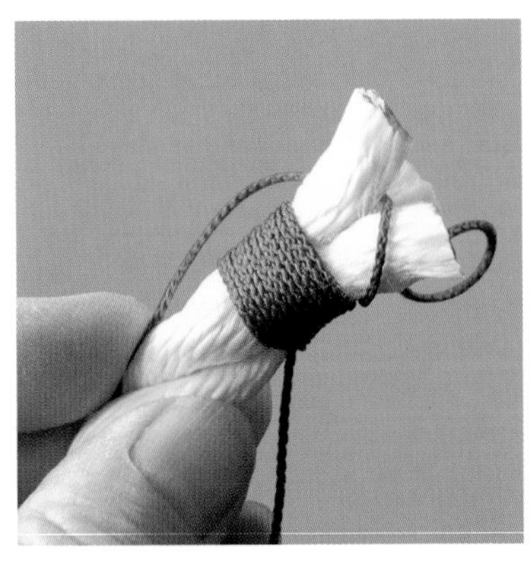

Palm and needle

A neater and even more secure result can be achieved with a sail maker's palm and needle. With a little modification based on common sense, this method has the benefit of being usable with braidline.

- Thread a couple of metres of whipping twine onto a sail needle, and push it twice through a strand of the rope to secure the bottom end, starting further back from the end of the rope than with other whippings, making sure the rope stays laid up.
- Now whip the twine around the rope towards the end, against the lay as usual.
- When your whipping is as long as the rope is wide, pass the needle under the same strand that it was bedded in at the bottom, now working with the lay.
- Next, pass the twine down the score, under the next strand, back up to the top, and so on until you have two sets of frapping turns.
- If there is any danger of the first loop around the rope strand slipping, pass the final frapping turn through it before proceeding to the bottom of the whipping for the last time.
- Use the needle to make a half-hitch around the strand at the bottom of the whipping, then 'sew' the end into the strand a couple of times to bury it for good. Trim off and cut the rope to length near the upper end of the whipping.

If this whipping is being made in braidline, each frapping turn is sewn deeply, so as to capture the rope core as well as the coat.

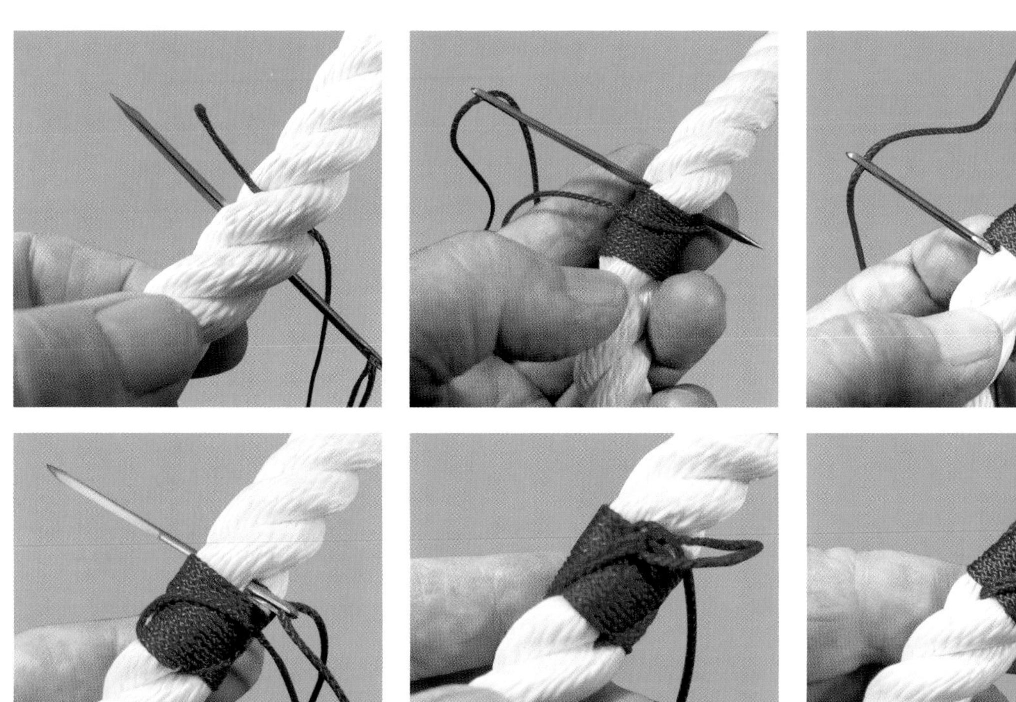

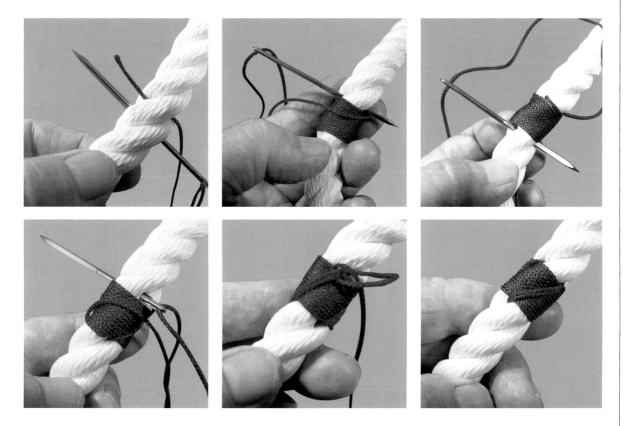

Securing lines

The world of leisure seafaring abounds in sloppy practice when it comes to securing lines. Shorelines in particular are often abused, leading to awkward handling and potentially dangerous situations. The way to get it right is not to stick slavishly to some specific system. There is more than one right way to do things. The important thing is to approach each situation with the attitude, 'What am I trying to achieve here? What could go wrong? And how can I make sure it doesn't?' Generally, the answers to these questions come down to two golden rules:

- Once secure, it must be impossible for the rope to slip, or even to come adrift altogether.
- When the time comes to ease or release the rope, it must be easy to do so under complete control, regardless of the load to which it has been or is being subjected.

Securing to a cleat

The ideal scenario

- Make sure that the rope is leading 'fair' onto the cleat, as in 'A'. This will enable it to run under control. If you force it around as in 'B', it can jam as you try to ease it, and may even lock up altogether.
- Having taken almost a full turn, lay on a figure of '8' as in 'C'.
- Follow this with a second figure of '8', then wrap a round turn around the whole cleat. 'D'. The line is now 'secure' if the cleat is for mooring, or 'belayed' if it is a running rigging such as a sheet or halyard.

Belaying pins

The traditional belaying pin relies on the same principles as the cleat, but it is somewhat easier to use and generally gives plenty of space on the pin to hang the coiled rope on if required.

Locking hitches

Notice that no locking hitches 'E' have been used in this classic belay. Traditionally, their use was frowned upon because wet natural-fibre cordage shrank and could end up locked semi-permanently. This is not so with modern ropes provided the hitch is made properly. If additional security is required – perhaps to prevent the possibility of a sea washing the rope off a cleat – there is absolutely no reason why you shouldn't use one.

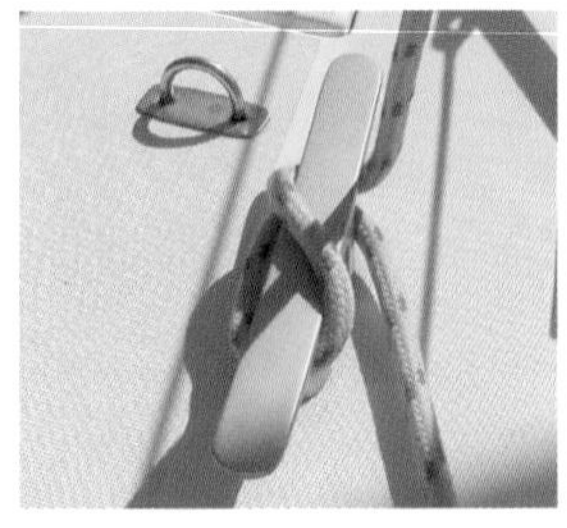

A

B

C

D

E

A locking hitch can also save the day where a cleat is too small to take a full 'belay'.

To make a locking hitch, first lay on at least one of the usual figures of '8'. As you go for the second (or ideally third), turn the rope over so that the working end comes out from beneath the last turn, as shown 'E'. The complete hitch should follow the neat figures of eight underneath it. If laid on the wrong way round, it not only looks unseamanlike, it is also less secure.

Resist any temptation to use a locking hitch without at least 1½ figures of '8' between it and the load. Clapping one on immediately after the first half-turn can give rise to a serious lock-up. Using more than one is a waste of time that might delay the release of a line needed in a hurry.

Securing to a post, a bollard or a winch barrel

Once again, the main issue is that the rope should be totally secure but that it must run under control when needed. It's very easy to get this one wrong – for example, by securing to a post with a clove hitch. Once the load is on, a clove hitch may slip or it might lock solid, leaving you either adrift without a paddle or looking for the ship's hacksaw. The same goes for a bowline, or any other knot that cannot be eased away when loaded, unless of course the other end can be reached and has been properly made up. Thus, it is perfectly acceptable to secure a dock line ashore with a bowline, so long as the bight is made fast sensibly aboard the boat.

If you have a Samson post on the foredeck for example, or are obliged to make up your springs onto cockpit winches, you will need a method that cannot lock and that won't fail either. At a pinch, you could use a round turn and two half hitches, but even these have been known to jam up under the sort of extreme loads that come on when a boat is left unattended on a falling tide and ends up hanging from her securing points. The answer is the 'tugboat hitch', sometimes called the 'bollard hitch'.

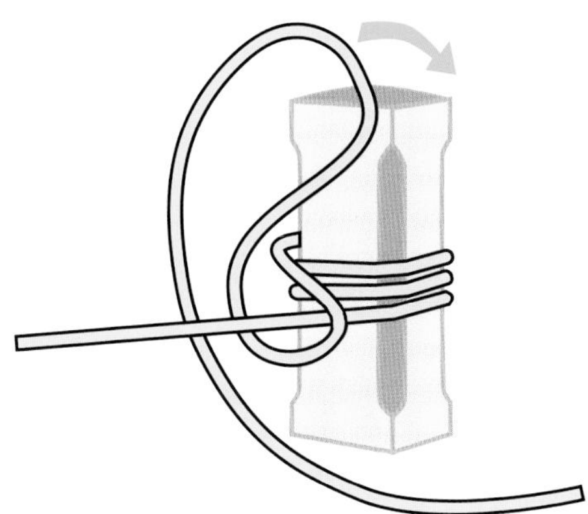

The tugboat hitch

This infinitely valuable hitch is made on a post or winch barrel as follows:

- Lead the rope fair onto the post, then take as many turns as is convenient, (at least two).
- The turns will actually hold the load. The remainder of the hitch is to make sure they don't come off and to supply a bit of friction to ensure they work as they should.
- Take a bight of the working end, pass it under the standing part and bring it back over the top of the post. Do not attempt to turn it or knot it in any way. Just lay it over.
- Now do the same thing once more, this time from the other side, again making sure to resist any temptation to turn the bight over into a locking hitch.
- This will usually be plenty, but if in doubt, lay on another bight.

  Be careful when releasing this if the rope is loaded. You may be surprised at how much pull there is. That's why you took so many turns in the first place.

The jammer

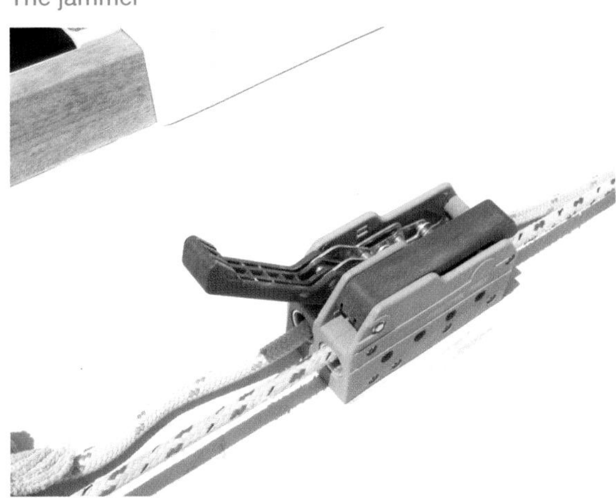

The jammer is in almost universal use in modern sailing craft. It stops off the bight of a line that may be under any load within its specification, so it can take the strain between the pull and the winch, releasing the winch for other duties. It is therefore common to see a multi-function winch backed up by a bank of jammers.

A jammer can be kept in the closed position as a line is winched through it, leaving the operator with nothing to do but walk away. However, two points must be borne in mind when releasing ropes that are jammed off.

- It's all or nothing with a jammer. If you are able to flip it open and loads are high, the rope will whip out of control if no steps are taken to contain its enthusiasm.
- Because of its cam action, a highly loaded jammer is often unwilling to open and release its rope. If this happens, forcing it will only mash the sheath of the rope. The answer is to winch the rope into the jammer by a few millimetres before throwing the jammer off. This not only allows the rope to be unjammed, it also leaves it under the control of the turns around the winch barrel.

Coiling and stowing

The clockwise coil

The basic manner for coiling a rope is to turn it clockwise or, as the process was once called – in the Northern Hemisphere – to turn it 'with the sun'. With three-strand rope, or a braidline with a laid-up core, this remains as important now as ever it was, because the lay of the rope makes it want to turn that way. Force it against its will and you leave it with bad memories and in a filthy temper. For days after such treatment it will kink, and be generally unwilling to run sweetly. It is perfectly true to say that a braid-on-braid rope can be properly coiled in either direction. The trouble is, if you get into the habit of coiling against the sun, you will end up doing it with three-strand line and the wrath of the ancient gods will descend. Examiners in the Yachtmaster scheme notice anti-clockwise coilers out of the corners of their eyes, and anyone who commits the atrocity becomes a marked man with a lot of slack to make up.

Start with the end that's made fast

Unless the rope is free, unattached and out of use, always coil from where it is made fast towards the loose end. Any kinks developed during the coiling process will then be shaken off. Coiling from the free end means that the kinks will be trapped, growing worse with the enlarging coil.

Coiling into the hand or onto the deck

However you intend to coil, it pays to flake a rope clear of kinks and obstructions before you start.

To coil into the hand, right-handed people should hold the coil in the left hand and pile up the turns with the right, applying half a twist to each one with thumb and forefinger to keep them lying smoothly. Most left-handers simply reverse the technique, except that the knack of applying the half-twist is for some reason more awkward to master.

If the rope is too hefty or too long to hold in one hand, coil it flat on the deck. Stand over the coil and, feeding the rope from your left hand into your right, spin it down into a flat coil. The turns should pile up on one another so that they can run without fouling.

Ready to run

Where a coil is being laid down so that the rope can run off it, make sure that the standing part is on top and the end underneath. That way, the rope peels sweetly off the top. Lay it down the other way and a snarl-up is certain. It also makes sense to ensure that the bitter end can't flip itself up between the coils as they are running. If it does, it will lead to one of life's more odious mess-ups, often at a time when you'd rather it didn't. Feed it out beyond one side of the coil to avoid this.

Flaking to run

When it is vital that a long rope runs cleanly, it pays to abandon the coil and 'flake' it down instead. This time you can work from the bitter end. Throw this onto the deck, then drop the rope into a series of natural figures of eight, one on top of the next, until you reach the cleat or belaying pin. The rope will run without a hitch. Some authorities refer to the process as 'faking'.

Flaked to run

Making up a big coil

Making up a coil

On a vertical cleat or belaying pin

a Hold the coil against the cleat in your left hand. Reach through it and take a bight from the top of the furthest turn of the coil into your right hand.
b Bring this towards you through the coil, putting in a half-twist as it comes.
c Now bring it up and over the top of the coil from your side. Drop it over the cleat to hang the coil for instant release.

a

b

c

On a horizontal cleat, or anywhere the rope has no obvious hanging point

There are many ways of achieving a reasonable stow on a free coil of line, but the most stable is to use a gasket coil hitch.

Right-handers coil into the left hand, working from the bight that is made fast. Leave a metre or two between you and the belay. When it's all coiled up, take the standing part around the coil, catching in its own turn. Now carry on four more turns, nice and tight, working towards the end of the coil. Finish by passing the bight through the coil and feeding it back over the top; then firm it up by pulling the coil against the standing part.

The gasket coil hitch can also be used on a free rope such as an unused sheet which is about to be tossed into a locker. It's easier to make when the coil is free, because the frapping turns won't tend to twist as awkwardly as they do when made on a working rope.

The soft option of just frapping a few turns round a coil and stuffing the end through is a poor alternative to the gasket hitch which, once mastered, is hugely superior.

Hanging a mainsheet

This is best done by a variant of the gasket coil hitch. Start from where the sheet is made fast and coil towards the bitter end. Make the gasket hitch with the last couple of metres, then pass a bight through the parts of the coil. Instead of continuing by bringing this back over the top and snugging it down, the end is passed through this bight and used to hang the coil from the boom end.

Big ropes

A really hefty rope is best stowed by means of 'stops', or short lengths of small stuff tied around it at either 90° or 120° intervals. This is an ideal system, but not convenient for a rope that is in frequent use. If it's not too huge, such a line can be stowed by passing an end twice round one part of the coil so as to form a clove hitch. For total security make a half hitch around the last coil, and then dump the rope into its locker.

The gasket coil hitch

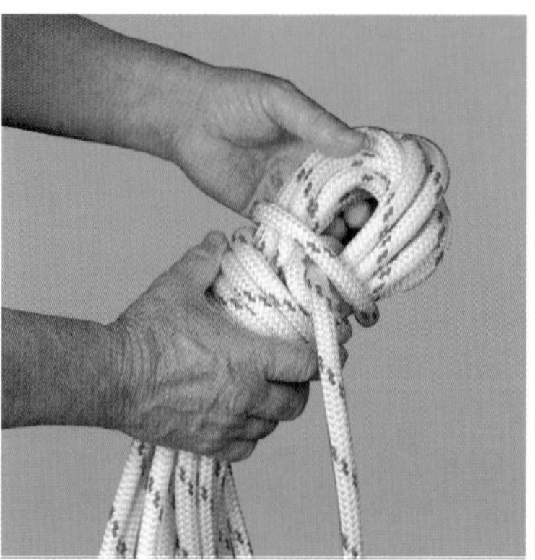

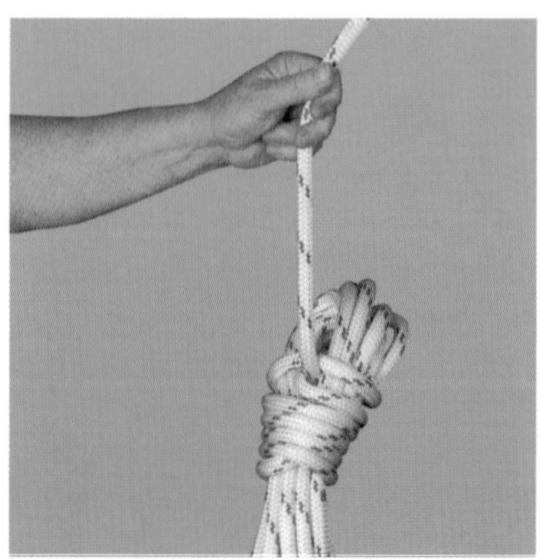

Creating power

Winching

A winch delivers additional power to the pull on a rope in two ways. First, there is the basic leverage aspect. If the winch barrel is 5cm in radius and the winch handle is 25cm long, a mechanical advantage is achieved equal to 25 ÷ 5, or five times. Most winches include a gearing system whereby the handle turns more times than the winch barrel for a given input of effort. This is called a velocity ratio and works in exactly the same way as gears on a pedal cycle. If you wind the winch round five times on the handle to gain a single turn of the barrel, the ratio is 5:1 and the power is commensurate. Factor in the handle length and you have a power delivery of 5 x 5, or 25 times what you are putting in with your strong arm. Many larger winches are two or even three-speed, with power rising accordingly.

The winch only works so long as there is enough friction to stop the rope slipping on the barrel. This is supplied by having an appropriate number of turns, and keeping them tensioned either by tailing the end as it comes off the winch, or by using a self-tailing winch top.

Loading a winch

Never use a winch without a full round turn on the barrel. Depending on how effective the lead onto the winch may be, you may or may not be able to apply more turns initially. If the lead is not good, extra turns may ride over one another and lock up. A good lead can allow up to four turns to be clapped on then rattled round as you gather in the slack. If in doubt, use a single turn to grab the slack, then lay on more turns as the load begins to build. Four turns is enough for most situations on all but the largest yachts.

Tailing manually

When you can no longer pull in the rope around the winch, it's time to begin winding. The tension on the turns must now be maintained. If you're strong enough, you can do this with one hand while winding with the other, working the tailing hand along the rope to keep it near the winch barrel. Where two hands are needed for full power, a second crew person must tail the winch, unless it is a 'self-tailer'.

Self-tailing winches

These have a circular device on the top to grab the bight of a rope fed into it off the barrel. The bight strips off after it has been round once, allowing the winch to feed continually through the 'jaws' of the self-tailer. It is common practice to leave a loaded line in a self-tailer rather than belay it on a cleat as one would with a conventional winch. This is slack practice, since it can be knocked out of the jaws. The best answer is to flip an additional 'safety turn' over the top once cranking has finished.

Self-tailing winch

Winding a winch

To achieve the maximum from what your body has to offer, place yourself over the top of a winch as you wind it, ideally, so that you are literally looking straight down the middle of the barrel. This may involve for a sheet winch the inconvenience of standing with one foot outside the cockpit coaming, but the alternative of trying to crank it at arm's length is a feeble substitute.

Easing rope around a loaded winch

If loading is light, you can safely take turns off a winch progressively until the rope can be eased by slackening up the tail and letting it slide round the barrel. Loads can build up surprisingly however, and trying to do this on a windy day with a genoa sheet is the road to trouble. The sheet will stay put as you start to slack up, then suddenly grab a foot or two, in the process of creating a riding turn or catching someone's fingers. The safe technique, known as 'cracking the sheet' because of the noise it makes; is to place the flat of one hand firmly on the turns while slacking away the tail with the other, perhaps helping them round the barrel with a cupped palm. Once the worst of the strain is off, turns can be removed sensibly as required.

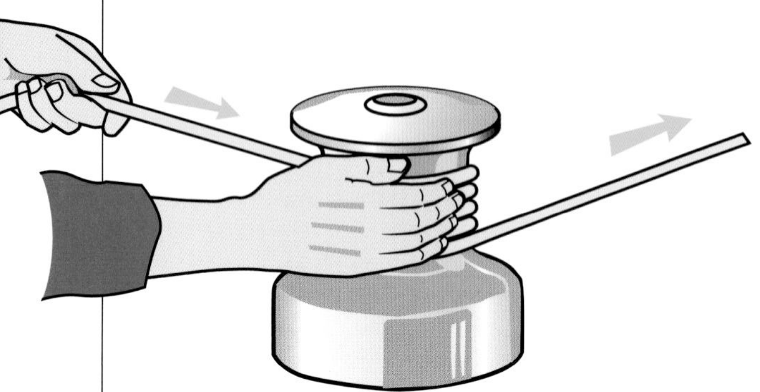

Powered winches

On larger yachts, many winches are driven by electric motors. The better ones have manual backup in case of battery failure. These winches are extremely powerful and the utmost care must be taken when using them. The global advice to watch the load not the winch lest you do damage is emphatically applicable here. If confronted by an electric winch, look for the activating switch which generally has a flip-up cover of some sort. If the winch is a self-tailer, even greater vigilance is needed. Winches can also be powered hydraulically, although these are rarer.

Riding turns

These come about when the neat turns on a winch barrel are forced over the top of one another so that neither end can be eased. Two solutions are common. The first is to take the bitter end to another winch and literally wind the riding turns out. The second is to hitch a stopper knot onto the bight of the loaded line using a rolling hitch (see page 41), take the strain on this, either by a winch or a tackle, and unwrap the mess once the load is off the winch.

Tackles

Unlike 'ground tackle' (anchors and chain) which is articulated as it is spelt, the pulley systems on ships were traditionally pronounced as 'tayckles'. In the days before the universal adoption of winches, they were the seaman's primary tool for upping the power. One end is fixed, the other is attached to the load and moves with the pull. Power is defined by the velocity ratio, just as it is with the teeth on a pair of gear wheels. In the case of the tackle, the ratio divides the distance moved by the load into the length of rope being pulled through the tackle. The ratio is equal to the number of parts of rope involved at the moving block. All tackles can be rove to advantage, in which case the block with the most parts is at the moving end, or to disadvantage with this block stationary.

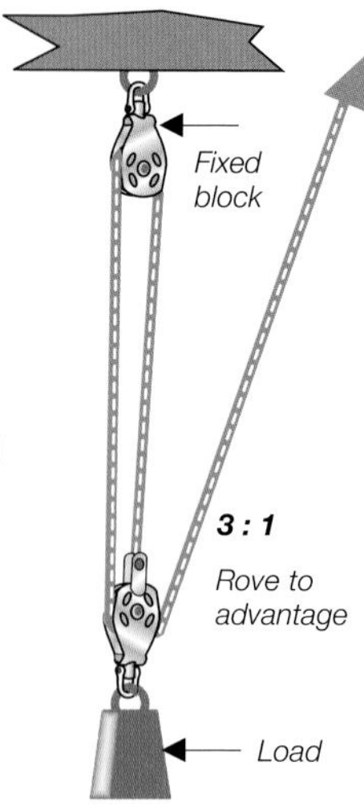

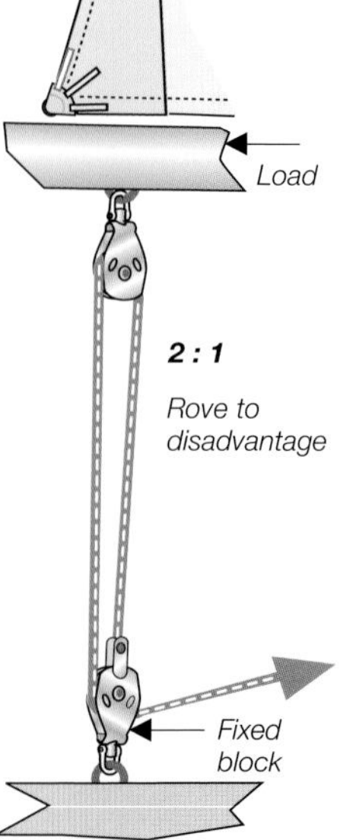

In theory, it is hard to imagine why anyone would reeve up a tackle to disadvantage, but in practice it often renders the pull more convenient or the end more readily made fast. A mainsheet on a cockpit traveller is a case in point. These are invariably rove to disadvantage because the bottom block needs to carry the jamming cleat, so the sheet must exit from the tackle here. If it were the other way up (rove to advantage) the hauling end would emanate from the block on the boom end and be unworkable. A typical kicking strap is another example.

Friction in tackles

The theoretical power of a tackle does not increase infinitely with the number of sheaves in the blocks. A certain amount of friction exists in even the simplest system and, as the sheaves multiply, this builds up with them until a traditional tackle begins to run out of steam at around 6 : 1. Modern bearings and floppy ropes have done much to ease this failing, but it still exists.

Climbing the mast

Except in specialised traditional craft, the days when sailors swarmed up to the yards on ratlines are over. Patent systems now exist to help singlehanders, and any boat where a crew member cannot be hoisted up the mast by a third party must investigate these. For the overwhelming majority, however, the way aloft is via a helping hoist and a bosun's chair.

The bosun's chair – Sitting in a bosun's chair is a self-explanatory affair. The chair is hoisted by means of a halyard that is generally shackled to its lifting ring. Try to avoid snap shackles if at all possible, but if there's no choice, tape it shut just to be sure. For obvious reasons, there is a long tradition that the person to be hoisted must rig his or her own chair.

The hoist – Choose a halyard which can somehow be led to a winch strong enough for the job. If a powered winch is available, so much the better, but where the power source is the anchor windlass some creative leading via turning blocks may be required to lead the tail to the barrel. Once the climber is as high as necessary, make the halyard fast with the greatest care, then stand by it in case someone who is not aware of what's going on should cast it off.

Safety line – If possible, also rig a spare halyard to the chair and take up the slack on this as the hoist progresses to provide a safety net against the unthinkable.

Take your weight – Winching a heavy person aloft is a tough job. Unless the winch is powered, whoever is winding it will be more than grateful for all the help they can get. The person going aloft should do all possible to assist by 'climbing' up a spare halyard, or the standing rigging.

Look aloft – The winch grinder must look aloft as much as possible while still maintaining full concentration to keep the turns safely on the winch. It is very easy to wind the climber into a diminishing gap where shrouds come in to the mast, especially with a powered winch.

Communicate – Maintain communication between wincher and climber. On a very tall mast, this might have to be by prearranged signals, but since both are engaged on the same job, they should work together.

Stand from under – Never hang around beneath a person working aloft, and if it's you up there and you drop something, hail the deck with the age-old cry, 'Stand from under!'

Boat handling

Drying out

Anyone sailing in tidal waters will sooner or later have to consider the option of floating the boat into a berth at High Water then letting her dry out as the water recedes. This process is simple for a boat without vulnerable projections and that's able to stand upright. However it demands careful planning and bold execution if the vessel is not a natural bottom-sitter. Certain issues are common to all craft taking the ground.

Nature of the bottom

Being forewarned about this is critical to any drying-out operation.

Soft mud If mud is soft enough and clear of submerged debris, almost any boat will sit down in it reasonably comfortably. Even a deep-keeled yacht will work herself into the bottom over a few tides so that she digs herself a snug berth. If you are anchoring and expect to be marginally placed for depth at Low Water, consider the bottom. Is it charted as mud? If so, you will probably sink in and lift off again with the rising tide, never knowing it's happened. If it is rock or gravel, go somewhere else!

Medium soft Many harbour bottoms have a layer of mud over sterner stuff, in which case ask locally or study a good pilot book to ascertain the real state of affairs.

Hard standing This means you can have confidence that the boat will not sink in beyond an inch or two, so full drying-out practices must be deployed. Hard standing is great for scrubbing the boat, inspecting stern gear, etc.

The dockside

For a boat that must lean against something, the nature of the dockside must be understood.

Walls A clean, unobstructed wall is the ideal, but this is not often found. Walls are commonly reinforced with piling, and the position and size of these must be taken into account when selecting a berth.

Free-standing piles In many places, stand-alone piles are driven into the half-tide foreshore specifically for boats to dry out against. In such berths, the tide may set across the boat as she is drying out, so care is needed to make sure she stays in place and does not slew round.

Shelter

Never dry out in a berth that might become an open lee shore. Serious damage can be done by pounding as the time approaches where you are irreversibly committed or, worse still, just before you finally float off. The same caveat applies to berths where motorboat wash may be excessive.

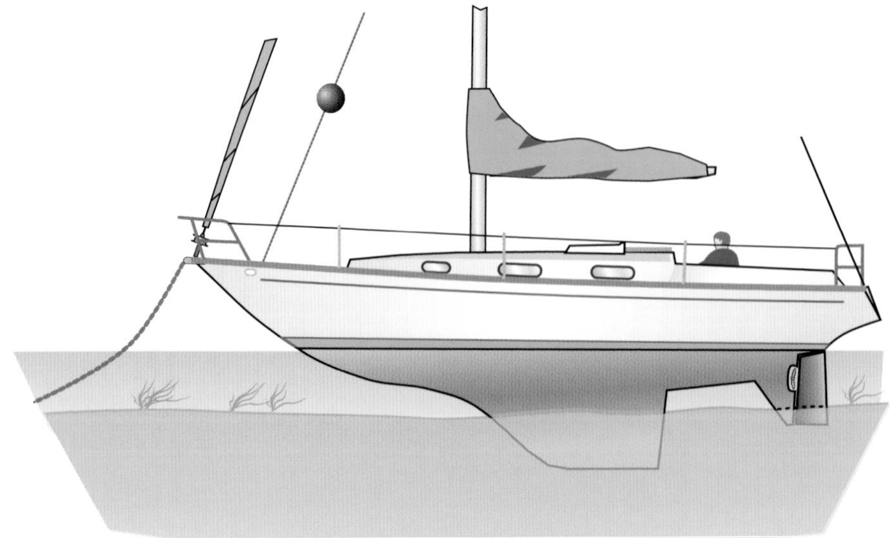

Half-dried out in soft mud at low water.

Power craft

There is no special magic about drying out most power craft, but it is vital to understand the nature of rudders and stern gear. Both may be vulnerable. Indeed, they may deter drying out at all. On some boats, however, the rudders are strongly mounted and protect the screws.

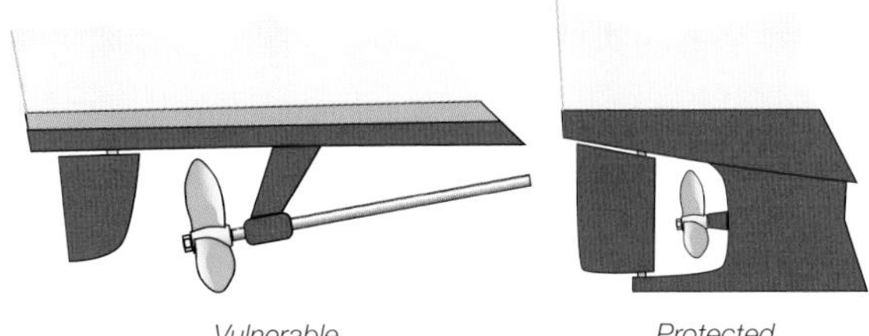

Vulnerable *Protected*

Bilge-keeled sailing yachts

Make sure the bottom is clear of obstructions, check that you can get ashore once the water has gone away, and that's it. The worst thing that can happen is that one keel finds a soft spot and you end up heeled over a little way.

Drying out alongside

Deep-keeled sailing yachts

With legs A deep-keeler with bolt-on beaching 'legs' is essentially the same as a bilge-keeler. Both can settle on any ground that is reasonably flat and of uniform firmness. However, the legs are there to keep the boat more or less upright on her keel and many prove inadequate to carry her full weight if she should lean hard over onto a single one. So long as care is taken about where to lie, this should not happen, but if you dry out beam-on to a steep slope, or with one leg in soft ground, the worst may come to pass. Wherever possible, it pays to inspect the bottom at Low Water before committing yourself.

Without legs Drying out a yacht leaning against a wall looks frightening, but in practice there is surprisingly little to it, given a strongly built craft with a long keel or reasonable fore-and-aft length along the base of the fin. The trick is to ensure that she leans in at a safe angle. Not enough will render her potentially unstable. Too much, and her weight will crush her toe rails and stanchions. Step-by-step, here's how it works:

- Bring the boat in near the top of the tide to give yourself time to prepare.
- Secure fore and aft; rig plenty of strong fenders.
- To induce a slight heel, run a halyard to the shore and take up all the slack. Alternatively, stack weight along the side deck nearest the wall. A deep-keeled motor fishing vessel type of yacht may not have adequate halyards, but much can be achieved by shifting anchors, cable and water cans into the right place.
- As the tide falls, keep taking up the slack on the halyard and tend the lines to hold the boat tight against the wall. If she lies too far off, she will incline in too much when dry.
- As soon as she touches, crank up the halyard and keep watching the lines. Most boats change their fore-and-aft trim as they dry out, so you may have to ease bow or stern. Maintain that close-in position. You'll get plenty of heel later as the fenders begin compressing.
- If the boat has a fin keel, there is a chance now that she will either 'pray' by nodding forward, or 'squat' by lowering herself aft onto her rudder. If this looks like a possibility, take lines up to the dock from a suitable strong point and bowse them bar taut. The loads will be substantial, but so long as the lines are set up onto something whose strength is above suspicion, all will be well. Fortunately, praying and squatting are by no means common.
- The boat should end up securely heeled at not much more than 5°. Keep the halyard made up for security, and stand by to tend it and the docklines as she floats off again, because they will have tightened them as she went down.

Towing

Any boat may sooner or later be involved with towing. The skills break down into those of the tug and the tow, with different arrangements required at sea and in harbour.

At sea

The main issues for towing at sea revolve around keeping snatch and chafe in the tow-line to a minimum. Steering also requires some consideration.

Snatch and tow length A rope is more likely to break under a snatch load than a steady heave, especially if its integrity has been eroded by chafe during a prolonged tow. Because of its high stretch potential and good overall strength, nylon makes by far the best towline. When it snatches, as it surely will from time to time, the spring in the line takes the sting out of the situation. Keeping the towrope as long as practicable also helps reduce the danger of snatching. If the longest suitable cordage available is proving too short, a weight such as a spare anchor strung onto it halfway between the two vessels may ease things, although care must be taken to avoid chafe from the hanging point. If need be, inspect this through binoculars racked right down for close-in work.

Passing the towline

Two vessels small enough to be thrown around by the waves should avoid coming alongside one another at sea, if possible. If there is no other way of passing the rope, rig all available fenders, then some extra padding. Sailing craft can often find a sail bag or two; power boats might consider cushions or whatever else they can find, but whatever is used must be big enough to stay put when the boats pitch around. Conventional fenders often pop out with expensive consequences. A better plan is to heave a light line which can then be used to pass the towrope. The boat doing the heaving should be to windward, and the ideal heaving line is light with a heavy knot on the end. In extreme conditions a floating line can sometimes be drifted down to a casualty, attaching a fender to provide extra windage.

Heaving lines

The way to heave any line, large or small, is as follows:

- Coil carefully clockwise, so that each coil is on top of the one before it.
- Either secure the bitter end or stand on it.
- Pick up the coil in two hands, dividing it about fifty-fifty.
- Right-handers throw the right-hand coil – 'underarm or overarm' technique to suit age and athleticism – releasing the other immediately afterwards. Left-handers vice-versa.
- The towrope is bent on with a single or double sheet (see page 42) bend and pulled across.

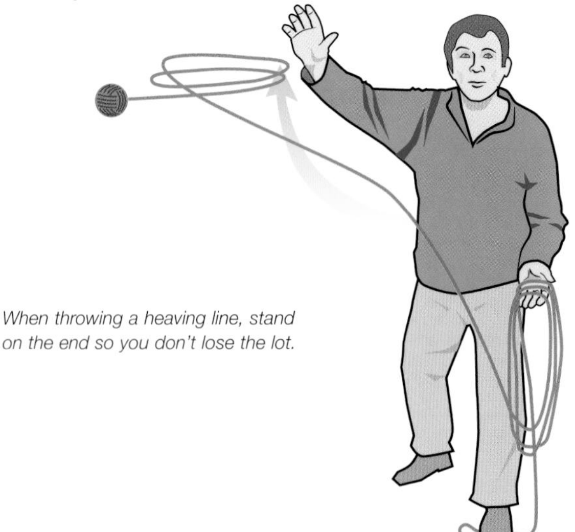

When throwing a heaving line, stand on the end so you don't lose the lot.

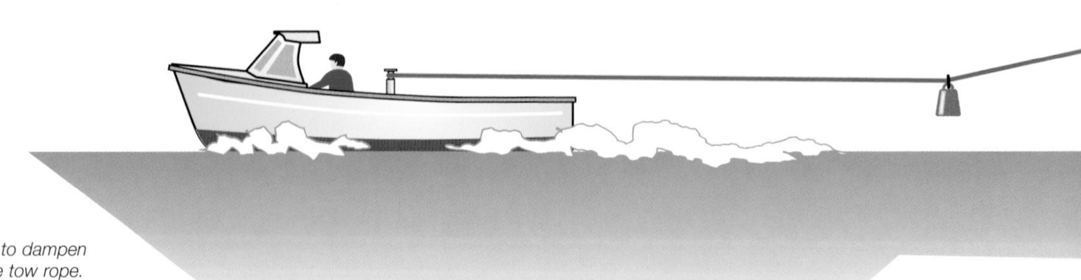

Using a weight to dampen snatching in the tow rope.

Securing the towline

On both vessels, the essentials for securing a line must be followed. Under tow it is doubly vital that the rope can be eased or slipped under a full working load.

An ideal towing point

Towing vessel

Attaching the tow All traditional single-screw tugboats from ocean salvage monsters to yard launches tow from a point around amidships. This allows their sterns to swivel in response to rudder movements, enabling them to steer unencumbered by the tow. Few non-dedicated small craft have such facilities, and steering is inevitably compromised by a single attachment point above or even abaft the rudder post. There is little to be done about this, but if you anticipate steering difficulties and understand them, you can use whatever possibilities exist to minimise the issue.

Modern sailing craft because of their backstays have no cleat or bollard amidships aft and many motorboats are similarly hampered. The answer is to rig a bridle from the quarters then attach the towline to the middle of it. If quarter fairleads are available, using these and leading the bridle ends to a pair of primary cockpit winches may do well. Whatever the towing points, it pays to share the load by passing a line forward from them to some secure point, then bowsing it taut.

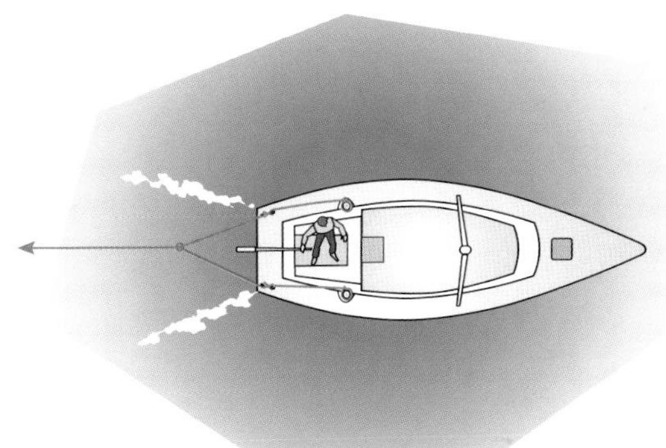

A good compromise - the towing bridle

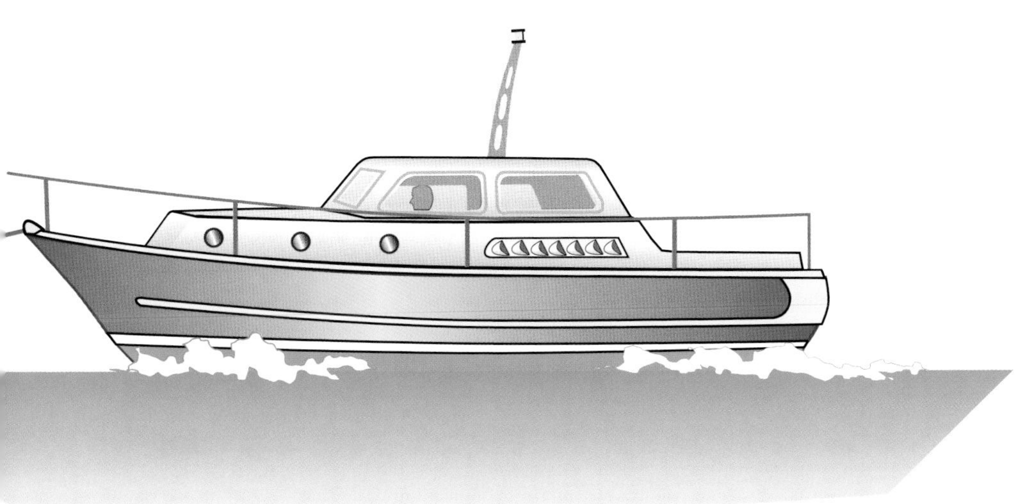

The towed vessel

Attaching the tow As in the 'tug', the tow must take all possible care to spread the load of the towline. If it is to be attached to a foredeck cleat, windlass or bollard, a sailing boat can do this easily by securing an additional line to the attachment point and cranking it aft with the sheet winches. Motorboats must think laterally. Sailing craft with the mast intact may choose to secure to this, but only if it is keel-stepped. Deck-stepped spars have been wrenched out of their tabernacles by loads for which they were never designed to take.

Chafe While chafe may affect the tug, it is the tow that takes the brunt of this number one enemy of successful towing. The towline will come aboard over the bow, typically through a roller or a fairlead. Whatever its lead, try to rig chafe protection of some sort. Ideally, slide a length of armoured plastic hose (such as is specified for cockpit drains or heads) over the bitter end and work it down to the fairlead. If the bight is already fast and under load, cut this in a spiral and slide it on that way, but although this is better than nothing, it will probably work loose and require regular attention. Heavy cloth can be used, or anything else you can contrive, but a well-found boat will always have a length of suitable hose for just such an emergency. Old-fashioned canvas / rubber fire hose is a workable alternative. If a bowsprit is making the lead impossible, try rigging a towing bridle from both sides of the bow (ensuring that it is secured for instant release), making the towline fast around the bight of this, then easing it far out ahead.

Under way

Towing vessel

- Take the strain as gently as possible, expect the tow to take a while to accelerate up to speed, and be ready for all sorts of snatching if a sea is running.
- Monitor the tow, the towline and its attachment at all times.
- Proceed at a sensible speed, bearing in mind the strains that the tow is putting on both craft. Never tow a boat at, or nearly at, its hull speed, especially if it is a powerful motorboat. A fair guide for a sailing yacht is around the speed she could probably make to windward, which will be about $^{3}/_{4}$ of her theoretical maximum – say 6 knots tow speed for a 40-footer. If the tow is a shallow-draught power vessel watch her wake. If the wave starts building up under the stern, slow down.

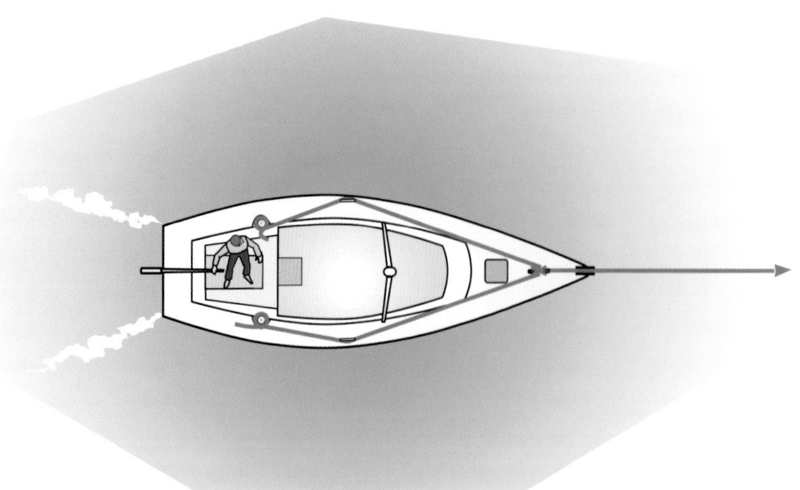

A forward cleat may not be strong enough. Lines taken back to sheet winches will help take the strain.

Towed vessel

- Monitor chafe.
- Note how the speed of the tow is proceeding, and communicate with the towing vessel if need be.
- In general, steer towards the stern of the towing vessel.
- In a following sea, steer with care because your vessel may well surge from side to side.
- Where the tow's rudder is lost or jammed she will probably yaw from side to side, sometimes violently. Dragging a drogue (either purpose-built or otherwise contrived) from her stern will help keep her in line. If things become impossible and the rudder has gone altogether, towing her slowly stern-first may solve the issue.
- Sailing dinghies should tow with the centreboard 'up'.

In harbour

Towing alongside

At sea, persuading a towed vessel to lose way is not a priority. In harbour it may be central to safety. The answer is to tow alongside, secured together in such a way that when the towing vessel takes off way by running her engine astern, the tow follows suit.

- Secure fore and aft with breast ropes and springs. Keep all lines tight. The springs take the strain, while the breasts serve to keep things in line.
- The secret of control is to rig the tug so that her stern projects beyond the casualty. If this is not done, manoeuvrability when turning is restricted by lack of leverage. If the tug is too short to do this realistically, at least be aware that steering will be less than ideal.
- As at sea, maintain communication. Both boats should steer together whether proceeding ahead or astern.

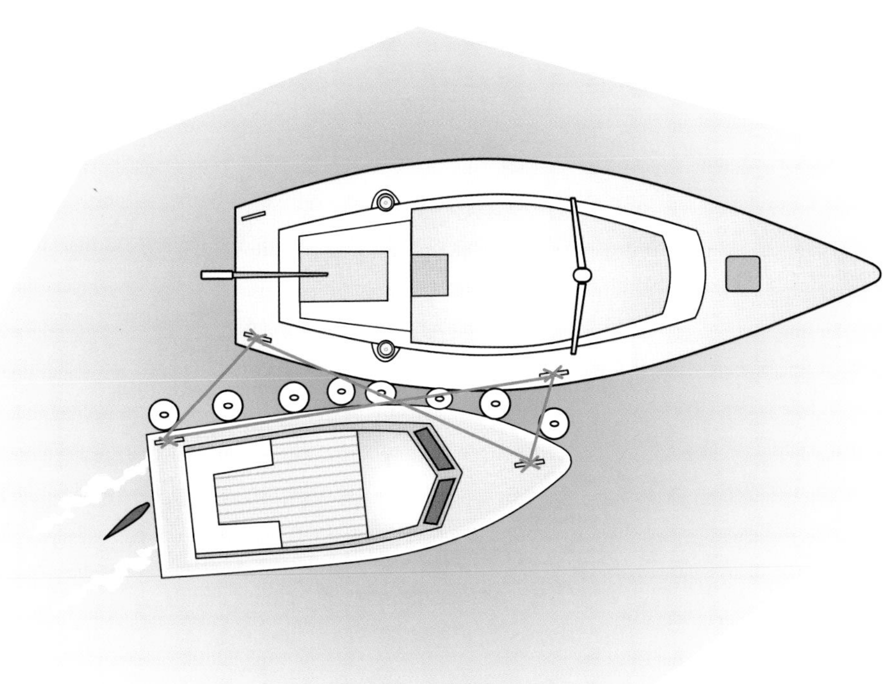

When towing from alongside rig really strong springs and use plenty of fenders.

Manoeuvring and berthing

The seaman's eye

The seaman's eye is hard to define, but if you don't have it, your exercises are doomed to failure in strong winds or tides. The success of any manoeuvre depends on the vessel going into it from the right place at a suitable speed. Unlike road vehicles which operate on a stable surface, a boat in a beam wind is stalled and skidding from the moment she leaves her berth until she has gained enough way for her keel to start working (see page 63). If the water is tidal or subject to currents, the whole 'road' is in motion, so she is not going where she is pointing even after she has gathered way. Understanding how much she will slide, how to use the tendency, how to prevent it, and knowing which is best, is half the battle. The rest is being able to judge any developing situations by eye.

Wind awareness and apparent wind

Knowing the wind's direction is always important. When a boat loses most of her way and it's blowing hard, it becomes vital. Everyone knows that you can find the wind direction by looking at a handy flag, but while this is true for bunting hoisted ashore or a burgee aboard an anchored vessel, on a moving boat it will give a false reading because of 'apparent wind'.

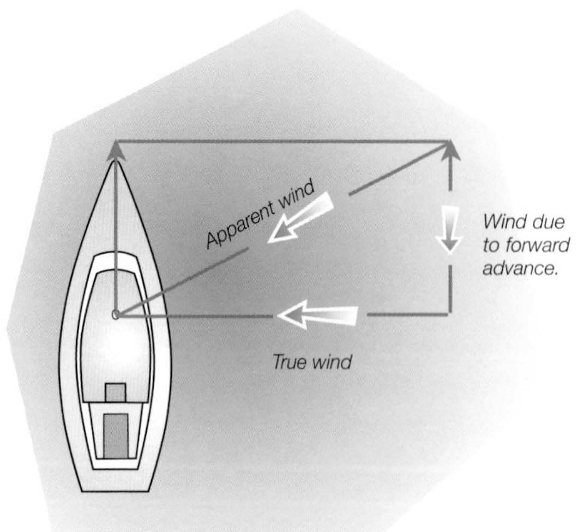

A boat motoring through still air generates an apparent wind across her deck, equal and opposite to her motion through the air. If a wind is blowing over the water, this combines with the wind created by the boat's motion to form a resultant apparent wind. Unless the boat is on a dead run, the apparent wind usually blows from forward of the true wind direction. Apparant wind is the wind registered by every flag or wind arrow on board, or by any electronic instrument whose readout has not been modified by a processor to deliver true wind speed and direction.

Being able to sort out true from apparent wind is important for sailing boats manoeuvring, but it can also be useful for high-speed motor boats taking off way in preparation for an awkward arrival alongside in a strong crosswind.

In the absence of direct evidence from the shore, the best way of detecting the true wind is by reading the small ripples it puffs onto the water — not the waves, which are subject to other forces. But like the ripples on a bowl of soup when you blow to cool it, the wind ripples run at right-angles to the airflow. Recognising them takes time and practice, but the time taken is very well spent.

Spotting the current or stream

'Mark 1 Eyeball' is the best instrument. Only resort to the tide tables when all else has failed.

Moored or alongside, just look over the rail. Manoeuvring free, note how moored vessels are lying. This is generally 'head-up' to the moving water, although a strong wind may modify their attitude. In the absence of other craft, check the 'bow waves' on piles, buoys or anything else attached to the seabed. If there aren't any 'bow waves' and the shore is reasonably close, lay the boat as nearly across the suspected current as you can. You'll spot your drift by noting how the immediate shore line appears to slip sideways against its background.

Stalling speed and bare pole performance

Any boat, power or sail, only fully resists sideways motion when under way. As she slows, there comes a point at which the keel or her general sideways resistance stalls. The velocity of this varies greatly between a deep-keeled, traditional yacht, a short-finned fast cruiser and a shoal-draught motor boat, but they all have a rate of knots at which the rudder in a cross wind stops working. Knowing this pace is vital for a neat manoeuvre on a windy day; understanding how fast she will slide to leeward is also valuable ground-base information. An awareness of how she will end up in relation to the wind if left to her own devices is also indispensable. Here's how to discover these factors:

- Pick a stretch of sheltered water with a bit of sea room and a stiff breeze blowing across it. Lay the boat square across the wind under power and take her out of gear so that she loses way steadily (*a*).
- Note the speed at which you have to steer 'up' to keep her straight, and how fast she's going when you can no longer prevent her falling off the wind. If you haven't a speed log, so much the better. Your relationship with the boat at this stage is more about feel than about numbers (*b*).
- Now see how little throttle you need apply to regain control using the rudder. This is the pivotal factor in slow manoeuvring (*c*).

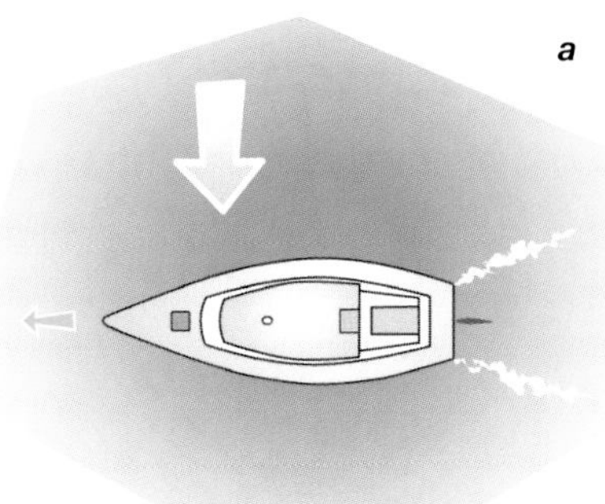

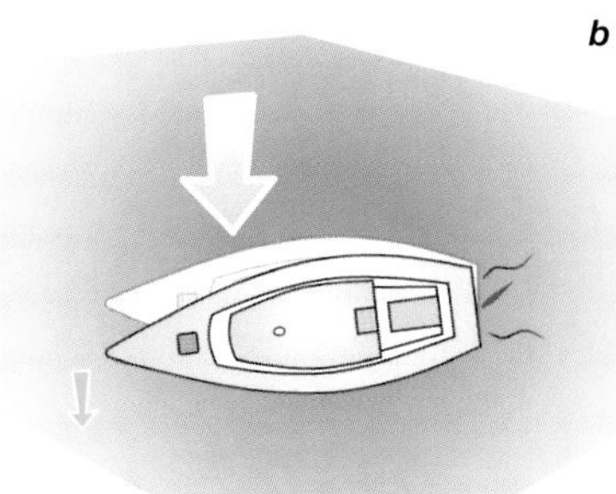

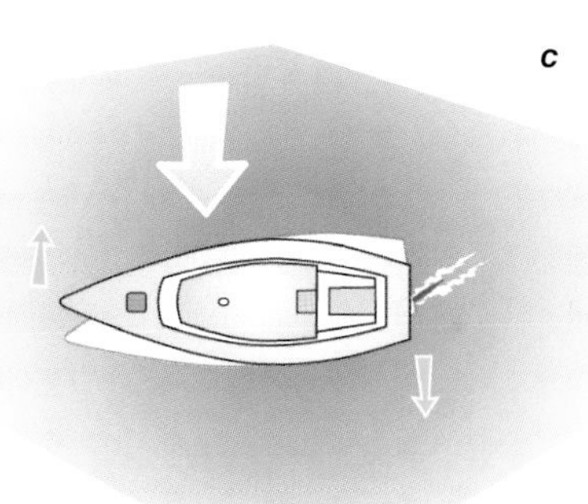

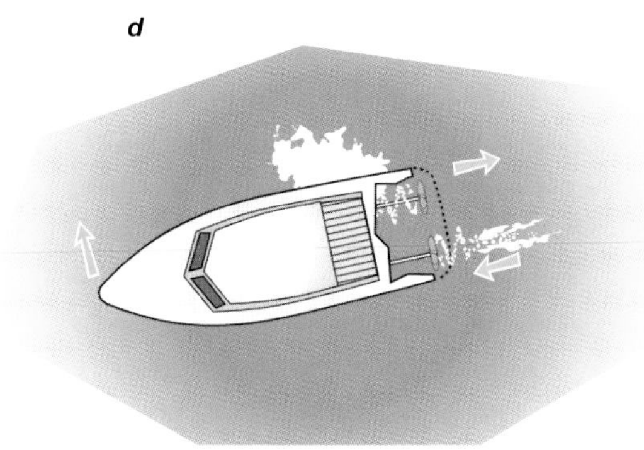

- A twin-screw vessel can achieve the same result with only modest application of ahead and astern on opposing engines, but be aware that while this may bring her back into line, it may not stop her sliding sideways unless she starts moving ahead a little (*d*).
- Next, try the same exercise with the bow pointing much closer to the wind and compare results.
- Finally, run the boat dead before the wind and take her out of gear. She may well go straight indefinitely under the windage of her superstructure. If so, take way off by running the engine astern and start again. See how far up towards the wind you can steer 'under bare poles' without having to resort to putting the engine into gear to hold control.

Berthing under power

Alongside

Berthing in any vessel short of a small ship relies in general upon the deployment of four lines. Depending on the length of dock available and the nature of the deck hardware, these may vary in detail. Note that the spring lines may be called by different names. The bow spring, for example, can be given the name 'backspring'. Some authorities describe a backspring as leading aft from a midships cleat or bollard, while others say it leads forward from aft. The 'fore spring / backspring' nomenclature is far from the universal favourite among small craft sailors although some with a naval background may prefer it. Whichever term you adopt, make sure the crew is in no doubt what you mean. The terminology in general used by small-boat and yacht seamen is set out below:

- Bow line — runs forward from near the bow to the dock. Its functions are to keep the boat alongside and to stop the boat moving aft.
- Stern line — leads aft from the stern, keeping the boat in and stopping her moving ahead.
- Bow spring — leads aft from the bow or 'shoulder' of the boat. Generally secured ashore somewhere abaft amidships, it serves to stop the boat surging ahead, helps to pin the bow in, and can also be used to help in manoeuvring.
- Stern spring — leads forward from the quarter, mirroring the bow spring.

This arrangement of lines allows full control of the boat whether alongside a pontoon in sheltered water or a tidal wall on a windy day.

Short docks

Where the length of available dock does not permit full-length bow and stern lines, 'breast lines' are used instead. The task of stopping the boat surging fore and aft is then taken by the springlines. The breasts serve merely to keep bow and stern in.

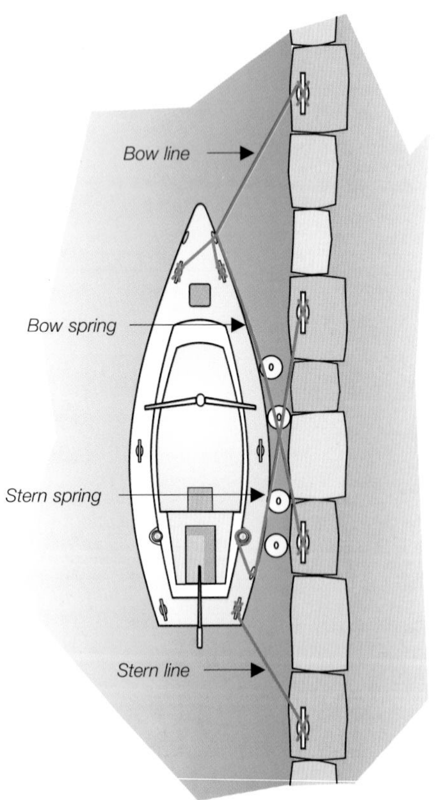

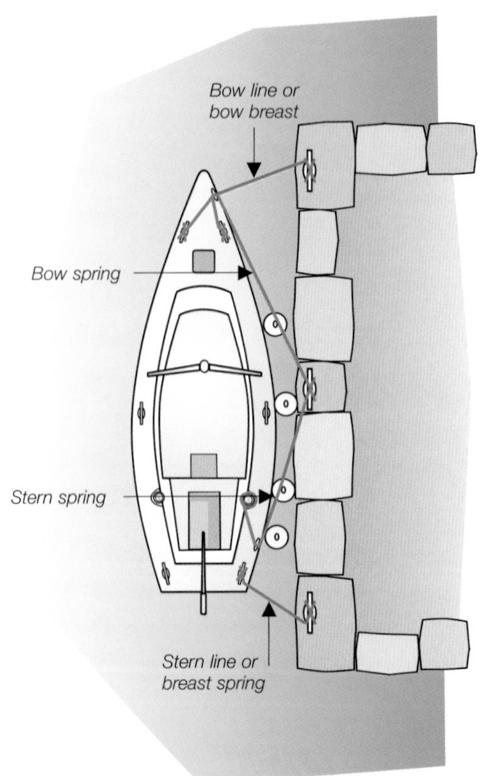

Short docks – the 'midships alternative'

Many yachts and motor boats have a midships cleat or fairlead. This has a number of uses, but it is often abused by the myth that its main purpose is to run springs. On a marina berth, leading spring lines from this cleat can stop the boat surging fore and aft perfectly well, so long as the bow and stern lines are rigged as breast ropes. Their additional inward pull will then compensate for the lack of springs to bow and quarter. In a livelier situation, a midships spring does not serve nearly so well as a full spring from forward or aft, because if bow and stern lines are rigged rather than breasts, it may prove impossible to persuade the boat to lie parallel to the dock.

A midships spring line is useless for manoeuvring a boat off a dock (see page 74), but a short line from amidships can be as good as an extra hand when used properly (see page 75).

Fendering

Fenders should be as large as you can carry. They are always a nuisance on board, and tiny ones may work after a fashion in a marina, but when fendering is really needed only serious ones will do. For an appropriately secured forty-footer, three between boat and dock should be plenty, with a fourth on stand-by for extreme conditions. The more the merrier, of course, but shipping four big ones is a much better than eight small ones.

Lanyards Fender lanyards should be long, strong, and light enough to knot easily. Ideally, they will be hitched to the guardrails in way of the stanchions so that the weight does not drag the wires down in unseemly bights. At least one fender should be capable of being strung from both ends to protect the vessel against piling when no fender boards are available.

Fender Boards Where yachts are obliged to lie against piled walls a 'fender board' must be rigged. This is secured to the boat, the fenders are hung inside it, and the board takes the rub. Harbour authorities sometimes offer boards to their customers, but in areas where such docks are commonplace it pays to carry your own.

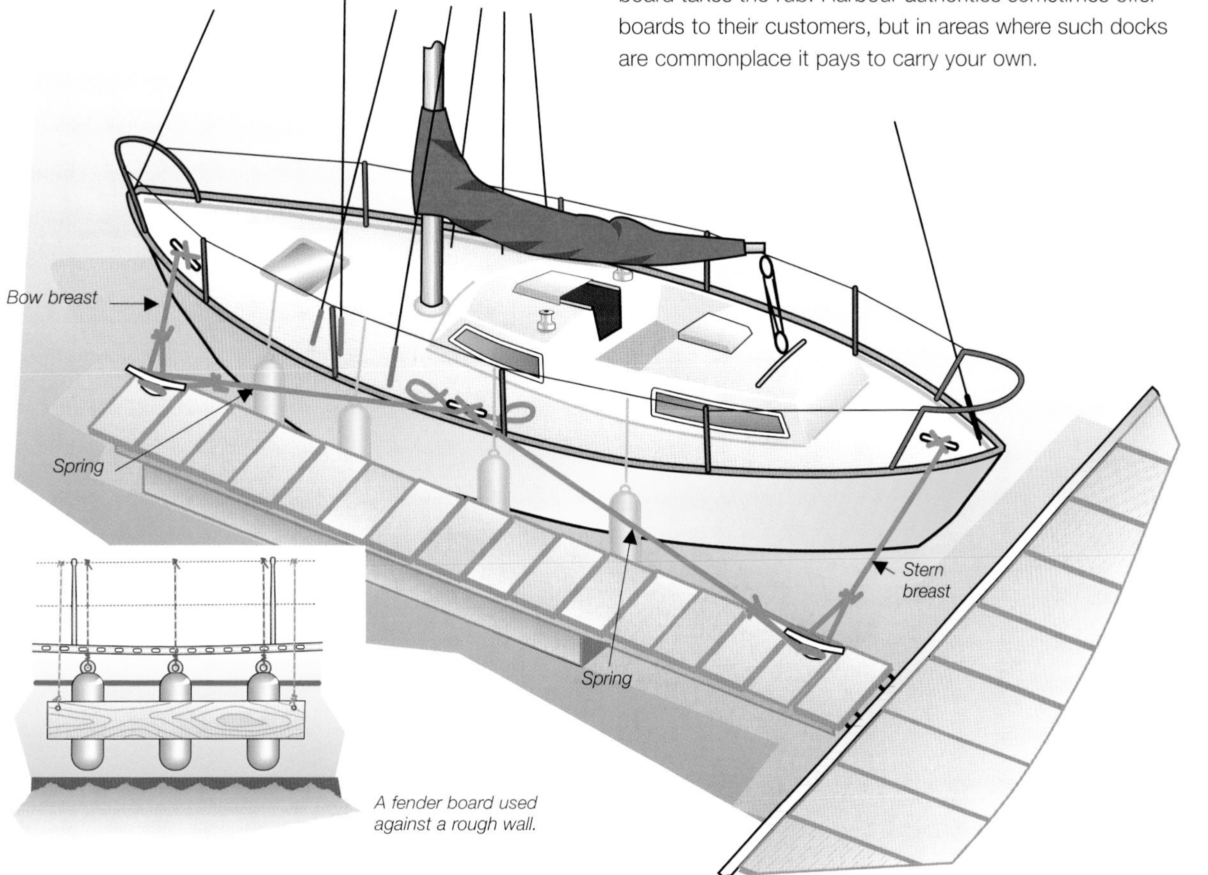

A fender board used against a rough wall.

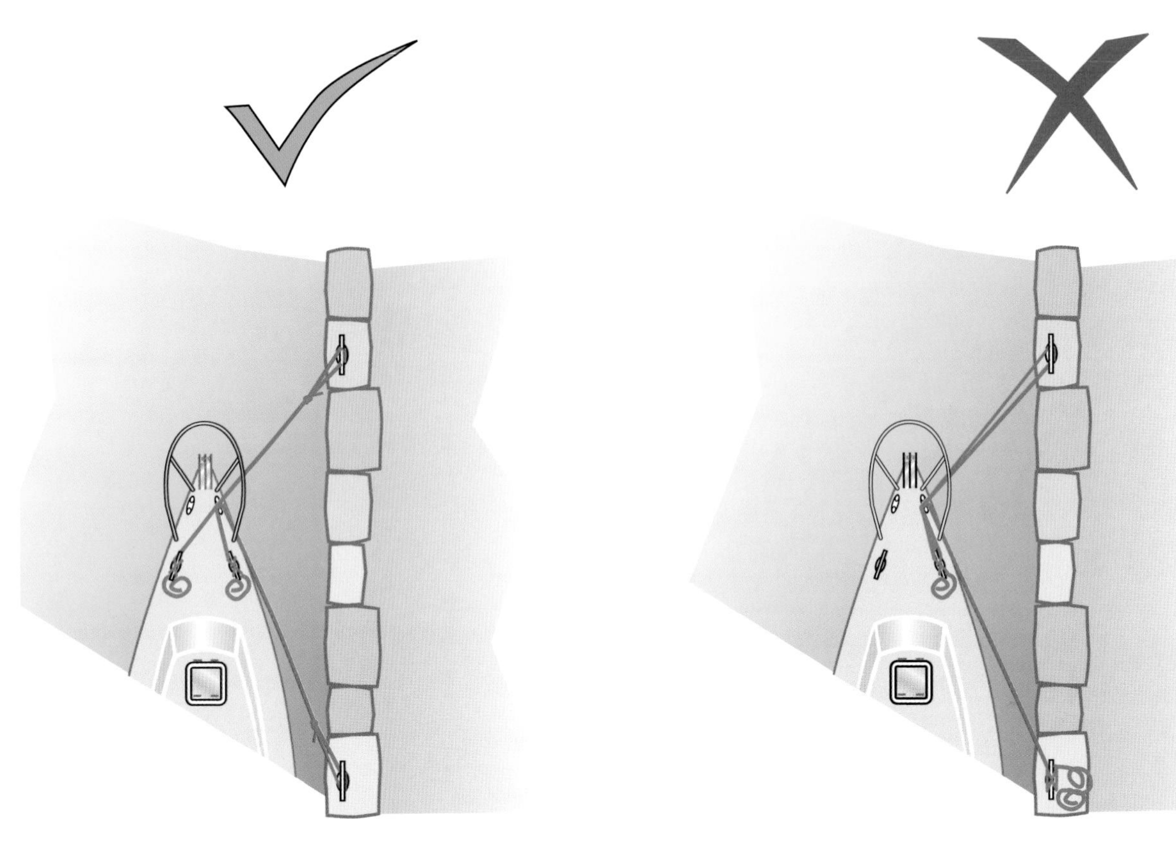

Rope handling

One cleat, one job – The practice of securing one rope on top of another on mooring cleats ashore or on board is to be avoided. It's even chances that when you need to adjust one of two ropes made up on the same cleat, yours will be the one underneath. If the upper line is loaded up, you're in an impossible situation. Always try to find a spare cleat, a winch barrel, a windlass drum, or anything else that is strong.

One rope, one job Using a rope to double as a bow line and bow spring, for example, is unseamanlike. It may be convenient, but it makes securing alongside far more cumbersome. When its bight is made fast, converting one shore line into two, all manner of nonsense results when one end is loaded and the other needs adjustment. 'One rope one job, one cleat one rope', and the boat is under perfect control no matter what may happen.

Ends ashore Big ships always take the ends of their mooring lines ashore. The reasons for doing this are equally sound for smaller craft. First, no untidy mess is left on the dock for people to trip over, to kick inadvertently into the water, or even to hack off and steal. Secondly, 'ends ashore' means that a single length of line secures the ship to that cleat or bollard. Third and perhaps most importantly, the end can be made up into a bowline and looped over the shore cleat. If more than one rope falls to the cleat, the loops can be dipped through one another which allows them to be lifted independently, however this cannot be done if they have been cleated off. To say that a bowline cannot be let off under load in this context is false because, so long as the bight of the line is secured on board in a seamanlike manner, it can always be tended, no matter what the conditions. By slacking this away, no circumstances exist where the bowline could not be lifted off.

Finally, and quite simply, once this system is in place and a crew understand and have practised it, it remains by far the easiest way to do the job.

Tidal walls

Securing alongside a marina berth is a set-piece. A wall with a substantial rise and fall of tide presents more of a challenge. Clearly, when the boat is high on the top of the tide, her lines will be shorter than when she has dropped down to Low Water. Extreme cases of this such as the mighty walls of the southern Channel Islands are now rare. Most areas of big tidal activity are served by at least some sort of floating pontoon arrangement. Nonetheless, twenty-foot ranges are still by no means unknown.

The essential step is to make your shorelines as long as you sensibly can. The geometry is simple, the further away the bollard, the less the line will change its angle as the tide falls. If rings are set into the wall near the High Water line, use these rather than dockside bollards to lessen the changing angle, but secure with a long bowline so that you can reach the knot if the ring may become submerged. Even a stout ladder rung can be pressed into service for a spring line, so long as it is carefully checked for structure and condition first. This also removes the chances of chafe where the line scuffs over the lip of the dock wall, but whatever your arrangements, you must stand by the boat as she drops down and be ready to slack away.

Sound practice in shore-line discipline now really pays off, because any one of them could come tight with several tons of yacht on the end of it. To be hung up by one's own lines is the final horror and embarrassment for many a sailor. Especially one who has failed to pay attention to how the lines are secured.

Neutralising a long shore-line Sometimes, finding a way of making some of the lines fast ashore below dock level (see illustration below) will ensure that no further tending is required. Even in this happy state, if the lines are long enough to accommodate her at Low Water she may still drift out from the wall at the top of the tide, perhaps damaging herself as her springs fail to function properly. In such instances, and in the absence of volunteer ship keepers, try rigging a weight such as a full water can halfway along the line to take up the slack. It may just suffice to give you 'all night in'.

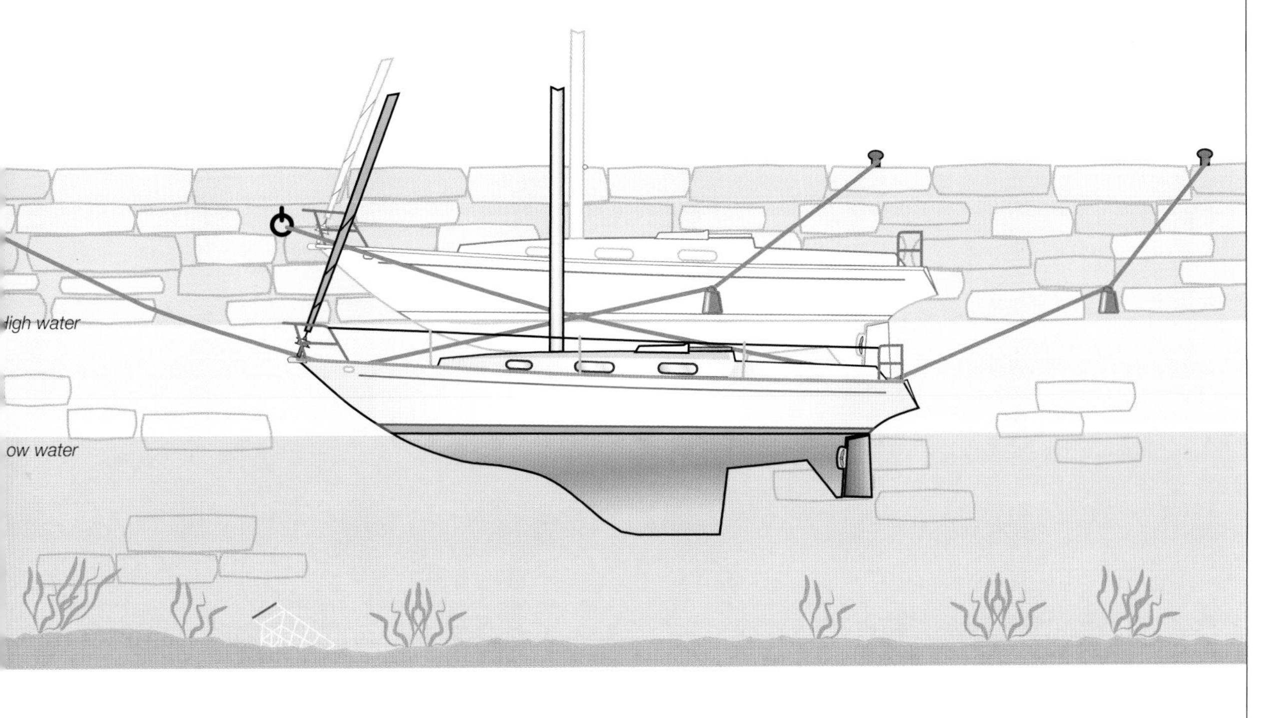

The dynamics of coming alongside

Fully crewed Remember, it's 'one rope, one cleat, one job', so rig at least the first two lines in advance with bowlines ready on the ends that will go ashore, if there are bollards or cleats. Consider how much line you'll need when the boat is secured, take half as much again, then make the bight fast aboard. Lead the lines through any fairleads, pulpits, guardrails etc, and pass them to the two 'jumpers', stationed around amidships. They will take the first pair of lines ashore as the boat swings in to lie alongside. Stepping onto the dock, they drop their bowlines over the respective cleats or secure to rings. Designated crew members take up the slack on board. In gentle conditions, there is no need to make the bights fast on board before stepping off. This is a safety precaution in case things go wrong and the person ashore needs to take a turn to hold the boat. The other two lines can now be run out.

Note that if the yacht needs pulling in to the dock, the end is still made up ashore and the heaving is done from aboard. It is bad manners to expect anyone else to haul your boat around.

Which lines first? In slack water, bow and stern lines are run first. If a strong stream is running and you are coming in bows-up, secure bow line and stern spring so that the boat can settle back evenly onto them. Keep steering straight ahead while you hand out the other two lines. It may help to run the engine gently astern against this first pair of lines to keep the boat stable until the final two are set.

Docking with a full crew.

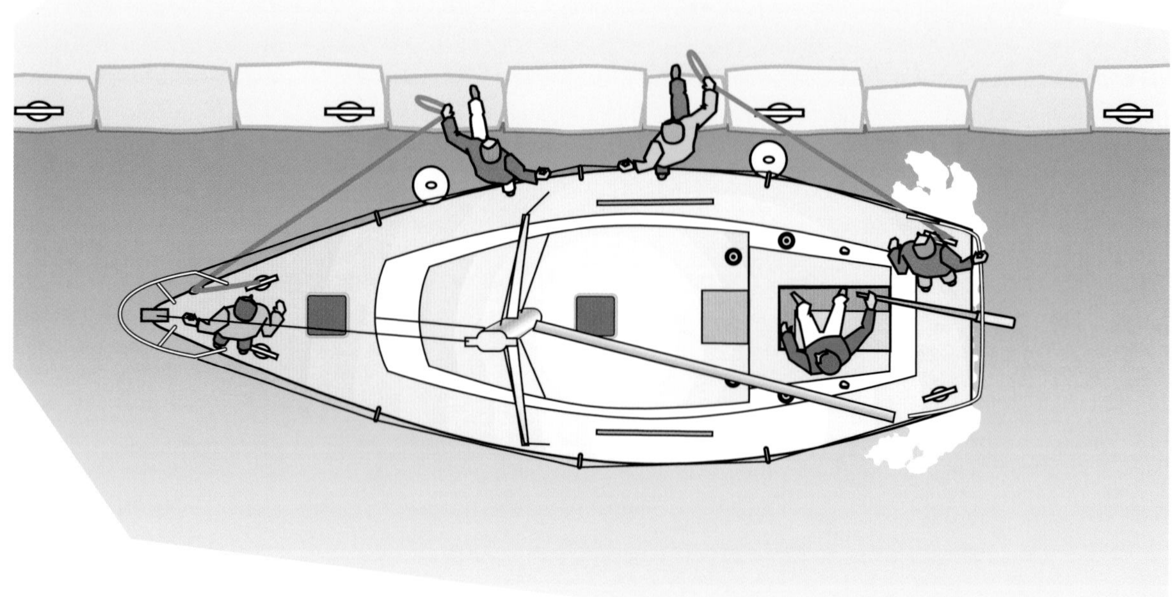

It is usually easiest to step ashore from the widest part of the boat. This is often near the mast where the shrouds provide convenient handholds.

Short-handed

When only two are aboard, the crew handles the bow line while the helm stands by to deal with the stern. The object of the exercise is initially to get two lines ashore secured as best they may be. Circumstances will dictate how this is achieved, but a well-tried system goes as follows:

- The bow line is treated as for a fully crewed boat with the bight well and truly secure on board and 'length plus 50%' in hand ready for action.
- The stern line is run out ready and draped over the guardrails amidships, or to some other convenient spot.
- When the boat is alongside, the crew hops ashore and secures the bight of the bow line on a cleat, taking up all the slack on the dock. This will leave a pile of rope by the cleat, but this is only temporary.
- The crew now walks smartly aft and either grabs the stern line from the guardrails or is handed the line by the helm. The crew drops the loop over a suitable cleat and the helm takes up the slack as though the boat were fully crewed.
- Both crew now walk forward to formalise the bow line. In gentle going, the bight ashore can be detached, the loop dropped quickly over the cleat and the slack snatched up on board. If it is blowing hard off the dock, it may be necessary to run a second line with its end ashore to hold the boat. The initial one can then be removed and freed up for other duties.
- Set the springs and the job is done.
- Choose which two lines to take ashore depending on the conditions as though the boat were fully crewed, but if you go for bow line and stern spring, don't be afraid to motor against them while setting up the others. The boat should lie very stably like this, giving you the time you need without stress.

Docking short-handed

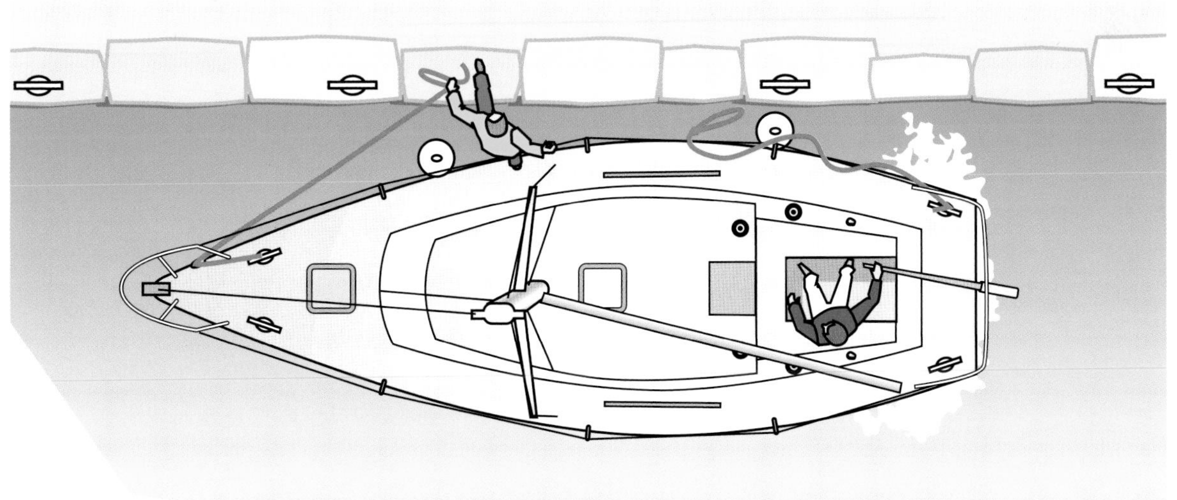

A stern line draped over the guardrails is usually retrievable by the crew from the dock. Sometimes the helm must hand it across.

The 'midships shortie'

In some circumstances, a useful trick is to secure initially from a midships cleat or fairlead with the shortest line you can contrive. If the cleat is in the right place – near the boat's pivot point (see page 72) – she will be unable to swing either her stern or her bow far out. One end will generally be favoured, however, and fenders rigged in anticipation. The boat is now temporarily under control while you run out the permanent shorelines.

Many boats will settle into a stable condition if motored ahead against a reasonably modest midships spring with the rudder set to swing the stern hard into the dock, in which case the line need not be especially short. If the boat goes 'bows-in' under this treatment, the cleat is forward of the pivot point. Try attaching the 'spring' to a cockpit winch or some other strong point further aft.

What can go wrong?

The dockside loafer If a helpful bystander offers to take your lines, make sure he drops the loop over the cleat and walks away. Too many people will pull a rope when given one, which is the last thing you want. They may even catch a turn, using the bow line as a spring line to stop you, thus stuffing your bow into the dock. Tell casual helpers clearly what you want, and be ready to repeat yourself reasonably politely if they appear too keen or not to understand.

The haystack lash-up Even though all big ships and large, professionally run yachts secure with the 'one-line-one-job' principle, some sailors insist on making up the end of a shoreline on board, then lugging the whole lot off the boat and trying to tie up with it. The results are bights on the dock, ends led back as springs, double head ropes, one line on top of another, and springs lashed up from a single rope with a bight secured ashore somewhere between bow and stern. Such methods are hateful to the seaman. They are cumbersome to apply, and the lines cannot be tended under load. Modern ropes are phenomenally strong, and any adequate shore line ought to be more than up to the job without doubling up. Nor is there any merit it making fast to perfectly good cleats with a round turn and two half hitches. If you're uncomfortable with bowlines or spliced loops, just cleat off and leave a locking hitch on top to make sure. Some people pass the bight of the loop through the cleat and bring it back over onto the horns to form a hitch like a gasket coil hitch (see page 52). This is a handy technique in circumstances where extreme snatching is expected, but the truth is that if all lines are properly made up, it is normally unheard of for a simple loop to fall off a cleat or bollard.

With a 'midships shortie' spring rigged and the rudder pushing the stern in towards the quay, a boat can be left to her own devices while the other shore lines are rigged.

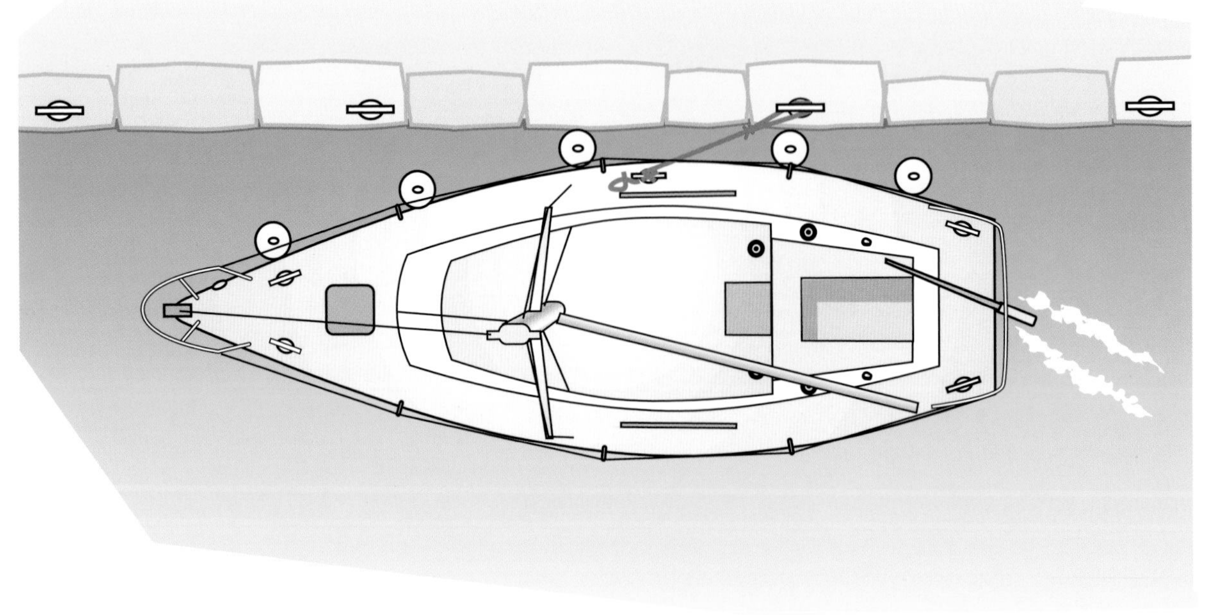

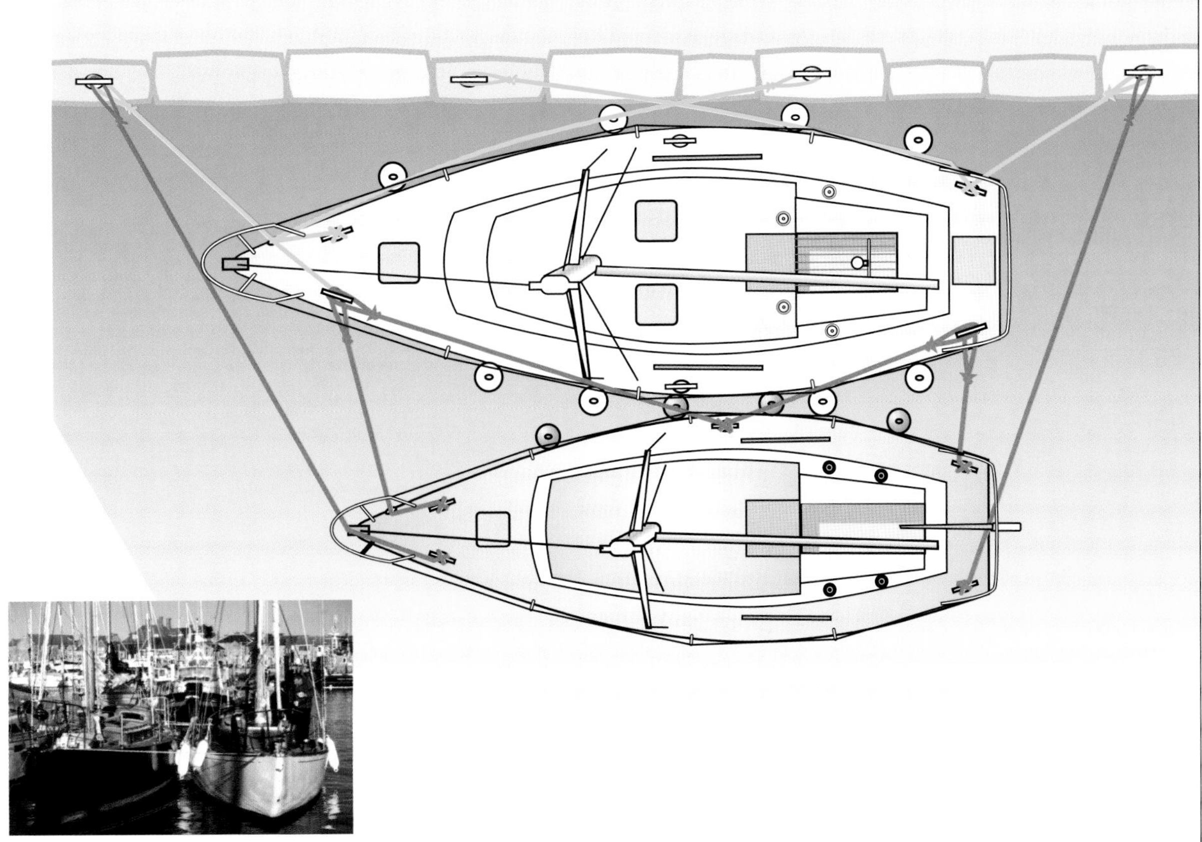

Rafting up

Good manners

The first person in a berth has all rights to it. Unless you are specifically ordered to raft up by the harbourmaster, or unless there is an established customary right, you can only lie alongside another boat with her skipper's agreement. The convention is therefore that before setting foot on another's deck, you ask.

'Ahoy Saucy Sue! OK if we lie alongside?' is the usual hail.

This may be met with a friendly affirmative, but don't take it personally if the response is less enthusiastic. If a crew plan to clear out early the following morning or even overnight they won't want you alongside; you won't want to be there either because when you raft up to another boat it is your responsibility not to impede her departure. Usually, this is sorted out by good communication, but if you raft up and the crew of the boat inside you is ashore you should either stay on board just until they return, or at least tuck a note in their companionway saying how you can be contacted.

'In Kings Head, back at 2300' would suffice, so long as the pub was close by.

Choose a boat of suitable size to raft up to. Bigger than you or the same length is the ideal.

Lines in a raft

First, secure to the inside boat with breast lines and springs. Now run shore lines to the dock, and take your own weight.

Watch your spreaders

Sailing boats need to make sure their spreaders are not next to one another. If they are, any wash that happens by can lead to a 'clash of heads' with expensive results.

Leaving from inside a raft

Ideally, the outside boats should release their lines and stand off while the inside boat leaves. If this isn't possible, let go the outer shorelines at the downwind or downtide end of the raft, then release the other lines so that the inside boat can slip out in that direction. The boat immediately outside the one leaving will lead her released shore line around the leaving boat so that it can be hove in smartly immediately she has cleared the raft. On no account, release shorelines from the up-tide end of the raft.

Basics

The pivot point We have seen (see page 63) how all vessels reducing way reach a speed at which they effectively stop steering with their rudders. Understanding this is essential when coming alongside. Equally important is to grasp the fact that when a boat's rudder steers her, it does so from the stern. The rudder is set one way and the stern is forced the other by the water flowing over the rudder blade. In fact, it is the aft part of the boat that is shoved away from the rudder. The forward part swivels the other way, with the boat effectively swivelling around a 'pivot point' in the vicinity of amidships.

Propeller torque A further issue is that when a propeller is running astern at low boat speeds, it pulls the stern one way or the other because of the torque of its circulation. Most single-screw boats have propellers which revolve clockwise when viewed from the stern as they drive ahead. This is called a right-hand propeller and it pulls the stern to port when it runs astern. A boat with a right-handed propeller therefore berths most tidily 'port side to', because as she takes way off by running her engine astern, she is naturally tending to swivel in towards the dock. If other forces such as tidal stream oblige her to berth starboard side to, so be it, but in the absence of extraneous factors, port side to is best. A boat with a left-handed propeller behaves the opposite way.

Because of these features, a right-handed boat is best brought into a port-side to berth at an angle of around 30° (a). When her bow is virtually hitting the dock, she steers to starboard and swings the stern in towards the wall (b). The engine is put astern at the same time so that the propeller will help pull the stern in. She should lose the last of her way neatly alongside, giving her crew ample time to step ashore with their lines (c).

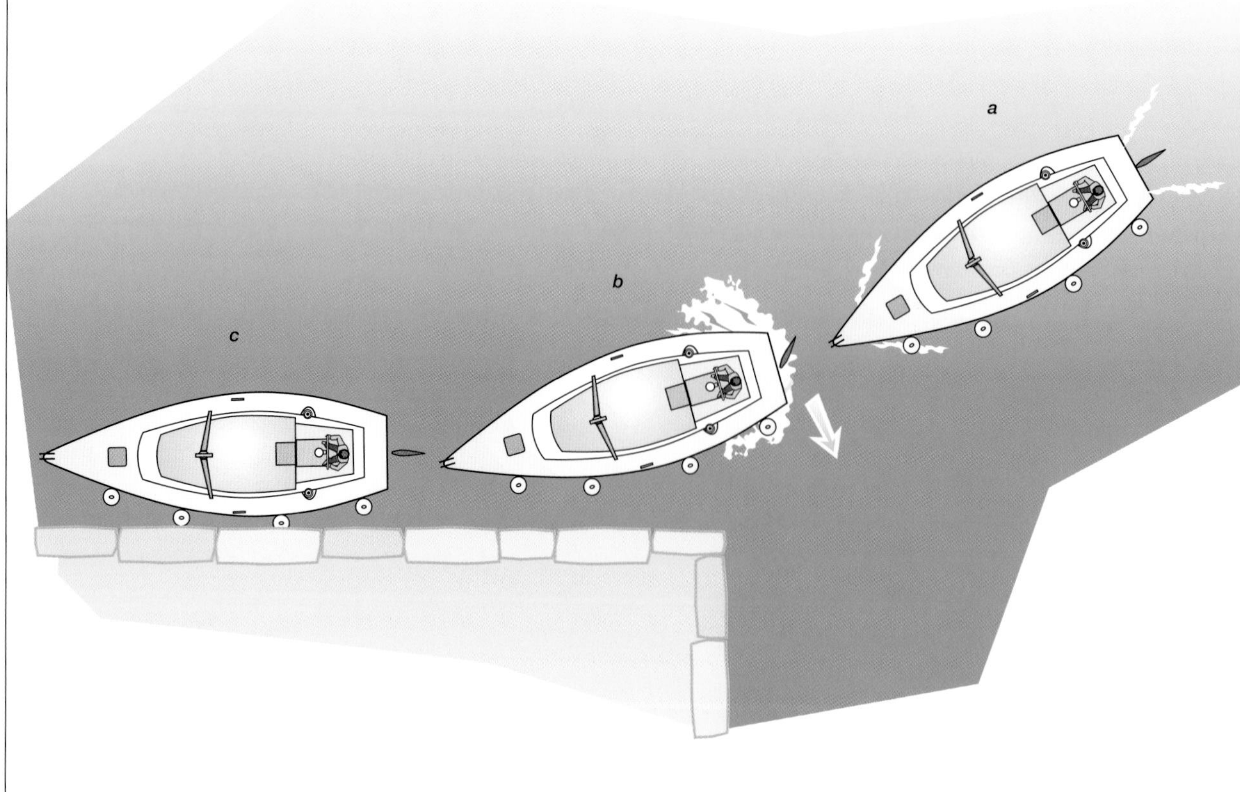

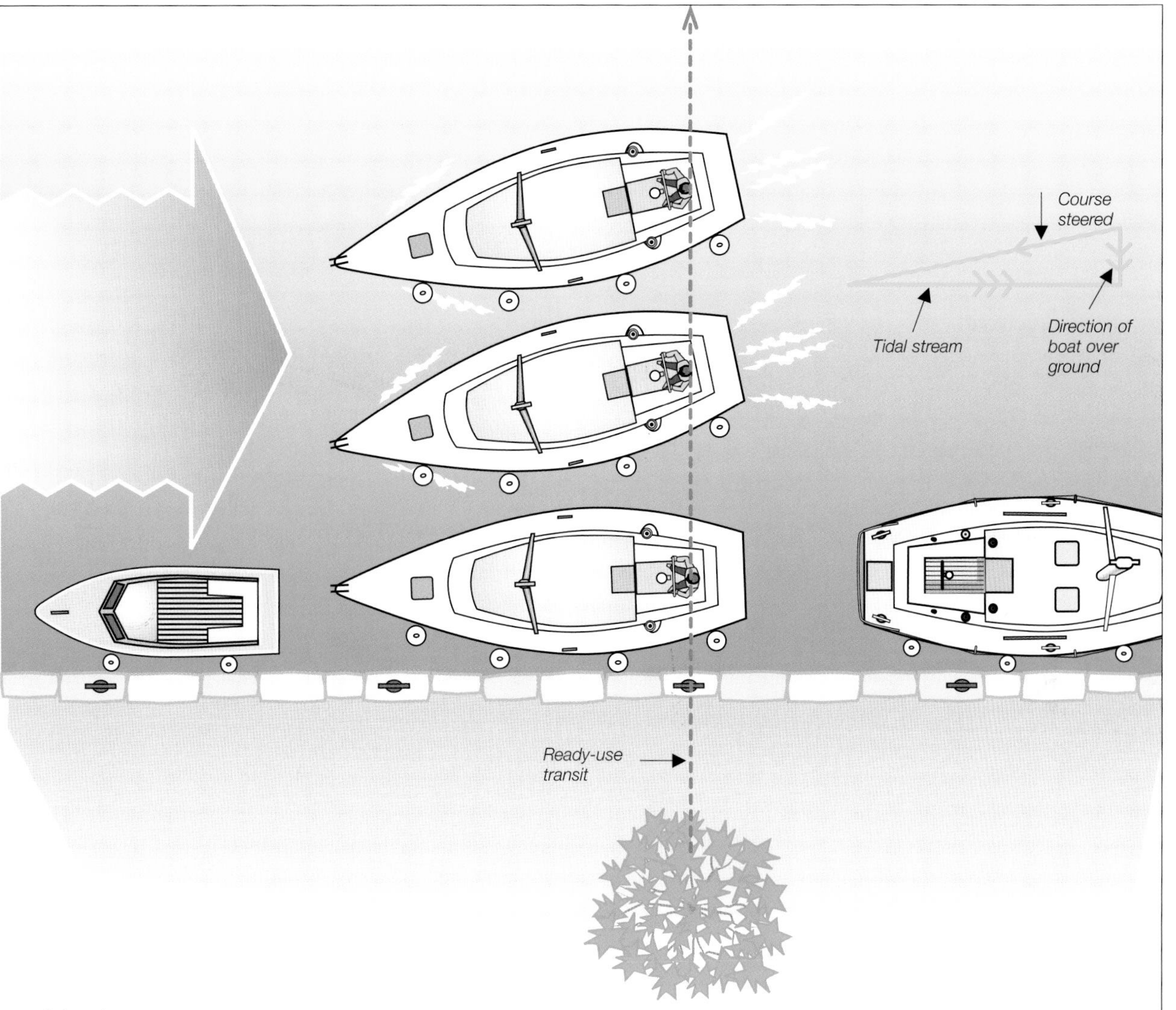

Other factors

Tide and current Where a current is running, it is essential to head into the berth up-stream unless, for some reason, you are obliged to come in stern first, in which case you will approach up-tide but making sternway. In either case, the same rules apply.

When berthing in strong currents, it is vital to bear in mind that the boat may not be going where she is pointing. Pick up a transit in the berth by lining up a bollard with something in the background, then keep the two objects in line as you approach. Adjust speed accordingly and don't be afraid of placing the boat almost parallel with the berth, then 'ferry-gliding' in with plenty of way on through the water, but moving sideways over the bottom as the current tries to sweep you backwards.

Blowing on When a strong wind is driving you onto a berth, a light boat – especially one with little inherent draught – will suddenly blow hard onto it when you reach the low-speed stalling point. Only by getting to know her can you predict with any certainty how violent this is likely to be, but it will happen to any boat given enough breeze. In general, keep as much way on as you dare then blast it off with astern propulsion when almost on top of the berth. This demands serious confidence in the engine and gearbox. If you have doubts about them, either go slow and prepare for a messy arrival, or exercise the seaman's option and go somewhere else.

Blowing off The same rules hold good for blowing off as on, with plenty of way being the answer if you must come alongside. When the gale makes this impossible, a sailing boat can often 'back up' to the wall going astern, sending her most agile crew member ashore with a line. Once one rope is on, a second can be passed and the boat hove alongside. Coming 'head-up' to the wall is a better option for a motor vessel which may well have more power and less windage, but the sailing yacht's natural tendency is to lie with her quarter or even her stern to the wind, so at slow speeds it is best not fight her.

The simple case

If there isn't a lot of wind or tide, the best way off a berth for a small yacht or boat is to drop her lines and shove her bow off. Unless she is 'houses high' like some motorboats or very large yachts, to do more than this is to be pedantic and to make work.

The weather berth (blowing onshore)

With strong onshore winds, only the smallest craft will be able to shove off effectively. The answer now lies in the spring lines. If all ropes but one spring are removed and the engine is run against that spring with a fender suitably in place, the opposite end of the boat will be levered off the dock. Thus, going astern against a stern spring forces the bow off, vice-versa with a bow spring. Once the relevant end is far enough away from the wall, the line can be taken in and the boat driven out (fig 1).

Spring Lines – Bow or stern? The advantage of a stern spring is that the boat steers out of the berth going ahead. She is thus immediately under full control. For most single-screw motor craft, this is therefore generally the best option. So too for sailing vessels, except that many of these have so much windage forward from the mast that it is hard to spring the bow off. For them a bow spring can be more effective. The bow spring has the additional advantage that water is being thrown at the rudder by the engine running ahead. This means you can steer the stern away from the dock, and double the effectiveness of the spring line.

It's 'horses for courses', but so long as you understand which line does what and their relative benefits, you won't go far wrong (fig 2).

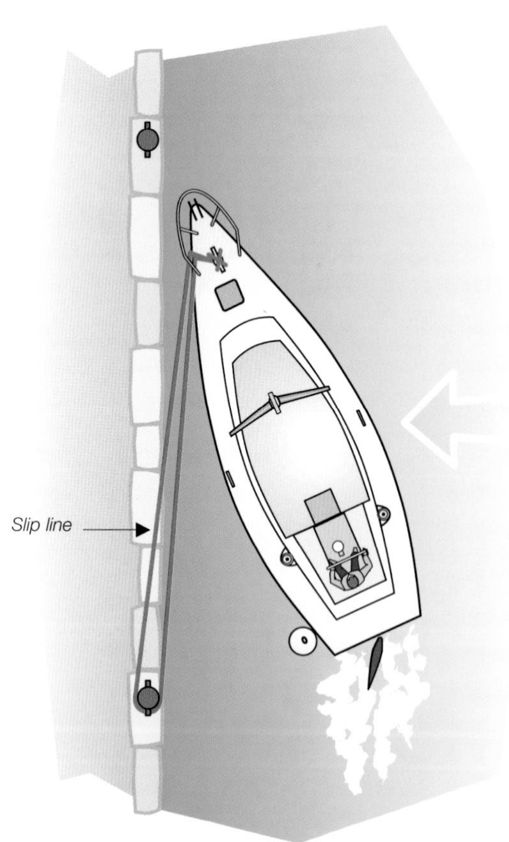

fig 1

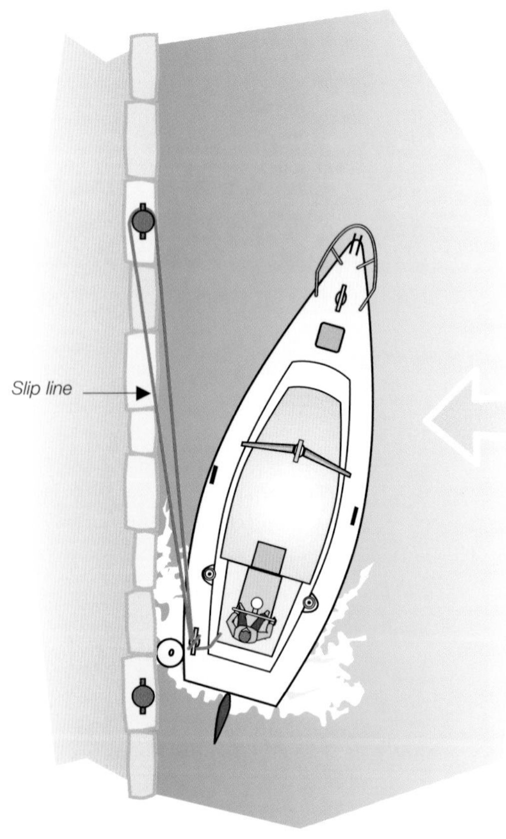

fig 2

Using twin screws to leave a weather berth – The twin-screw yacht has a huge advantage in this most awkward of situations because she can run one engine against the other to 'twist' herself off the dock. Take in all lines – except the bow spring where space is tight. Set fenders up forward, now steer 'in' to the dock with the rudders. Go slow ahead on the outside engine and slow astern on the inside one until the stern is far enough off the dock to reverse out safely. If you adopt the same technique with an offshore wind, the boat will literally move sideways out of the berth.

The lee berth (blowing offshore)

Getting a boat off a lee berth is not generally a problem, but leaving crew behind as the vessel peels off quicker than expected can be a serious nuisance.

Slip ropes – When the boat is being blown hard enough off the dock to make stranding the crew a real possibility, slip ropes that can be released with all hands aboard should be used. The same applies in any conditions for boats of exceptionally high freeboard whose crew cannot simply hop aboard after letting go.

A slip rope is rigged by making one end of the rope fast aboard, leading it around the dock cleat, bollard or ring, then back aboard again, where the bight is made fast. When it's time to leave, the shorter end is let off and the rope pulled on board. The engine should not be gunned until it is certain the rope has been slipped successfully.

A single slip rope, or maybe two, is usually enough. The process is time-consuming and more are rarely necessary. If the wind is so strong that you're unwilling to take the weight off a rope to rig it as a slip, set up the slip rope alongside it and release the original 'overnight' rope afterwards. This process of relieving one load by taking the strain on another is the essence of seamanship.

Slip ropes are not generally required in an onshore breeze or light going. They should be treated with the same philosophy as making a rope up on a cleat. Consider the issues and what is to be achieved, then decide how to proceed. This will show whether or not slip-ropes are needed. The practice of using them as a matter of course is to be discouraged.

Anchoring

How an anchor works

Anchors do their business by digging into the seabed. With the right anchor and a good holding ground, the power can be remarkable, but to achieve full performance the ground tackle must be given every chance. All anchors are designed to plough into the bottom as they are pulled along more or less horizontally. It follows that if they are dangling straight below the bows, they have little hope of success. Rather, they should be let out on as long a 'scope' as possible. The further they are from the boat, the more horizontal their pull will be and the better opportunity they will have of doing their best. In good holding and moderate weather a boat anchoring with a sensible anchor and chain cable will want a scope of four times the depth of water (generally written as 4 : 1), although three may be adequate depending on the boat and her gear. Nylon rope, or 'rode', calls for a greater scope of up to seven to one. Whatever you are using, the more scope the better, so long as you don't swing ashore or into another boat.

Parts of an anchor

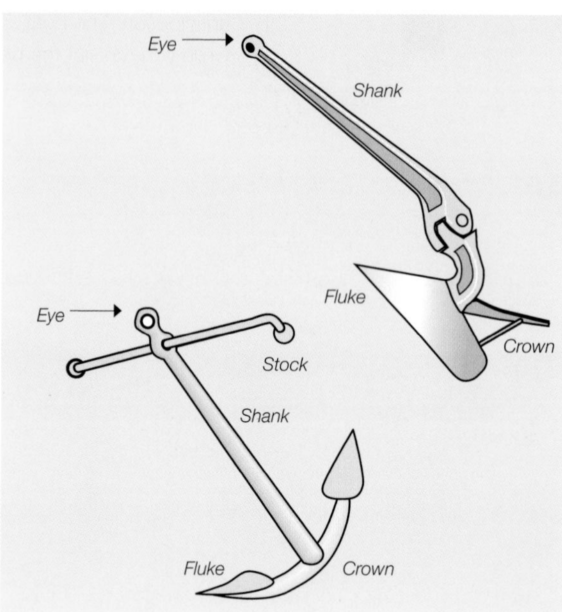

Types of anchor

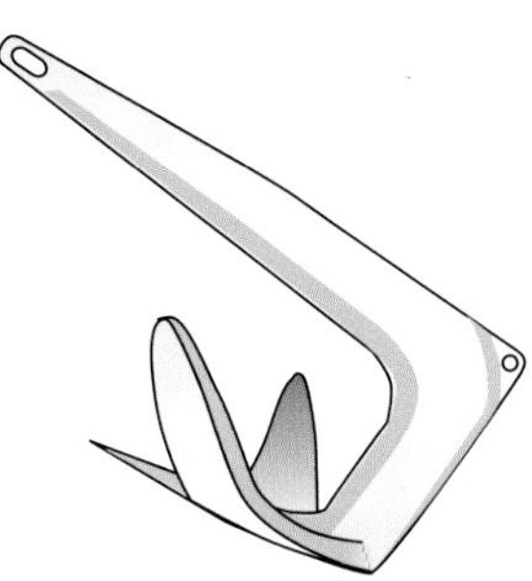

Bruce Developed for oil rigs, it has remarkable holding power, a short shank and no moving parts. Convenient for self-stowing bow arrangements.

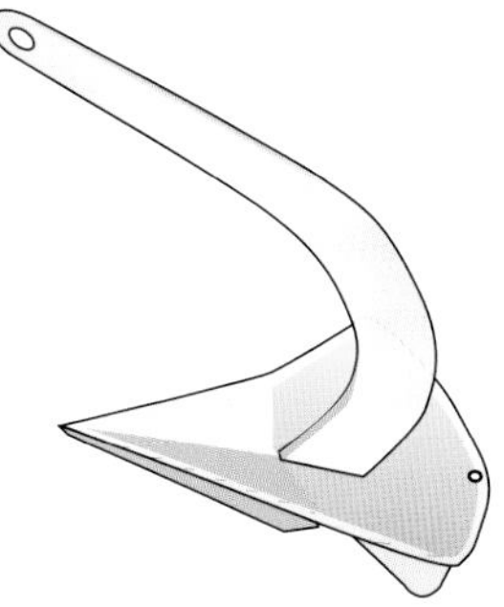

Spade A first-class self-burying, self-stowing anchor of remarkable power. Stows conveniently in a bow roller and the shank is dismountable for storing below.

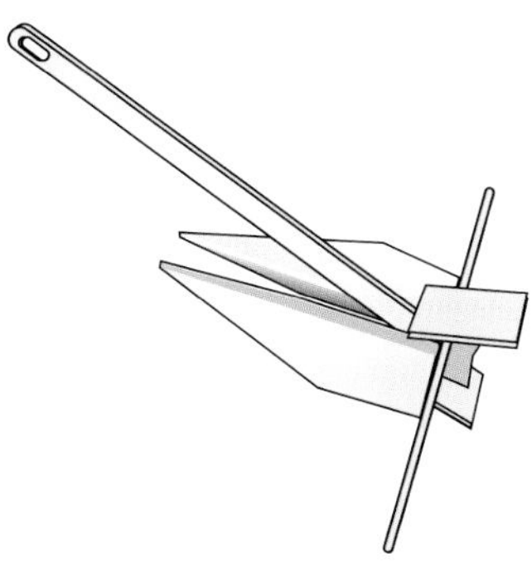

Danforth Stows flat, good on clean sand, useless in kelp. The moving flukes are notorious finger-breakers.

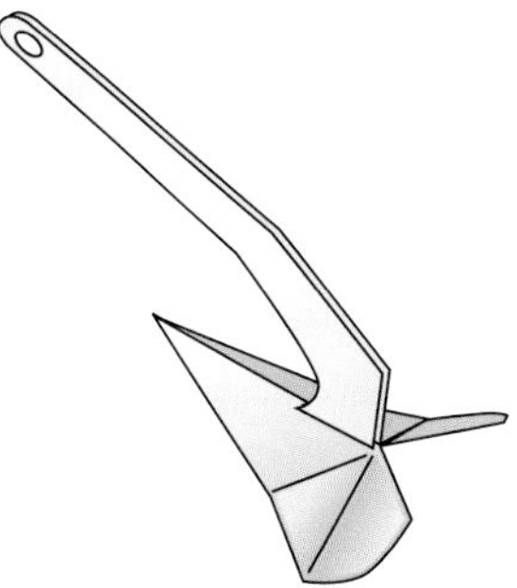

Delta Said by many to equal the CQR, it has no moving parts and so is easier to handle.

Fisherman Given a bad reputation by tiny replicas on sale in chandlers, a Fisherman of 70lb or more works superbly on lifeboats and on many traditional yachts as well. It must have heavy chain and be of large proportions, but it will set in any bottom and even works in kelp. Stowage for ready deployment can be a challenge until a suitable system has been developed.

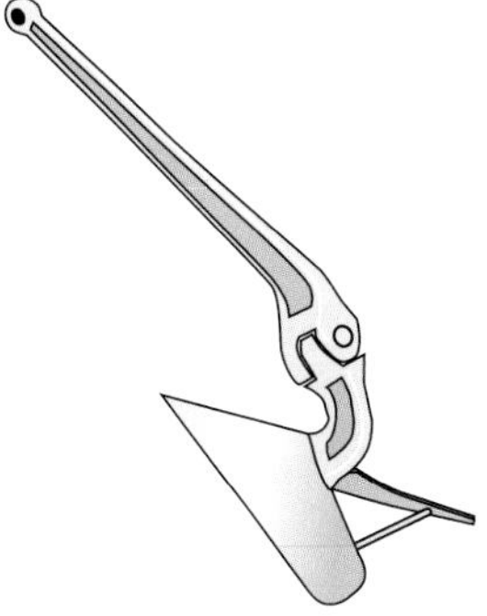

CQR Plough-shaped anchor that churns its way into most bottoms effectively, although not good in mixed stones and kelp. Good holding for its weight. An excellent all-purpose option but it must be the genuine article. Some imitations have been known to fail. The plough-share part swivels on the end of the shank which assists stowage and helps holding power at awkward angles, but can trap the fingers of the unwary.

Warp or chain?

Warp and chain both have their protagonists, so we will not offer an opinion here as to which may ultimately be better.

Chain — the benefits

- Chain is totally chafe resistant both at the stem head and on the sea bed.
  Its weight confers four further advantages:
- Holds it down in a deep curve, applying a more horizontal pull for less scope, making it handier in tight or crowded anchorages.
- Helps damp the tendency of an anchored vessel to surge around.
- Encourages it to enter the water at a near-vertical angle unless it's blowing hard, making it less vulnerable to passing vessels.
- Assists it to self-stow readily.

Chain — the drawbacks

- Heavy to stow if it doesn't live in a deep, self-stowing chain locker.
- Heavy to handle unless assisted by a windlass.
- Potentially dangerous at cleats if care is not taken to protect fingers etc. Again, this danger is removed by a windlass.
- Comparatively expensive.

Warp — the benefits

- Light to use.
- Holds as well as chain, given enough scope and a good anchor.
- Easier to handle on a boat with no windlass.
- Light weight is a benefit for light displacement craft where stowing heavy chain can produce trim issues.
- Springy nature helps absorb shock loads in extreme conditions.

Warp — the drawbacks

- Stem-head chafe is an ever-present danger that must be neutralised.
- At least 5 metres of chain are required between rode and anchor to prevent sea-bed chafe and to improve pull angle.
- Large scope means wide swinging circles.
- More easily fouled by other vessels.
- Long length can create stowage issues. Consider stowing on a reel.
- Comparatively inconvenient on windlasses for larger craft.

Anchoring - warp v chain

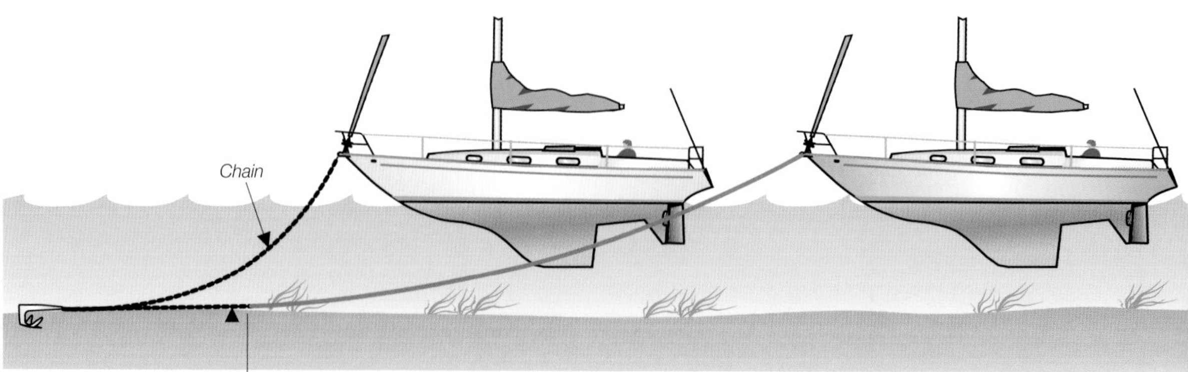

Choosing an anchorage

Strategic considerations

Shelter Few things are as satisfying as a quiet night anchored free of charge in a peaceful bay or river. Little is so stress-mongering as a bad night hanging on in poor holding ground on a lee shore. An anchorage should always be selected with shelter in mind. Consider what the wind may do while you are anchored, then find a spot where you will lie in a good lee. Give thought to the sea state. Protection from the wind may ensure safety, but rolling around in a slop hooking into the berth from outside is a wretched business.

Holding ground A chart of the appropriate scale will usually carry a symbol to indicate the nature of the bottom anywhere you are likely to anchor. It may even show an 'anchor' symbol enticing you to 'let go here'. However, these are sometimes for the information of ships not boats, so treat them with caution.

Most anchors hold best in clay ('cy' on the chart) or firm mud ('m'). Sand ('s') is surprisingly good also. Avoid areas where kelp and other weeds ('wd') are charted; only anchor in rocky ground if you have no other option because it is likely that your hook won't hold at all. Even if it does, it may foul and be lost. The so-called 'Chart 5011' is really a booklet containing all the symbols used on UKHO charts. If in doubt about the letters relating to the sea bed, looking it up in 'Chart 5011' will resolve the question. Be especially aware of the dangers of 'foul ground'. Often this will refer to old mooring chains and the like which can snag an anchor, making recovery difficult or impossible (see page 83).

Tactical considerations

Crowded anchorages When the available space is well populated, try to deduce where the neighbours' anchors may be lying before laying your own. If the other vessels are all wind-rode, it is generally safe to anchor so that you bring up three or four boats' lengths away from the next yacht. Where wind and tide combine to create an ambiguous situation, the only sure policy is to assess likely swinging circles (are the neighbours on chain or rope?), and anchor so they cannot overlap.

Swinging ashore It is always tempting to tuck in as close as you dare under the lee of the available shelter. Make certain that if the wind should change you are far enough to seaward to be able to swing through 180° and remain afloat.

Tidal height When anchoring on a rising tide, be sure to allow extra scope so that you don't drift off at High Water after plucking the hook out. The penalty for miscalculating a falling tide fits the crime. A sailing boat ends up on her side, and a motorboat risks propeller damage amongst other hazards. Fortunately, the arithmetic to avoid this could not be simpler:

- Calculate the height of tide when you intend to anchor *(a)*.
- Note the height of Low Water *(b)*.
- Subtract the Low Water height from the present height to find how much the tide will fall.
- Add this to the depth you wish to lie in at Low Water, sound in until you reach this depth, then let go.
- Reading the chart to find the depth is not only a waste of time, it may be inaccurate, because the depths given are spot soundings and may not coincide with where you end up lying.

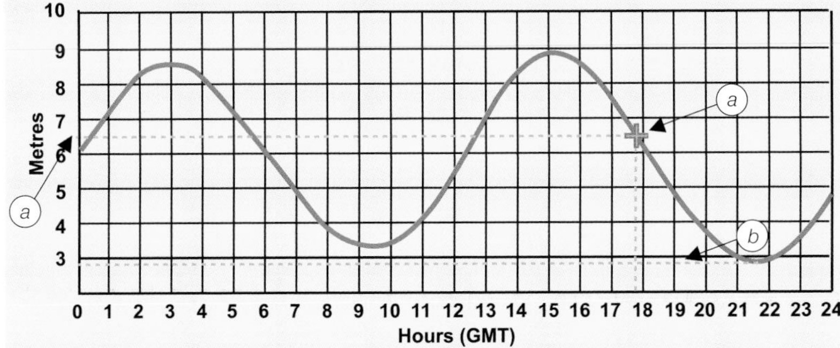

a *Height of tide at arrival time*
b *Height of tide at low water*

Laying an anchor

There's more to laying an anchor successfully than heaving it over the side on the end of a length of chain or warp. Here's how to make sure it holds:

- Take all way off.
- Foredeck crew lowers the anchor steadily over the bow if possible, or lets go if it's too heavy.
- Crew signals when it hits the bottom and makes sure the cable stops running out.
- Helm motors away slowly astern in the direction the boat will end up lying.
- Crew lets the agreed scope of cable run out under control so that it lies in a straight line between the boat and the anchor.
- When the cable is nearly all run, the engine is shoved out of gear. The boat will carry her way until her weight gives the anchor an initial bite on the seabed.
- As her head starts to swing to the cable, put her slow astern once more. The crew now monitors the cable as it rises from the water. Expect it to dip at least once as the anchor takes a secure hold.
- When the boat stops moving again so that she is 'hanging' on the hook, increase power to 'half astern'. The crew watches the cable to see if it falters while the helm notes a transit abeam. If this stays still and the foredeck reports no movement on the cable, you are well and truly anchored.
- It only remains to throttle back somewhat to let the boat creep ahead under the weight of the cable if it's chain, or the spring of a nylon rode. Wait until the situation stabilises before putting the engine into neutral and shutting it down, otherwise the boat will surge ahead over her anchor and leave an untidy mess on the bottom which won't be so conducive to good holding as a straight line.

The snubber

Many serious cruising boats attach a short length of nylon line to the cable, then lower it away over the stem head until the join is near the water. The inboard end of this 'snubber' is made fast and the anchor cable slacked away again. Lying to the snubber removes noise when anchoring on chain and protects the main rode against chafe if it is rope. Either way, it is sound practice.

The anchor weight

The holding power of a given scope can be maximised by lowering a weight down the cable. This serves to increase the catenary and delivers a more horizontal pull to the anchor. The technique is useful in crowded anchorages where laying a long scope may be impracticable. Sometimes called a 'chum' or an 'angel', suitable shackles for running down a chain or rope can be purchased from specialist chandlers. Without one of these, care must be taken lest any make-shift arrangement chafes the cable.

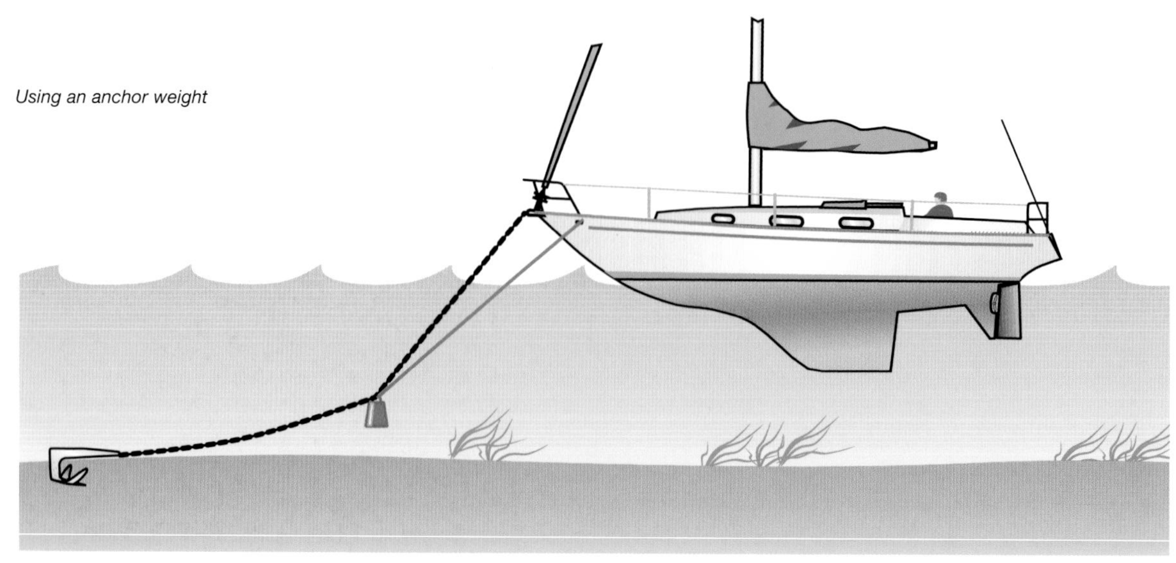

Using an anchor weight

Dragging anchor

The first sign that a vessel is dragging her anchor is when her head fails to pull back to weather at the end of a swing. If she isn't looking up to the wind from time to time, she is either dragging or about to drag. The best way to be certain your anchor is holding is to find and keep checking a casual transit (two bushes, one behind the other, would be fine) that lies abeam of the direction in which you would drag. In a wind-rode berth, the transit line would run square across the breeze. If no transit is available, a compass bearing on a single object is a poor but acceptable substitute, but the object should be sensibly close, because any change in bearing lessens with range. At 3 miles, a shift of 1° might mean you have already dragged 100 yards.

Dragging anchor

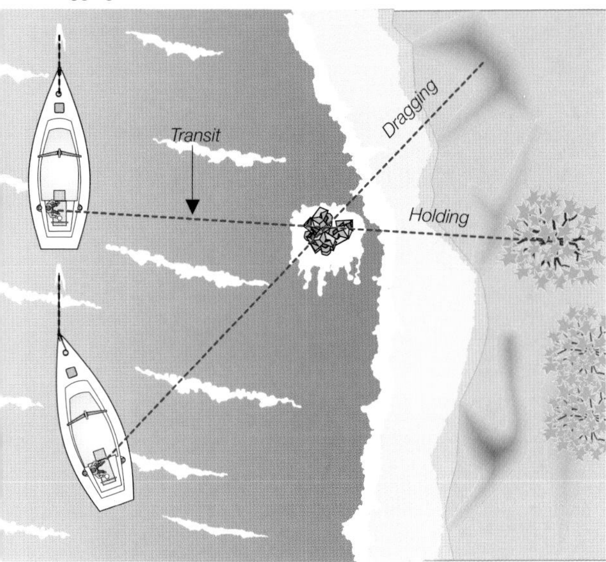

Many GPS receivers can be set to emit a sound signal if your position changes more than a selected distance. On a dark night with not even a compass bearing to help you this is of some use, but it cannot approach a transit for practical value. If you set it to a small enough circle to tell you when you start moving, it will challenge your sanity by going off every time you swing. Set it to a wider circle, and it may not advise what's happening until it's too late.

Lying to two anchors

Wind-rode

Vessels with plenty of hefty ground tackle will only rarely be obliged to resort to extra anchors, but there comes a time when everyone needs additional reassurance and all the holding that's available. If wind-rode, the most effective way is to lay out a second anchor in a 'Y' form from the bows. Anchored on warp, this can be done by motoring up to where you want to lay the second hook, gathering slack on the first cable as you go, then dropping the 'pick' and falling back onto both anchors, but it is often simpler to do the job as you would if your first anchor were laid on chain.

Here, the second anchor (sometimes called the 'kedge'), is lowered into the dinghy. All the cable you intend to lay is lowered in with it and the bight made fast on board. This is vital if the kedge is on chain, but you may get away with paying a rode out over the yacht's bow. As you move away from the boat in the dinghy, pay the cable out behind you until it is all gone, then drop the anchor carefully over the side. This can be a dangerous manoeuvre because of the possibility of becoming snagged with the anchor and carried down with it, so care needs to be taken.

Once back on board, heave up on the new anchor until the catenary of the original one begins to drop, showing that both anchors are taking the strain.

Wind-against-tide

At best this is an uneasy scenario at anchor. At worst, it can give rise to the direst of circumstances as the boat tries to lie head-up to the tide and stern to the wind, then starts sailing ahead under bare poles straight over her anchor, perhaps even tripping it out. The situation is exacerbated when several boats are lying close together. Disparate characteristics can make them career into one another; even similar craft can get into trouble.

Bowsprit and bull rope A further aggravation caused by wind-against-tide anchoring is that the cable crunches along the topsides as the boat sails over the hook. This is a particular nuisance for plumb-stemmed traditional yachts, but fortunately these generally have bowsprits. They can save their day by rigging a bull rope through a block on the bowsprit end and securing it to the bight of the cable a few feet below the stem. Hauling the cable forward with this miraculously quietens matters down. In less demanding circumstances, a bull rope is worth rigging just to take the place of a snubber.

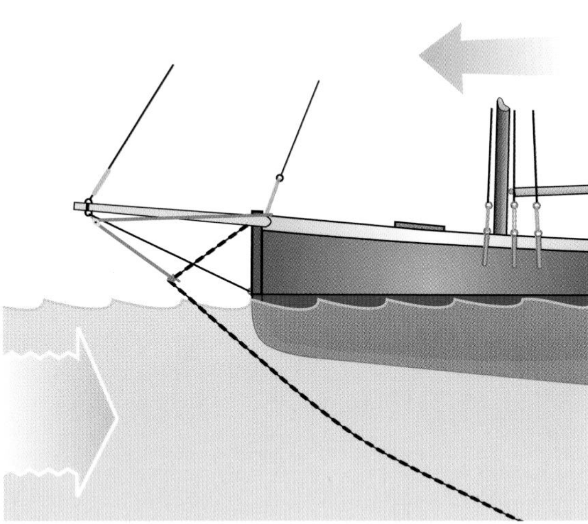

Fore-and-aft anchoring Where swinging room is seriously limited or a wind-against-tide situation becomes intolerable, the vessel's position can be pinned down tightly by lying between two anchors. To achieve this state, there is no law against simply hanging well back from the bower which will be set from the bow, and dropping the kedge over the stern. The bower is then shortened up as the kedge cable is paid out, until you can even up between the two. The trouble with this is that the boat will lie stern to the tide for at least some of the time. A more seamanlike solution is to lay the kedge well astern by using the dinghy and dig it in by pulling hard. The kedge warp is then taken forward 'outside everything' and bent to the main bower cable with a rolling hitch. A few extra metres of bower cable are surged out so that the rolling hitch is well below the surface. The boat is now effectively moored fore and aft but is still able to swing head to the stream.

The main drawback with this 'Bahamian Moor' method is that if the boat swings through too many tides and goes the same way each time, she can wrap herself up in a pretty mess of twisted cables. The classical solution to this dilemma is to join the cables with a swivel, but the practicalities of this lie far beyond most yachts and small motor craft. The realistic answer is to use the rolling hitch, but keep an eye on it.

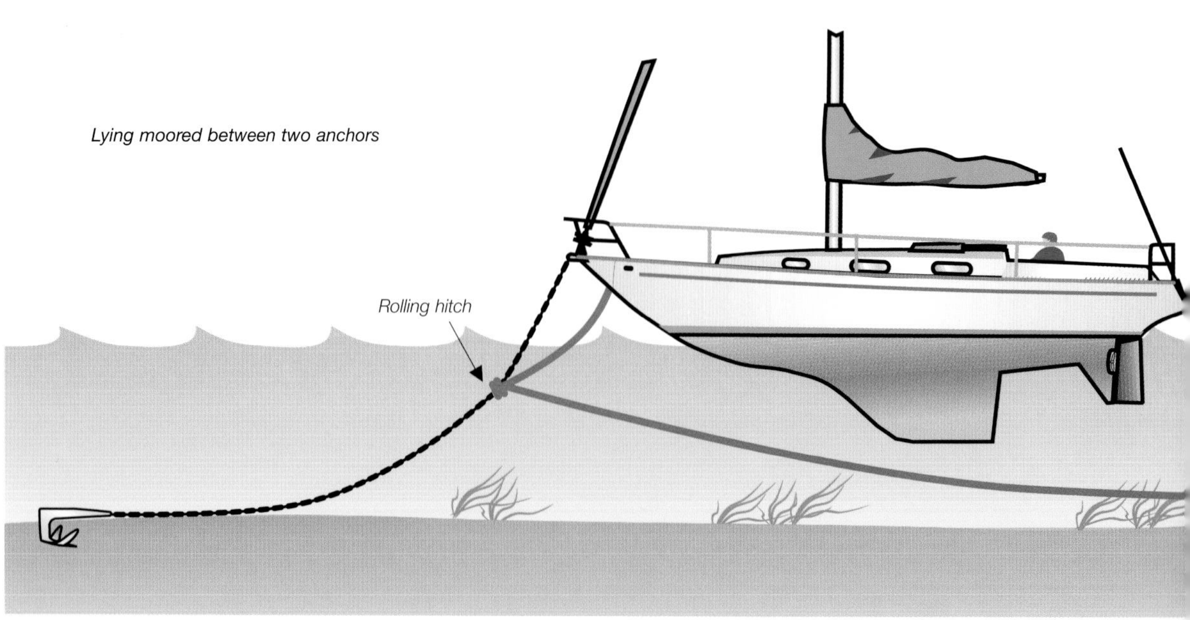

Lying moored between two anchors

Setting up a sheer

When a strong tide is running past an anchored vessel, she can change the location where she lies by lashing the helm across. The water flowing past the rudder gives her stern a cant, the keel is presented at an angle to the stream and she ferry-glides away as far as her cable will allow. Very often, she will lie stably in the new position. This can be most useful in a crowded anchorage or when anchored close to a river bank, but care must be taken in a reversing tide, because the sheer which gave you comfort in one direction may set you ashore in the other.

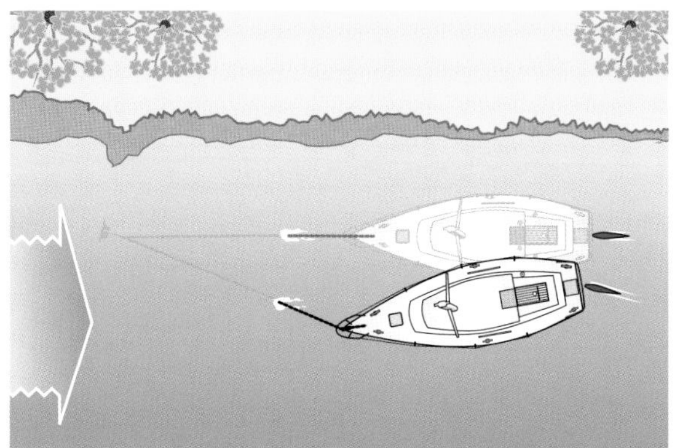

Weighing anchor

Bringing an anchor back on board is generally just a matter of shortening the cable until it is 'up-and-down', motoring hard against it to break it out, then heaving it up. The conventional method is to motor ahead over the shortened cable, which trips out the anchor efficiently, but if you're uneasy about going ahead over a rope or a chain, motoring hard astern is almost as effective and involves fewer potential dramas.

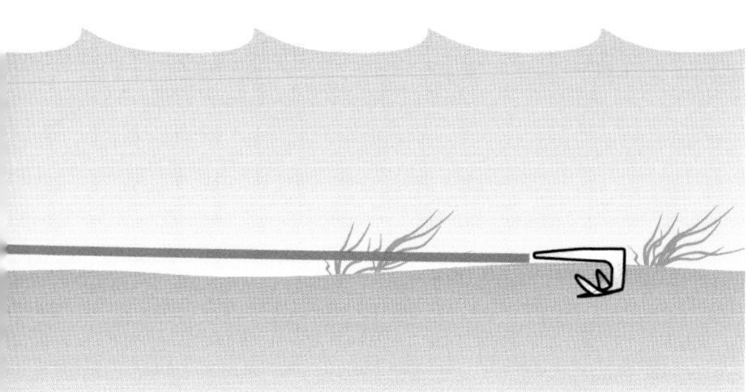

Weighing under sail, the trick is to allow the head to pay off with the mainsail hoisted and the sheet set for a close reach. Not trying to point too high, the boat now sails as far as she can on one tack. When the cable snubs her up, tack and sail back near towards the anchor as possible, heaving in the slack cable as you go. As it comes tight, catch a turn, tack again, repeating the operation until the hook breaks out.

Fouled anchors

Fouling the anchor is usually predictable and can be avoided by not bringing up where the bottom is known to be littered with debris. Occasionally sheer bad luck pays a call and we are left with no choice but to try and clear it. If it's not too cold or too deep, the ideal answer is to don the ship's mask and snorkel (all should carry one), take the plunge and unhook the fluke from its snare. If this is not possible, use whatever power you have to heave the anchor up to within reach of the surface. A windlass is best, but failing this, you may be able to lead a messenger line to a primary winch. When you can get a hand to it, you will probably find that the fluke is around an old ground chain. Pass a line beneath this, make it fast, then slack away the anchor which, duly relieved, should fall free. This is the favoured technique in crowded Mediterranean harbours where many boats anchored stern-to can foul one another's cables. If it doesn't work, or the obstruction is too heavy to lift, try passing a small bight of chain under the anchor cable with a rope on each end and using the dinghy to 'worry' it down to the anchor. When it's there, heave up and away from the boat as hard as you can. With luck, it'll trip out the fluke. If this fails, buoy the cable with a fender, slip it, and return with a diver to retrieve your gear.

Anchor buoy If you must anchor in dubious ground, attach a tripping line to the crown of the anchor and float it to the surface with a pickup buoy or an old fender. If the hook fouls, you can capsize it clear by heaving directly up on the line. This simple ruse works almost every time and is a highly worthwhile precaution.

Mooring

The anatomy of a mooring

A mooring is a permanent attachment to the seabed. It may take the form of two or more heavy anchors interconnected by massive chain, or it may be a single large block, often of concrete. It connects to the surface via a 'riser' of chain or nylon attached at its upper end to a buoy. Boats moor up either by securing to the buoy if it is designed for this purpose, or by picking up and lying to a strop attached to the riser. This is usually attached immediately below the buoy. If no strop is evident and the buoy has a ring on top, it is generally safe to secure to that. A strop is often evidenced by a small 'pickup buoy' with a plastic handle which can be grabbed with a boat hook. The pickup is attached to the strop with a light line. Do not attempt to put any weight on this. Pull it in until the strop itself is in hand, then lie to this if it appears to be adequate for your vessel. If you have reason to doubt the suitability of a mooring, assume the worst.

Picking up a mooring

The process Approach up-tide just as though coming alongside a berth. If there is no tide, come in up-wind; if the tide is weak and the wind strong, it may be necessary to make some sensible compromise. If in doubt, inspect the way other boats in the vicinity are lying. If there are no boats the situation might be less than crystal clear, but there is generally plenty of room for error.

If you see a pickup buoy, use the boat hook to grab the bight of light line that joins it to the mooring strop. This is far easier than trying to grapple the little buoy itself. When you have the pickup line in hand, use it to bring the strop aboard. This may be chain or rope, but either usually ends in a loop which you can drop over your foredeck mooring fitting. If it's too short or the loop is inappropriate, pass a rope through it and make this fast instead.

Securing to a mooring A mooring with no strop usually has a ring on top of the buoy. Grab this with the boat hook and secure it with a line led out through the bow roller or fairlead. You might pass the line as a slip rope if you're not stopping long. The convenience of this both for picking up and letting go is obvious. The technique is also convenient if loads are high and you need to secure rapidly. Don't be tempted to lie to a slip rope overnight, because there is nothing to stop the rope worrying at the ring and chafing. At best, your line will be weakened right in the middle. At worst, it will wear through and away you will go.

The solution is to pass a slip initially then secure more permanently using a round turn and a long bowline. The slip can be left on as backup and the round turn takes out any tendency to chafe. You might expect that two half hitches would be recommended, but while this might be acceptable, the bowline has a couple of advantages:

First, because the loop can be as long as you like, it can ride well clear of the buoy. Should a sea get up, your

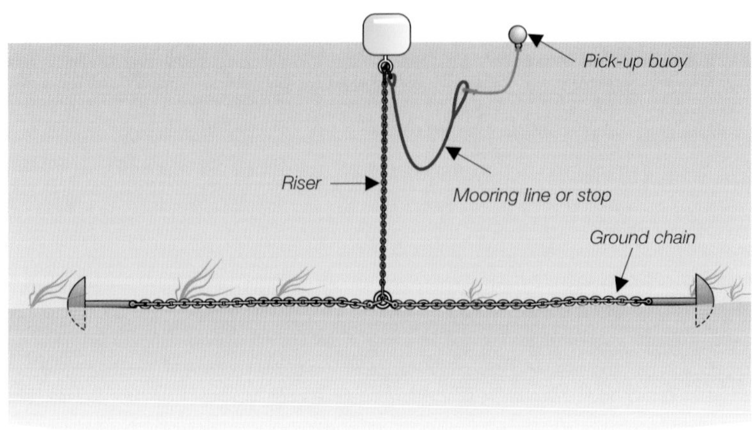

fingers are away from the action. Secondly, you can bring the knot back aboard so that nobody has to lean precariously over the bow to undo it. Crew members with bad backs will be grateful for this.

If the boat seems likely to surge around on the buoy and you are in any doubt at all about the effectiveness of your fairlead, think 'chafe', and slide a length of armoured hose onto the rope where it passes over the bow, just as you would for towing (see page 58).

If chafe looks a potential issue, perhaps when the tide turns and blows against the wind, you may even choose to unshackle your chain cable from the anchor and take it to the ring on the buoy. Your troubles are now at an end, but anyone sleeping up forward on a wild night may have their repose disturbed by the rattling and snubbing. The same is true for chain mooring strops.

When it's time to let go, shorten up the slip rope and ease away the main mooring before untying the bowline or unshackling the chain. If you've no slip, motor up slowly to relieve the load.

The lasso Where there is no pickup and it proves impossible to grab the ring, the last resort for making initial contact with a buoy is to lasso it. Secure both ends of a rope to either side of the bow, leading the bight forward, outside everything. Experience and practice will show how long the bight should be on differing occasions, but deploying it is a knack worth developing. Take off all way with the bow over the buoy and drop the bight so that it sinks into the water beyond it. When it is well down, pull up the slack on one end. The bight will catch on the riser immediately below the buoy and stay there until you have secured in a more permanent manner.

Never lie to a lasso. It is clearly less safe than other means of making fast; it is also unpopular with harbourmasters because it chafes the riser.

To use the lasso as a matter of course when a better method of attaching to a buoy presents itself is unseamanlike. Compared with a boat hook and a pickup it will always be a hit-and-miss affair.

Wind against tide – traditional craft

The bull rope Lying to a mooring with wind against tide causes chafe and noise on any boat as she 'sails' past the mooring and is brought up short by the strop. Boats with serious bowsprits have an inherent advantage in these circumstances because they can rig a bull rope as they might also do for anchoring (see page 82). In this context it is secured to the buoy (usually with a long bowline) rather than to the bight of the anchor cable, then led back to the deck to hold the buoy clear, via a turning block or bullseye at the bowsprit end.

Bobstays and moorings The bull rope also helps to keep the mooring or anchor chain clear of the bowsprit's bobstay, which will otherwise chafe and cause stress all round. However, in addition to enjoying the benefits of the bull rope, the classical 'English cutter' whose mast does not rely on headgear rigged to the bowsprit to hold it up can tension the bobstay with a wire tackle which can be eased off when anchored or moored. The bobstay is then triced up, taking it right out of the way.

Securing between piles Piles generally have iron staples, or 'horses' on their inner sides, with a ring that can slide up and down to compensate for tide. When securing to these rings, the same rules apply as to mooring rings on buoys. A slip is useful, but should not be used overnight unless conditions are guaranteed to be quiet. When rigging the round turn and bowline, make the bowline as long as possible, because it is not unknown for the ring to jam at the bottom, especially when a number of boats are lying on the same piles. The skipper who called for two half hitches will then be left very embarrassed.

Rafting on piles Arrange your lines as though rafting up in an alongside berth (see page 71). The pile ropes substitute for the shore lines. As in the dockside situation, hail before rafting, then come alongside. When all is stable, use the dinghy to run your pile lines.

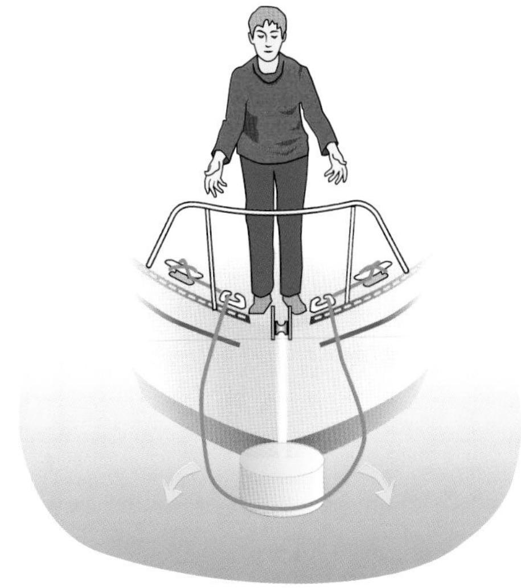

"The Lasso"

Heavy Weather

General issues

Definition
Heavy weather can be defined as conditions severe enough to cause a vessel on passage to consider modifying her plans, or to make a boat in harbour change her mind about putting to sea. Clearly, this point will vary from boat to boat and from crew to crew. A powerful, well-handled displacement power yacht may be perfectly safe offshore in force 9 winds, while an inexperienced crew with a 22ft bilge-keeled sailing yacht might justifiably be unhappy in force 5. It is up to all skippers to know the limits of comfort and most especially safety. If necessary, steps must be taken to discover what these may be.

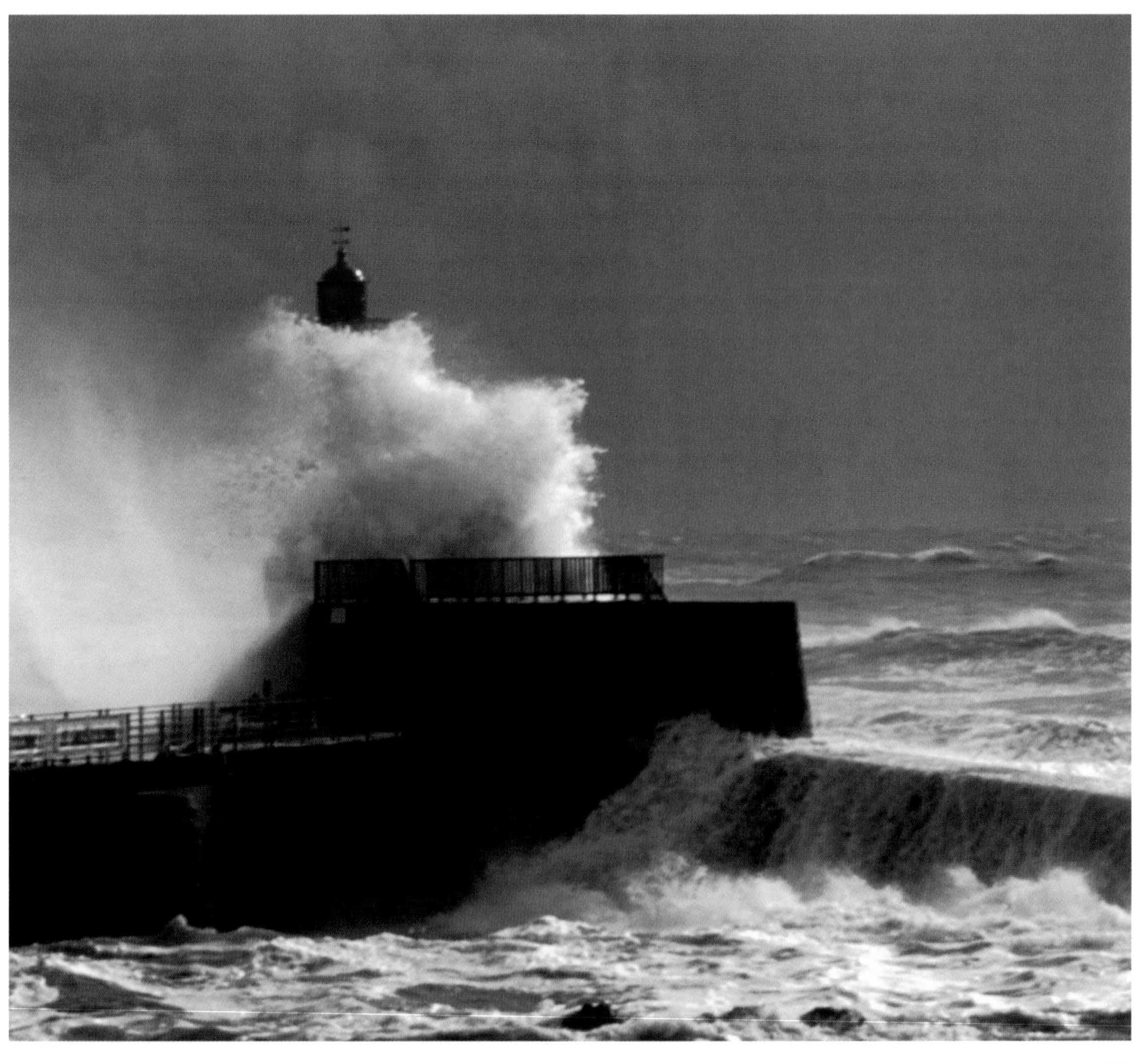

Weather gauge and the lee shore

Apart from the possibility of being overwhelmed in open water, the greatest danger at sea is being unable to claw free of a lee shore. In the days of square rig when some ships would struggle to make to windward at all, the lee shore was always potentially deadly. For modern yachts and power craft with strong engines and close-winded rigs, it only becomes so in tough conditions. However, a competent skipper is always aware of lee shores and develops an instinctive respect for them. In heavy weather, keeping strategically out of their way is vital, lest a vessel that seems to be managing fine is suddenly disabled by an unforeseen contingency. In the absence of traffic, an instinctive skipper will always steer up the weather side of a river on a windy day, and the very idea of cruising close in to a beach with the waves breaking on it is anathema. A seamanship examiner always notes how his candidates set themselves up to deal with lee shores. Keeping well clear is known as maintaining a weather gauge.

Strategic options

When overtaken by heavy weather at sea, it is important to look at the options, prioritise, then act. Strategy will depend on the direction of wind and wave in relation to the course desired. It will also be affected by sea room and crew condition amongst other factors. However, the following options will be considered:

- Continue with the passage – If things are not too severe, it may be possible to carry on regardless, taking due note of sea conditions for a motor vessel, or reefing down appropriately under sail.
- Keep to the sea and survive – The greatest danger at sea generally comes from the proximity of land. Unless the boat is likely to be thrown down by the waves she is not in any immediate danger from the water, but the land can smash her up in minutes. Once again, the main issue is the lee shore. Unless the boat is in mid-ocean and beyond reach of realistic shelter, it is often unpopular for a skipper to decide to remain at sea, but far more boats have been lost running for shelter than by staying out in open water. Keep well clear of areas of known wave disturbance, such as offshore shoals, tide rips, or zones of high current activity typified by the Gulf Stream of the eastern US. It is also important to have studied the survival tactics that are suitable for your boat, because the time to experiment randomly is not when it is blowing so hard you have to crawl up the deck to avoid being swept overboard.
- Seek shelter – If the vessel is at risk and shelter can safely be approached, this is the preferred option. When assessing the risk of exchanging searoom for the perceived security of a harbour or anchorage, the following points may be considered:

Downwind Running downwind for shelter under sail has the great advantage that the passage will be less dire for the crew and will place less stress on the boat. Even motor craft can benefit from this to some extent, despite the high skill levels required to drive faster craft. For every vessel, however, the coast that beckons will be a lee shore with all the attendant perils.

Upwind The opposite applies to an upwind refuge. Getting there may be gruelling, but by the time you arrive, you should be under the lee of a weather shore and essentially safe.

Assessing harbours of refuge If a harbour is to be attempted to leeward in storm conditions, its entrance must be impossible to mistake and wide enough to allow for any loss of control that may arise from a deteriorated sea state. Consider the way the bottom shoals. Anything sudden is likely to give rise to heavy seas just when you don't want them. Is a river involved? If so, avoid the ebb tide because it may cut up the sea cruelly. What is the disposition of any harbour walls? Will you have to make a hard turn in the entrance, perhaps for the first time since deciding to run for shelter? If so, is your vessel going to be powerful enough? Will there be wave bounce-back from the walls? And so on.

Notwithstanding all this, harbours do exist which are genuinely 'all-weather'. They are not common, but they are beyond price to the storm-tossed sailor.

Almost any refuge that lies to windward with a sheltering shoreline behind it can be entered in a gale. The only problem is getting 'up' there in the first place.

Broaching in a powered vessel

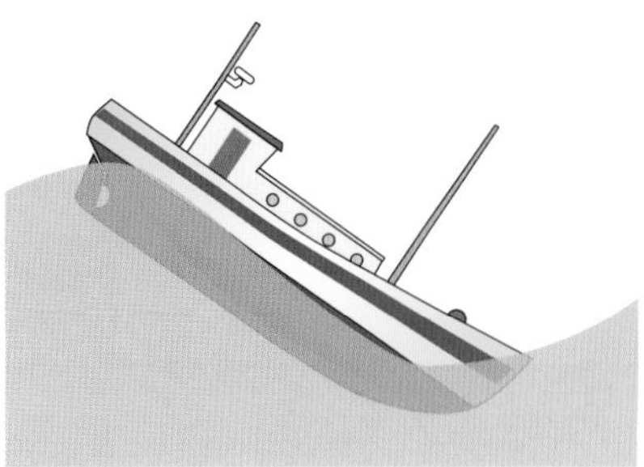

Bow buries in wave trough

Boat broaches

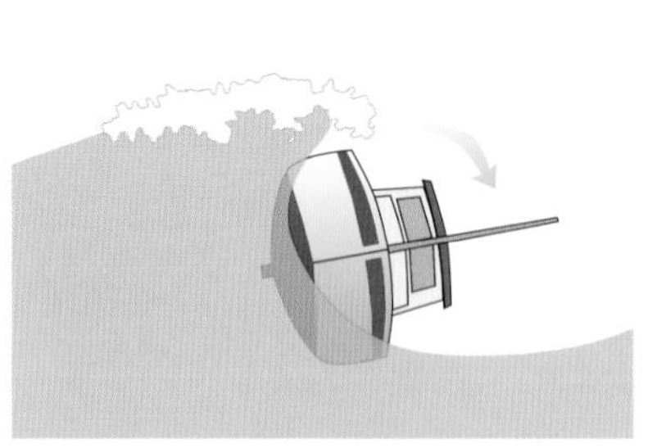

Leaving her beam on to the waves

Handling power craft in heavy weather

Watertight integrity

When the weather deteriorates badly, boats with large windows are at risk of having their watertight integrity breached. If one window is smashed and it is humanly possible to place it away from the weather, adjust your course and your plans accordingly. For example, if a forward wheelhouse window is smashed, consider seeking shelter downwind if this can safely be attained. Meanwhile, block the hole by any available means including mattresses, and advise the coastguard by radio or mobile phone.

Slow-speed motor boats without trim adjustment

Vessels in this category have no special technology to assist them as weather deteriorates. As with all power-driven craft, the seas are the danger rather than the wind, especially if they break in open water.

Upwind

Control speed to avoid slamming into the trough as you proceed over each succeeding wave top.

The beam sea

Not only is a beam sea uncomfortable for motor boats, a steep one that breaks from time to time is potentially dangerous. A study of the pages on sailing craft in heavy weather will show how any boat beam-on to the seas is vulnerable, while one that can keep herself more or less end-on is far better placed to deal with her situation. A wave does not have to be mountainous to throw your boat down or even roll her clean over. Any breaking sea higher than half her length places you seriously at risk.

If the direct course to your destination puts big steep seas on the beam, look for strategic ways to improve matters. You might perhaps steer closer to the wind and waves for a while in order to gain a lee from land lying to windward. This would exchange the beam sea for one on the bow until the boat was in calmer water, at which time she could bear away from the wind back onto course. She could then take what remains of the waves on the beam with little more than inconvenience.

If no way of avoiding the beam seas presents itself, you must make a decision about whether it is safe to continue, or if you should go into 'survival mode' (see pages 103-109) until the weather improves.

Dodging – Fishing vessels of the traditional displacement form use this technique to survive in seas that are otherwise too big or steep to handle safely. Others can do far worse than follow their example.

If you have a small mizzen riding sail, sheet it right in. If you haven't one, you may be obliged to work harder at the wheel. Head the boat up into the seas and throttle back until you are just making steerage way. In daylight, watch the waves coming as you rise to the crests. If a steep one that could break seems to be heading your way, put some power on and try to avoid it, then slow down again and continue jogging upwind. After dark, you are left with only luck and intuition on your side, but a well-found boat of reasonable size will generally manage. The surface drift of the gale will drive you back almost as much as the propeller is pushing you ahead, so your position may change surprisingly little.

Downwind

Keep sufficient way on to avoid being broached by a following sea. Broaching occurs when a wave picks up the stern and throws it round, generating centrifugal force which exaggerates the turn and takes it out of control. The boat may well heel over heavily under the same forces, and this can render the rudder less effective, or even useless. If you broach beam-on to the face of a steep wave the boat may be knocked down or even capsized, especially if the wave is breaking. For a displacement motor boat, probably the best way of avoiding a broach is to keep a sensible amount of way on. The propeller will then be throwing water past the rudder, counteracting the tendency for temporary steering failure near the crest caused by the circulation of water within the wave (see pages 148 to 150). Only experimentation can tell what is best for your boat on the day, but if heavy weather seems a likely outcome of your cruising you could consider shipping a drogue. Towing this astern on a rope of suitable length often confers the additional control to keep the stern in line. If you've no drogue, try tying every rope on board together then streaming the whole lot in a bight secured at either quarter.

Fore-and-aft trim

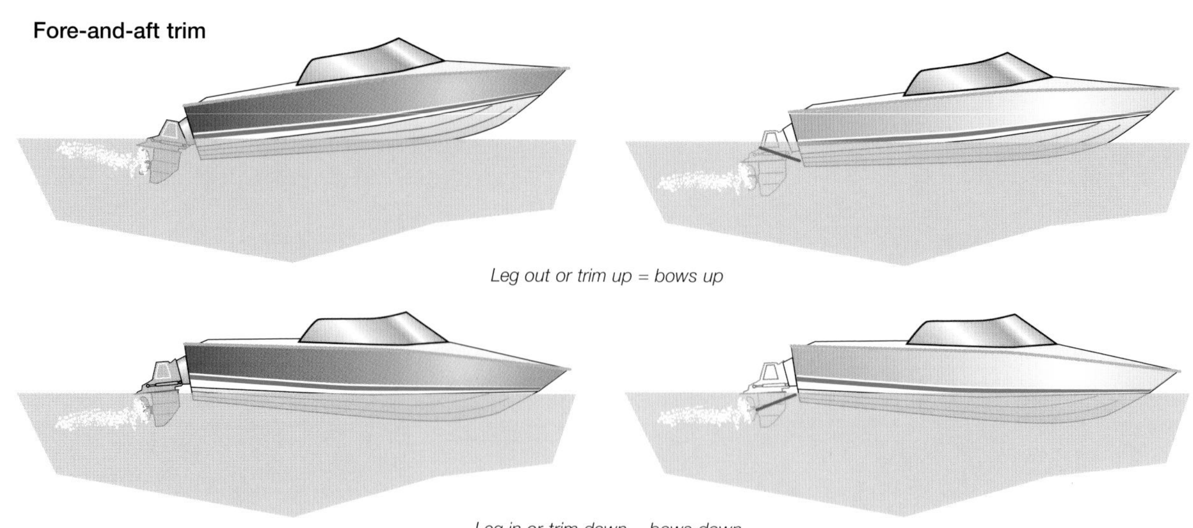

Leg out or trim up = bows up

Leg in or trim down = bows down

Faster power craft

Trim

Most planing power yachts and semi-displacement fast cruisers have the facility to adjust their fore-and-aft trim mechanically. This is achieved either by varying the angle of an out-drive or outboard, or applying trim tabs sited right aft, one on either side.

'Leg in' or 'trim down' keeps the bow down. 'Leg out' or 'trim up' encourages the bow to rise. 'Trim down' on one side only will persuade that side of the boat to ride high, discouraging rolling and helping her to deal with a beam sea.

Stowage – The motion of a fast motorboat driving into a head sea can be literally shocking. There is a certain amount the helm can do about this, but it's inevitable that both boat and crew are going to submit to something of a beating. Anything up forward is going to be well scrambled, so extra care needs to be taken to stow lockers tightly, pack crockery and glasses with towels, and generally make sure that nothing that could conceivably break loose has any chance of doing so. Crew must also be ready for a tough ride.

Head sea

A boat powering into a head sea, especially if she is planing, will try to take off on the wave crests and may plough into the trough so badly as to lose control. Fortunately, most boats today are of the deep-vee hull form. So long as the bow can be kept down to use as much of the waterline length as possible, the sharp sections will minimise any tendency to slam. This is achieved by trimming down or trimming the leg hard in. Throttle back as you climb the front of the approaching wave to prevent the boat taking to the air over the top, then power up down the back to keep the bows high and stop them nose-diving as you enter the trough.

Wave length – All of the above can be readily expedited if the wave length is long enough for such luxuries. Often, however, the seas are steep enough to create a challenge without being far enough apart for ideal set-piece manoeuvring. In such a case the best plan is to come off a dead upwind heading by anything from 30° to 45°, taking the seas broad on the bow instead. After a measured length of time, alter course to put the weather on the other bow and plug on until you have made up the difference. This tactic can make for a surprisingly comfortable ride, and the additional distance is far less than you might imagine, especially at only 30°.

Beam sea

Trim down on the upwind trim tab to raise this side of the boat a little and help ease the rolling. Assess the nature of the seas and in particular their regularity to decide how much way to keep on. Very often, a sea is confused and you may have to opt for a compromise between beam-sea tactics and those for a head or a following sea. The danger, as for the slower motor boat, is that you'll be rolled by a breaker. With your extra speed, however, you have some capacity to see a bad one coming and take avoiding action by steering to pass to one side or the other. If taking a breaker becomes inevitable, either turn into it or swing away to try and outrun it; don't just sit there like a duck in a shooting gallery and do nothing.

Downwind

This is the most dangerous state of sea for a power boat. She is vulnerable to a breaking wave crest giving her rudder nothing to bite on, leaving her wide open to a broach. She may also lose control by digging her nose into the back of a wave she is overtaking. In either case, knock-down is a real possibility. The best response to these perils is to adjust your speed positively to be slower or faster than the waves, and to overtake them where appropriate with circumspection. Trim up (leg out) to raise the bow and keep it from ploughing into the trough, and watch out at the crest for foaming water if the wave is breaking. Avoid these wherever you can. If a breaker looks like catching you up, power on and accelerate away ahead of it. Not only does the rudder become inefficient in the breaking water of the crest, the propeller may cavitate and deliver less drive. Be prepared to throttle back smartly if the engine starts racing. This will give the screw a better grip than letting it thrash around in the air bubbles.

If things get too 'hairy' for comfort, don't forget there are always other options, such as choosing a different destination or turning up into the wind and dodging.

Handling sailing craft on passage in heavy weather

The techniques of storm survival at sea for sailing boats are dealt with later, but there is much that can be done to help a boat perform while still on passage.

Weatherliness

It has been said with some justification that a well-handled bath tub will sail downwind. The issues arise when the wind is forward of the beam. A boat that can work to windward in hard going is called 'weatherly'. It is possible to say without risk of generalisation that larger craft perform better in this respect than equivalent smaller ones. A long waterline handles waves with greater readiness, while additional ballast and displacement render a rig more powerful. All sailing craft have a frontier beyond which they cannot be driven to windward and an extreme limit at which they can no longer maintain even their weather gauge. It's not easy to predict what these parameters might be, but skippers should take every opportunity to expand their knowledge of their boats.

Sail combinations

A poorly set-up rig with a roller reefing genoa furled in to 10 rolls or more will not perform nearly as well as a tautly prepared smaller boat whose headsails are setting properly. The roller-reefing compromise that is so attractive in moderate conditions becomes a nightmare when you really need the sail to perform.

Some serious cruisers and short-handed race boats use a choice of permanently hoisted headsails — generally two. On a typical 40-footer, one might be a full genoa that sets adequately with some rolls in up to force 5. The second is a 'yankee' – a full-hoist jib with a high-cut clew of less than 100% of the area of the fore triangle, usually set up close abaft the genoa. Its luff may well have an area of foam sewn into it. All these things militate towards satisfactory reefing of a sail designed for maximum efficiency fully unfurled upwind in force 5. At near-gale and beyond, even the yankee will have run out of steam upwind. It is replaced by a traditional storm sail hanked onto a stay which may need to be set up for the occasion (see page 94).

In more moderate going, the yankee is chosen for any short-tacking, because the genoa is too much like hard work and struggles to pass between its own stay and the yankee's.

The cutter – A simpler solution is to rig the boat as a modern cutter. The cutter's jib should be high cut for more effective roller reefing. The staysail set inside it is on a permanent forestay with running backstays for heavier going. This sail might also be on a roller, but there is much to be said for keeping it on deck and hoisting it when required. It can be made 'self-tacking' by means of a boom on a traveller, or by a single sheet led aft via a turning block well up the mast. The staysail can be set inside the jib to power up the fore triangle or used alone in heavier going. The boat probably won't point quite so high with both sails drawing, but she will smash through heavy seas more powerfully. Since no yacht points at her highest in such conditions, little is lost and much can be gained. In survival extremes a cutter retains the option to substitute the staysail for a storm jib and, like any other yacht, she can set a trysail (page 94).

The sad fact is that most cruisers do not have sail wardrobes like these and must manage as best they can with a single roller genoa. For such a boat working upwind towards safety in severe conditions, the only satisfactory answer is to motorsail. Reef the mainsail as deeply as possible and haul it out flat; sheet it hard in and motor to windward at between 30° and 45° as the seas dictate.

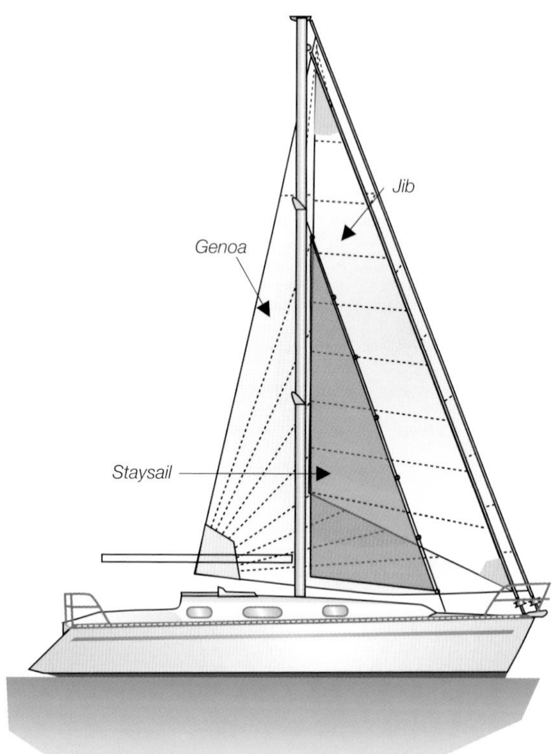

Headsail arrangement for modern cutter.
Note: The high-cut jib alternative to the Genoa.

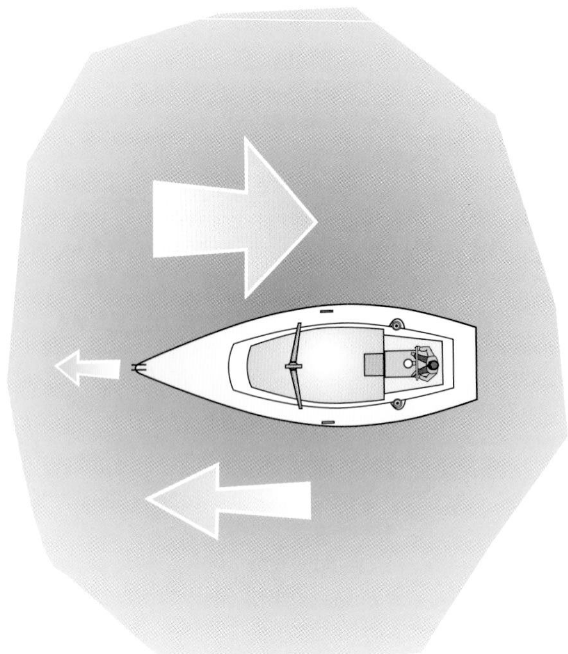
Boat heading to windward will experience a much stronger apparent wind than one going downwind.

True and apparent wind in heavy weather

A yacht running downwind at 6 knots with an apparent wind speed of 30 knots will, should she be obliged to turn instead to windward, find herself battling with over 40 knots. This is a full gale. The force exerted by wind on canvas increases as the square of the wind speed, so at 40 knots she'll be suffering not far off double the load she was coping with in 30 knots. In boats without anemometers, this is an easy mistake to make and every experienced sailor has received a nasty shock from it at some time or other. Even if you have a dial to put numbers to what you can see with your own eyes, it still may not prepare you for the full effect of the difference. Therefore, if you find yourself on a broad reach or a run, knowing that after rounding some corner or offlying hazard your course will come up higher onto the wind, you'll need to make any necessary preparations before it happens. Even if you don't anticipate having to alter course, there is still the possibility of some unforeseen emergency demanding that you round up. The bottom line of this advice is that it is rarely prudent to drive too hard downwind in a blow. If you're racing you'll have to make peace with your conscience, but a cruising skipper should always be second-guessing the odds.

Controlling apparent wind for safety

The fact that the forces on a boat are so much diminished by running downwind often makes this the manoeuvre of choice when boat or crew are being tested severely. If something carries away or there is a foul-up — perhaps in a roller reefing headsail gear — the natural tendency of anyone trained in dinghies is to turn into the wind and take the force out of the sails by letting them flap. The trouble with this in a larger boat is that they don't flap, they flog, and pity help anyone caught in their way. In a gale of wind, an innocent bowline on an uncontrolled headsail clew can become as dangerous as a baseball bat, and many's the black eye they have dished up. Such strains also put huge stresses on the boat's gear.

One way and another, luffing up often makes a crisis out of what began as a mere inconvenience. On the other hand, running off diminishes the apparent wind; it also lets the boat take the seas more easily. If there is a problem on the foredeck, the mainsail of a typical yacht eased right out can be used to provide a degree of shelter from the wind while the matter is dealt with. In a serious blow, therefore, running off is usually a better option, always assuming that lack of searoom is not a factor.

Shortening sail

The physical techniques of reefing and shortening sail in general lie beyond the scope of this manual, but manoeuvres for rendering the process safer come within its brief.

'Spilling' off way – This delivers not only the benefit of reducing apparent wind, it also lessens the effect of the sea. Steer onto a close reach with the true wind about 65° off the bow. Now ease the main and headsail sheets just enough to spill a little wind without undue flogging. Fine-tuning is done with the helm. Steer upwind to lose more way, steer to leeward if you feel the boat stalling. Stalling is to be avoided because the boat's head will fall away heavily to leeward. This fills the mainsail which, of course, cannot be spilled with the wind on or abaft the beam. Because the yacht is almost at a standstill, the wind hits the sail flat-on which makes her stagger and heel alarmingly.

This technique is useful when crew are moving forward to reef the main at the mast, or to change a hanked headsail. While the reefing is going on, the boat can be sailed on the half-lifting headsail alone to keep motion and wind to a minimum.

Spilling wind to take off way

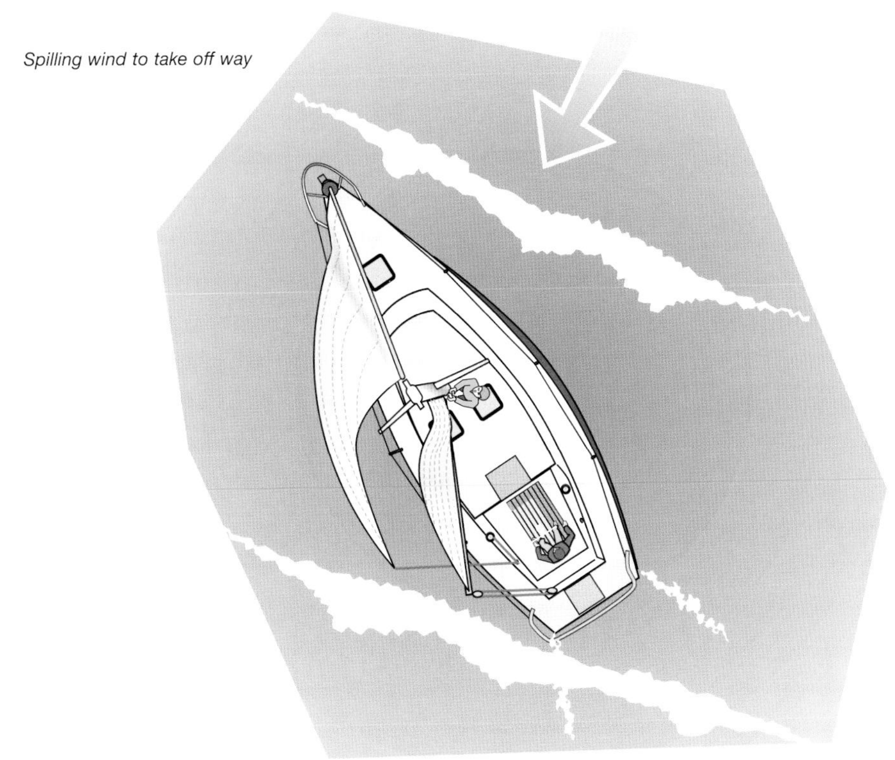

Storm canvas

Storm jibs

A storm jib is a small, flat-cut, high-clewed jib that is virtually bullet-proof. If the yacht sets her headsails by hanking them to a forestay or by feeding them into a groove, shortening down to it is simply a matter of taking down the next sail above it in size, bending on the storm jib and hoisting away. Unfortunately, the headstays of most modern yachts are taken up with permanently rigged roller reefing headsails which do not even pretend to set in gale force winds. For a storm jib to be useful it must be easy to deploy, and the best method of achieving this is an additional headstay inboard of the existing forestay. Usually, these removable stays are permanently attached aloft and stored at the shrouds to be brought forward and attached to the deck when it matters. They may also require running backstays which wait out of the way until their moment of glory. Storm forestays can be successfully tensioned with a tackle, perhaps assisted by a winch, but more often than not they have some sort of lever instead. Once in place, the sail is hanked on and the sheets led aft. Care is needed over the sheeting arrangements, bearing in mind that the boat is not going to point very high under this rig.

Any boat with roller headsails going properly offshore must have some such arrangement.

Trysails

The storm trysail has three advantages over the deep-reefed mainsail:

- It is rarely used and so can generally be relied upon not to blow out.
- It does not use the boom, and is therefore untroubled if this spar or its gooseneck attachment point has been damaged.
- Its tack is well above the gooseneck, keeping it clearer of any heavy seas breaking over the deck.

A trysail is set as shown in the diagram below. The luff is attached to the mast, ideally on a dedicated secondary track, but otherwise it is slid into the mainsail track through a gate above the stowed main. It is tacked down to some convenient point and hoisted by the main halyard. The two sheets are led via turning blocks on the quarters to spare cockpit winches. It is not sheeted to the end of the main boom.

Trysails set excellently closehauled or reaching. They are not good on a dead run because without a boom to settle them, they tend to gybe themselves. While this may not be dangerous in itself, the jarring on the gear and mast in 40 or 50 knots of wind is not to be countenanced.

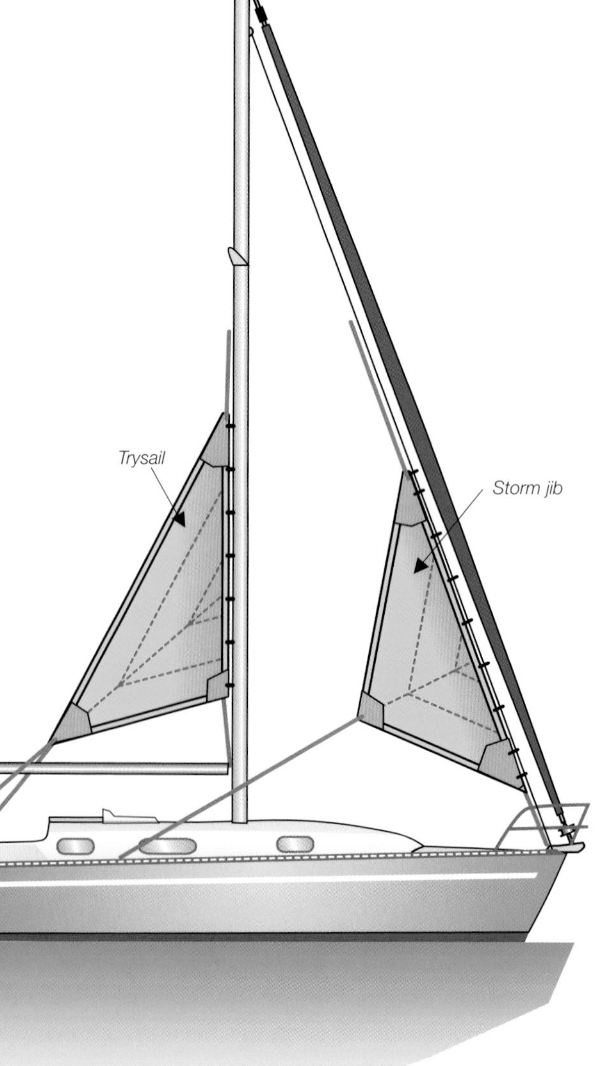

Making life easier

Running Off As described on the previous page, running off is a great way of defusing a windy situation. If a headsail is to be changed on an upwind passage and searoom is plentiful, it is far better to run off and let the sail collapse 'behind' the main than to keep plugging in to weather. Even where searoom is an issue, it is often worth running off just for a brief period to let the crew get up to the foredeck and douse the sail safely. The boat can then be sailed slowly to windward under main alone while they are changing it for the next one.

Running off is also the best way of taking the sting out of a big reefing genoa that is proving a struggle to roll. If you just let go the sheet, especially with the breeze well forward, the flogging sail will create enough drag to give you a hard time even though it isn't full and driving. Kill it behind the main on a run and it will come in like a lamb to the fold.

Heaving to (pages 106-107 for a description of this manoeuvre). For the right boat, heaving to can be another useful method of taking off way to tackle any job on deck. It is often the best method for defusing a sail-shortening exercise. For many modern yachts with a cut-away forefoot, however, the equilibrium of the hove-to state is too radically disturbed when one or more sails are adjusted. Letting off the mainsheet to reef the sail, for example, can allow the boat's head to pay off, filling the half-reefed canvas in a most undesirable way. If the boat is sufficiently stable hove-to, however, your crew will relish the prospect of going forward in greater safety than can otherwise be achieved.

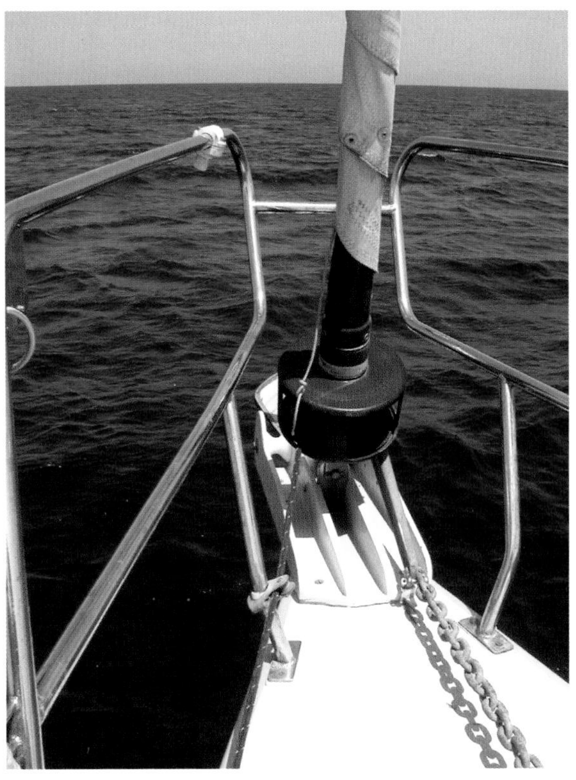

The loads on headsail roller reefing gears can be greatly reduced by running off the wind.

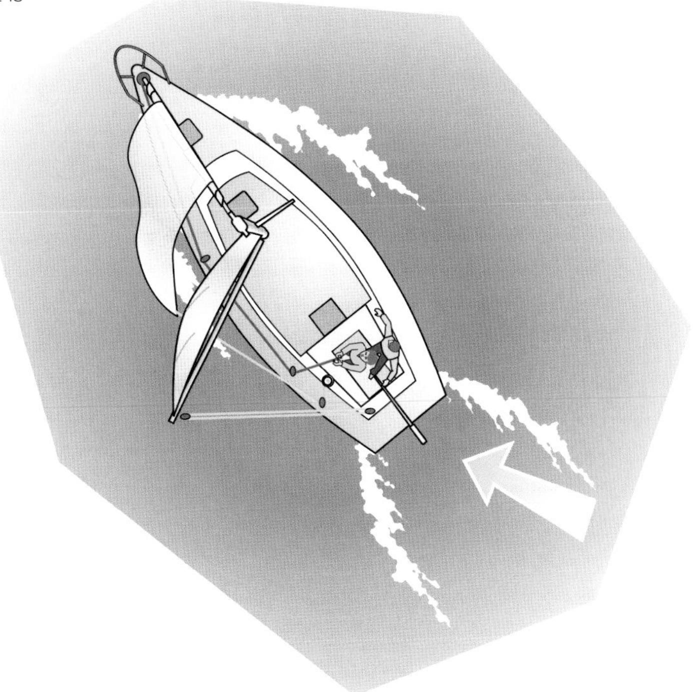

Steering in waves

Upwind

Steering a sailing boat upwind in flat water demands only one essential skill – the ability to keep the boat driving as close to the wind as she is able. Techniques vary with the type and size of boat, but the general rule is not to try to point too high in a seaway. Cracking off the theoretical closest angle by 5° or so can pay handsome dividends. In serious conditions, the angle may be wider still.

Long-keeled, heavy craft Such yachts are generally steady on the helm with an appreciable delay in reaction between applying rudder and any alteration in heading. In practice, this means that the waves make little difference to the technique. Just keep her 'in the groove' as best you can and let the boat's inertia carry her through the wave-tops as she smashes into them. There will come times, however, especially with smaller craft, where one wave slows the boat appreciably and the next stops her dead in the water. She will then sit there nodding, or 'going up and down in the same hole'. Her bow will also fall off the wind and as the sails fill, she will stall, sliding off to leeward until she has gathered enough way for her keel to grip again. This is not only counter-productive, it is also mighty depressing. In skilled hands, however, it rarely happens because the person at the helm has sensed the first wave by its steepness and borne away from the wind 10° or 20° as the boat passes over the top of it. This 'slacker' heading is maintained as she rushes down into the trough to face the stopper. The extra way she has gathered and the fact that she is not meeting the wave so near to head-on allow her to sail over the top of it without being checked. Once clear of the rough patch, she is brought back onto the wind and away she goes again. For such craft, pounding is rarely an issue.

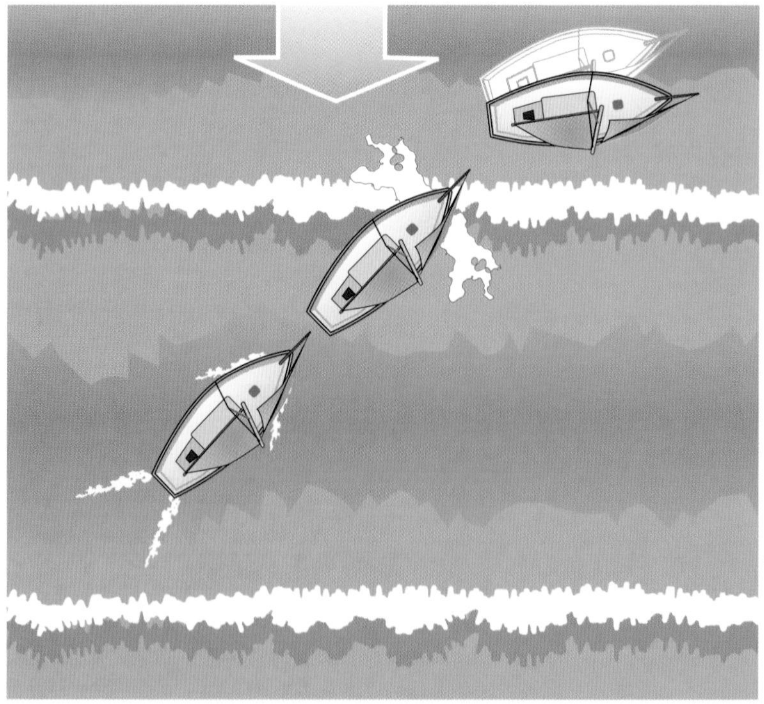

Although a heavy boat will usually punch through the waves, she can be slowed enough to lose her momentum in which case the bow may fall off to leeward and the boat will wallow. Bear away and maintain momentum before this happens.

Shorter-keeled, lighter craft Because this type of yacht reacts more quickly to helm movements it is often possible to steer rapidly off the wind as the boat comes to the crest of each wave. This will stop her plunging straight over the top, falling into the trough and pounding. Pounding not only jars the crew's teeth and increases risk of structural damage, it also slows the boat badly. If she is sailing powerfully, she can be luffed slightly above her best course without losing too much way as she climbs the back of the next wave. This process gives a mean course of closehauled, or a touch below. It's effective but tiring. Sailing on autopilot, of course, no such sophistication will be available, so if this is your choice try to reduce the pounding by not pointing too high.

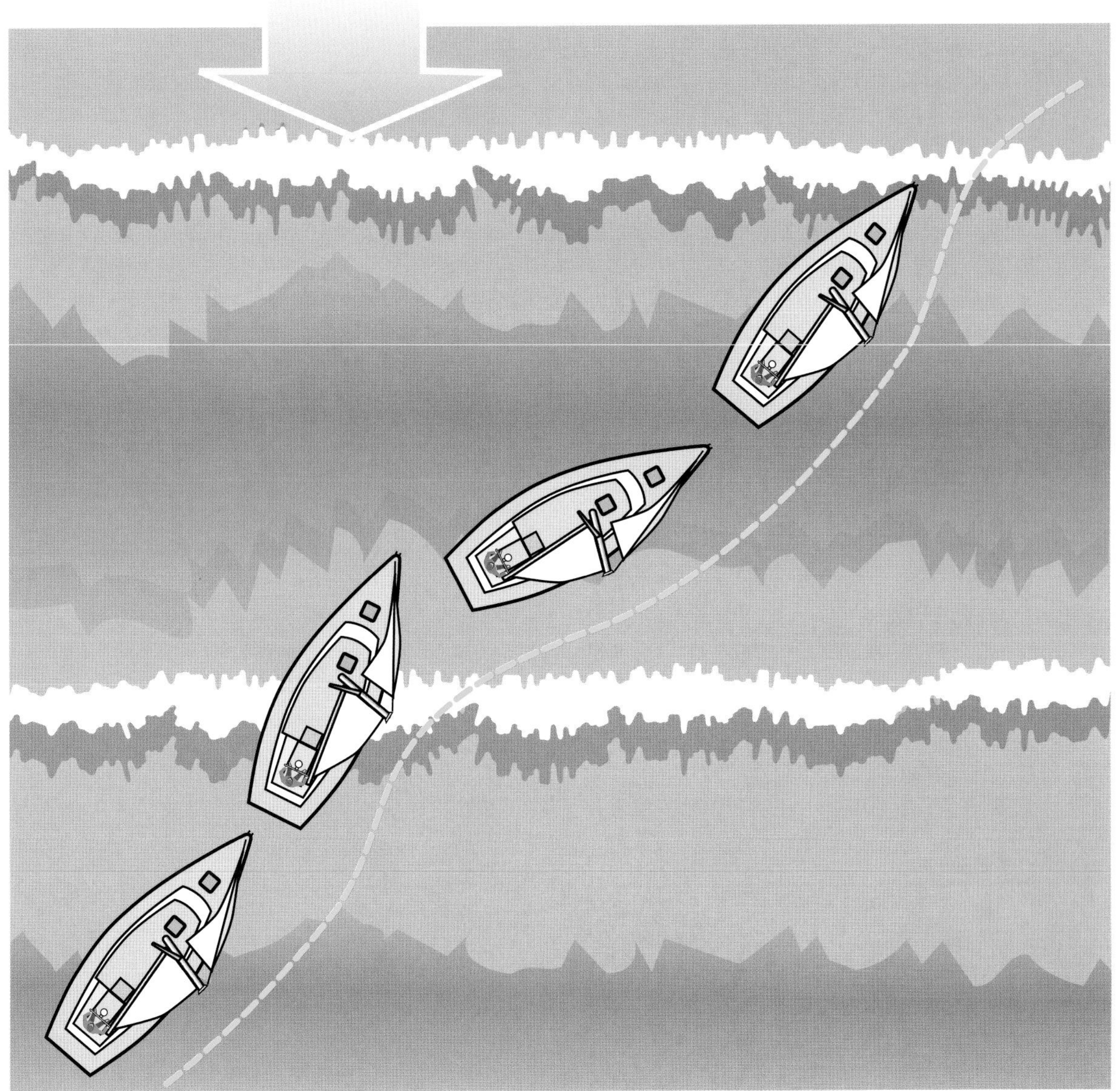

By bearing away after she breasts each wave, a light boat can build up sufficient speed to deal with the next one.

Downwind

Sailing downwind safely in moderately heavy weather is a matter of controlling speed so that the boat can be steered without drama, which means not being overcanvassed. There is no specific difference between the various types of yacht, except that lighter craft, especially those with flat sections aft, are more ready to pick up their skirts and start surfing. A century and more ago, the greatest danger faced by huge square-riggers running round the world in the Southern Ocean was that of broaching. Nothing has changed. The broach is still the ogre waiting to pounce on today's yachts as we power downwind in heavy weather.

Anatomy of a broach If you're unsure about what a broach really is, you'll know when you suffer one because the rudder will stop working and you'll end up defenceless, stalled right out and beam-on to the weather. Here's how it happens:

- Unlike a boat on a reach or closehauled, a yacht running is not receiving much steadying influence from her sails. This means there is little to stop her rolling and roll she will, to a greater or lesser extent.
- As she rolls, two things happen:
  - Her rig swings out far to one side of her pivot point and her rudder. If she rolls to starboard, this will tend to make her swivel to port.
  - The shape of her immersed hull alters putting a 'fat' section into the water on the side to which she is rolling. The other side will be relatively flat. The result of this imbalance is a tendency to turn away from the fat sections, so that if the boat rolls to starboard, she wants to round up to port.

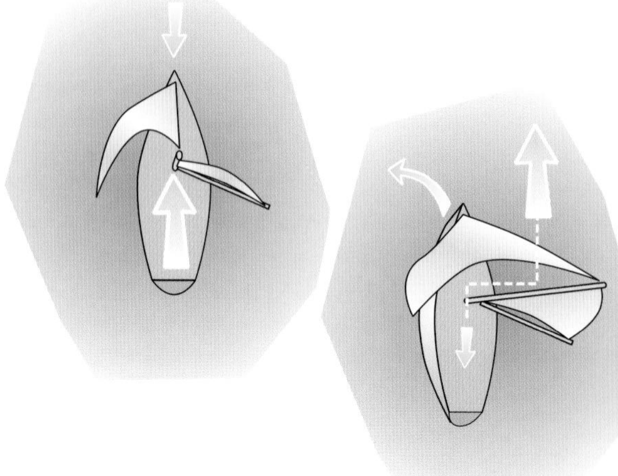

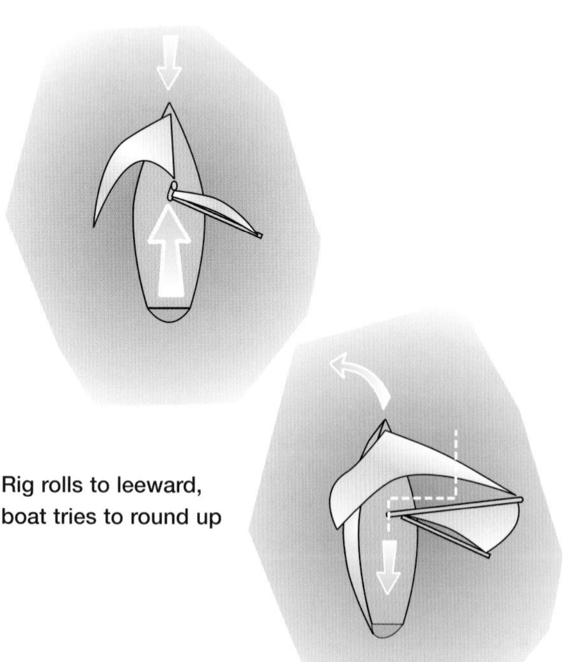

Rig rolls to leeward, boat tries to round up

The broach to windward

- With rig and hull working together to generate imbalance, it follows that as a boat rolls to leeward (the side the mainsail is set), she will try to swing round into the wind.
- If she is allowed to do this she will roll even more heavily to leeward as she starts to round up, by virtue of the centrifugal force of the sharp turn and by increased wind pressure on the sails which are not yet spilling wind.
- As the heel angle increases to eccentric proportions, the rudder becomes less effective, partly because it is trying to raise the stern rather than shove it sideways, and partly because it may well be half out of the water. Very likely it is already stalled and no longer functioning properly at all.
- A broach is now inevitable. Hang on and hope you are able to bear away back onto course without damage.

The gybe broach

- As a boat heels to windward on a heavy roll, the hull imbalance starts its mischief.
- The rig is displaced to windward by the roll and contributes to the tendency to swerve round to leeward.
- The swerve takes charge as centrifugal force kicks in, the rudder stalls and the boat broaches to leeward, gybing all-standing as she goes.

Prevention against the broach

In fast, light, modern yachts, all issues of broaching must be seen in the context of surfing (see photograph below), but two points cover the prevention of all broaches:

Keeping speed down You are far less likely to broach if you can keep your speed within sensible limits. The ideal is around that magical rate of knots your boat can make to windward in calm water. This will never be anywhere near the boat's hull speed, but it is the rate of knots at which she is not making big waves. As hull speed is approached and the waves increase, the strains on the rudder rise heavily. Unless surfing is contemplated, check her enthusiasm by shortening sail.

Keep her on her feet If a boat is allowed to wander from her straight course, the tendency to roll increases because the yawing will add centrifugal force to the mix of factors unavoidably already present. A good helmsman develops a feel for an incipient broach and checks the tendency to turn almost before it has begun. Proactive steering will help a boat stay 'on her feet' in awkward circumstances. Merely reacting to yawing that is already well under way is simply not good enough. Keep her going as straight as you can.

Surfing

Any sailing boat except the heaviest is capable of surfing down the face of a wave at speeds well in excess of her theoretical maximum. She does not have to be ultra-light, although it helps. Once surfing, it is vital to keep any boat on her feet, because at such speeds one can rarely argue with the centrifugal forces if she starts to spin round. Some race boats designed for long periods of downwind work in heavy weather are exceptionally light, wide and flat aft to encourage stable surfing. The extreme beam renders their rudders liable to lift out of the water when they heel heavily, so deep spade rudders are standard. Twin rudders ensure that the leeward one is kept in the water.

Surfing not only diminishes passage times, it is also extremely exciting, but it makes huge demands on crew at the helm and even greater ones of an autopilot. The average cruising boat is unlikely to surf for any length of time, but whatever the boat, the key to safety lies firmly in the driver's hands. Anticipation is everything if the yacht is not to run out of control and broach. The initial tweaking of the helm as the yacht takes off down the wave is not unlike what happens when a dinghy breaks out onto a plane. A firm touch of weather helm to start with as the wind grabs her and she tries to round up to windward, then a readiness to steer hard the other way as she accelerates and thinks about broaching to leeward. Only feel can tell you what to do, and practice makes perfect. There is no need to be intimidated, however. A good helm will soon be managing fine in a boat that is not being driven to the edge. The exhilaration is highly rewarding.

Mike Golding in Open 60.

Storm Survival

Like heavy weather in general, the definition of a 'survival' storm is decided by the ability of the boat and crew involved. Although notable exceptions arise from time to time, modern weather forecasting has reached such a high level of availability and reliability that true survival storms are rarely encountered by small craft on voyages of less than 48 hours duration. Indeed, it could be said that barring serious misfortune any prudent skipper using forecasts properly could cruise the coasts for a lifetime without meeting one. It is only when engaged in medium or long voyages far from potential refuge that a boat may find herself in the path of weather from which there is no escape.

In mid-ocean, or even a hundred or two miles from land, outside assistance may be beyond realistic call-out. The boat must therefore be assumed to be thrown entirely on her own devices with rescue only a remote contingency. It has been shown unambiguously that crews abandoning damaged vessels whose watertight integrity has not been breached are in greater danger than those who opt to sit tight and tough it through. At such times, searoom is unlikely to be an issue, so all the tactical options to protect her and her crew will be available.

Anyone undertaking voyages where survival tactics may be required should be fully cognisant with the choices. Because these may well be specific to the type of boat and her crew's stamina and technical ability, it is not enough to be vaguely aware that 'so-and-so did this or that'. Any relevant equipment must be aboard. It should be conveniently stowed, and will have already been tried and tested. The crew of a sailing boat carrying a para anchor must know to work it when the only safe way of approaching the foredeck is to crawl. If an engine is involved in a survival strategy, the worst must be assumed because it is when the boat is standing on her ends that it will stop. Sludge in fuel tanks, for example, can lie around for years, but you can be sure that it will arise and clog the filters when the waves are steep and life is threatened. Spares for these and the ability of someone on board to instal them quickly are therefore of critical importance. Whatever the boat, power or sail, if she is to go offshore any part of her that may fail in extreme circumstances must be checked and addressed prior to going to sea.

This section of the manual will consider the main sources of danger created by open-water heavy weather, and list the steps which may be taken by the crews of both motor boats and sailing craft to mitigate them. Since many factors straddle the divide between the two disciplines, readers whose interests may lie in one area are encouraged to consider the whole section.

Power

Open ocean storm survival for power craft:
Most of today's power yachts are constrained by the range of their fuel tanks. Given this inherent limitation on how far they can steam from a safe haven, they generally have sufficient speed available to outrun truly severe weather so long as forecasts are regularly monitored and sensibly interpreted.

Power craft undertaking prolonged ocean passages are few. Usually they are comparatively large. The super-high-speed variety invariably carry specialised crew who are trained and experienced to cope with their particular circumstances. Skippers of slower vessels, especially those operating solely in the displacement mode, would do well to study the sections of this manual dealing with sailing boat storm survival. The principles of stability, capsize and shunning a beam-on situation are very similar.

For all those who aspire only to well-planned shorter passages, matters should never go beyond the essentials of power-boat handling in rough water (as described on pages 88 to 91). However, it cannot be over-stressed that anyone undertaking extended voyages to the limits of the boat's fuel endurance should have total confidence in the maintenance and reliability of the engines – in particular the fuel system and the cleanliness of the tanks. Seaworthy covers for large windows are an absolute must. So long as the power keeps on coming, the water stays outside the boat and the weather has been anticipated, a safe arrival should be assured.

Sail

By far the greatest hazard for sailing craft in heavy weather offshore is that of being knocked down or even capsized by a high, steep sea. Occasionally, boats are pitch-poled (thrown end-over-end), but here the question of stability hardly arises, since the boat is literally picked up and tossed onto her deck. This is not to say that steps cannot be taken to avoid it, but it is a rare event that comes about in only the most extreme circumstances. Most knock-downs are the result of being caught beam-on to a sea, and it is this condition that is conventionally considered when assessing capsize potential. An understanding of the essential theory is a great help to a skipper when deciding how best to handle a given situation and a specific boat.

Static Stability

When a yacht is floating upright, her centre of buoyancy ('B') is midships, as is her centre of gravity ('G'). When she heels, her immersed shape alters and B moves outboard relative to the centreline, away from G which, because it is made up of all the immovable weight in the boat, does not shift at all. We will call the vertical position of shifted centre of buoyancy 'Z'. While this is pushing up under the forces of floatation (see the illustration), G is being pulled downwards by gravity. The effect is that the boat tries to come upright. If she is rolling freely she will do so. If she is under the influence of some outside force, such as her sails, she will reach a point of equilibrium whereby she remains at that angle because the force of the wind equals her capacity to self-right.

The horizontal distance between G and Z ('GZ') is a major contributing factor to capsize resistance. As the hull heels progressively, its length increases up to a maximum, decreasing once more as heel angle rises beyond normal sailing angles. At some point, the shifting centre of buoyancy will actually pass 'under' the centre of gravity and out the other side. The boat is now in dire peril because the buoyancy is still pushing up while the centre of gravity continues to pull down. These values relate to the global gravitational system rather than to any ideas the boat may have about 'this side up', and the result is 'negative GZ'. The boat is trying to invert and stay there.

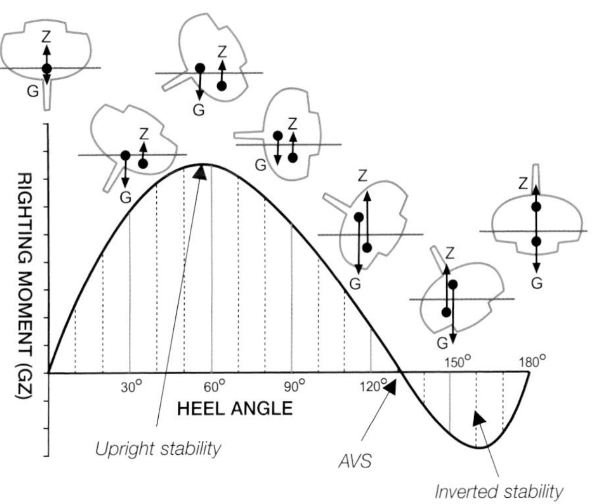

Angle of vanishing stability

A GZ curve can be projected for any craft, and all builders of yachts with offshore potential should make them available to owners who ask. Inspection shows how far the boat must heel to cross the point of zero GZ. Below the zero line, GZ has a minus value, and the boat is negatively stable. The degree of heel at which this takes place is called 'the angle of vanishing stability' ('AVS').

The greater the area of graph below the line, the more stable the yacht will be upside down. Fortunately, when a boat is knocked over, the water is invariably extremely rough and it is more than likely that the next wave will flick her upright again. Nonetheless, a high value of inverted stability renders this less likely. The obvious and extreme example would be a typical catamaran which cannot recover from capsize unassisted, but such craft come under rather different criteria.

By comparing AVS angles from various boats, you can build up some idea of how your own vessel is likely to stand up to capsizing forces, but it is important to realise that the GZ curve is only a starting point.

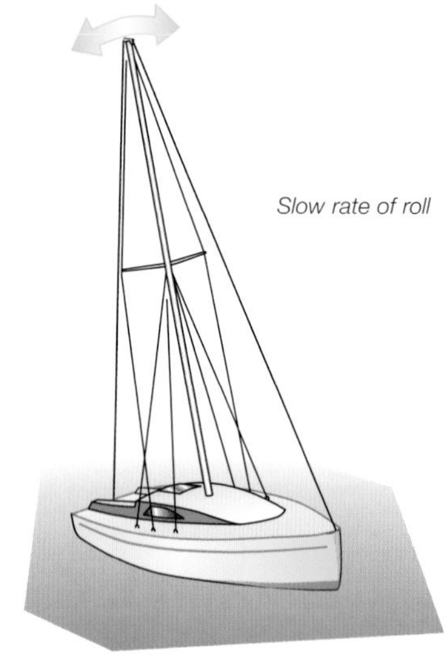
Slow rate of roll

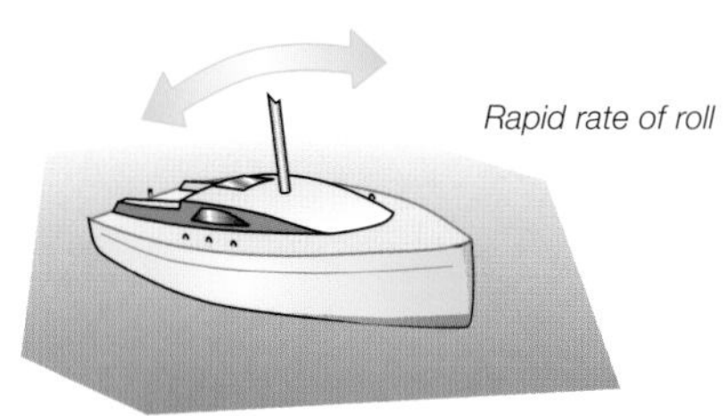
Rapid rate of roll

Further essential factors in capsize resistance

- ***Displacement*** In any mathematical formula of capsize resistance, displacement is a multiple factor. A heavier boat will, if all other factors are equal, perform better than a lighter one.
- ***Roll inertia*** This is a second element ignored by the GZ curve, but it has major significance in the dynamics of capsize. The further a parcel of weight is displaced from the centre of roll of the boat, the greater will be the arm of the roll resistance generated by its inertia. More weight means more inertia. More distance means a longer arm, or 'moment', hence greater effect. A tall, heavy mast supplies a surprising amount of opposition to the capsizing punch of a passing wave. This is surely contrary to what you might expect, but since it is already built into the centre of gravity with ballast to counterbalance it, its effect on the GZ curve is pre-ordained and may not be destructive. A heavy mast as part of the equation is a powerful safety feature in the real world outside the laboratory.

  The authority for this proposition is the Technical Committee of the Cruising Club of America, and these two factors explain why traditional, inside-ballasted sailing vessels such as smacks and pilot cutters were so spectacularly safe despite unimpressive GZ curves. They would have fared poorly if they ever capsized, but they almost never did.
- ***Beam*** High beam ratios in light, flat-floored craft confer substantial initial stability by virtue of the long righting arm as the centre of buoyancy moves outboard. The downside is that the same feature delivers a high value of inverted stability once the AVS is passed.
- ***Freeboard and coach roof*** High freeboard in itself does not appear to increase capsize risk, although it raises the deck and its associated weight and must therefore affect the position of the centre of gravity. However, a watertight coachroof supplies an unexpected reserve of buoyancy. A 'bump' in the GZ curve for the supremely stable Contessa 32 at the angle of heel when it becomes immersed shows this effect clearly. In terms of ultimate stability therefore, there is something to be said for the old-fashioned coachroof.
- ***Long / short keel*** Where all factors of beam, height of centre of gravity, depth of ballast etc, are equal, a longer keel shows no specific advantage over a short one in terms of theoretical stability. In practice, however, long keels are often associated with wholesome hull forms, moderate beam, heavy displacement, and many of the other ancillary factors adding up to better stability characteristics.

Multihull stability

Without going into too much detail, it can be said that while many monohulls of between 30ft and 50ft have an AVS of between 115° and 150°, a typical multihulled cruiser becomes negatively stable at around 90° of heel. This might not sound attractive, but it must be borne in mind that such craft enjoy huge 'form stability' by virtue of their beam and the buoyancy of the leeward hull. Their initial resistance to heeling (and hence knockdown by a passing wave) is therefore much higher. A graph of the righting energy required to capsize a monohull and a multihull of equivalent length reveals that up to around 65°, a catamaran requires a bigger slam to knock her over than an equivalent monohull even though she is little over half the displacement. If a multihull does suffer capsize, of course, her negative stability is total and she is unlikely to right again without outside assistance.

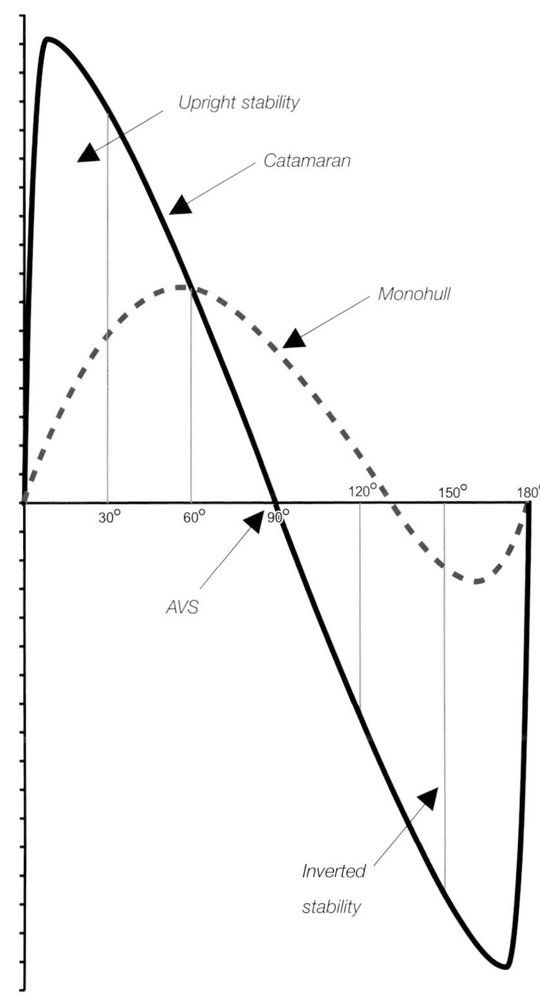

Survival options in open water

Open ocean storm survival for sailing craft

Sailing boats caught out in survival conditions can opt to operate either passively or actively. Generally speaking, unless deploying special gear, lighter vessels with flat-floored hulls need to be actively sailed, while heavier craft with longer keels are better placed to look after themselves without help from their crews. Developments with drogues and para anchors have in part mitigated this situation.

The possibility of knuckling down and carrying on with a passage in heavy weather has been considered earlier, but unless your destination lies far to leeward and you decide to run as a tactic to keep your boat end-on to the waves, to continue steering towards your goal is unlikely to be an option in survival conditions.

Keeping end-on

By far the easiest way for a boat to be thrown down or capsized is to be rolled beam-on by a steep or breaking wave. It follows that all survival tactics should aim to avoid this situation. The exception is lying a'hull which, as we shall see, is only an option for heavy displacement vessels in something short of ultimate conditions. Here are the accepted methods of achieving the right result:

Running off

Running before a gale has two great advantages: it keeps the boat stern-on to the action, thus stopping her from falling across the waves; it also decreases the apparent wind and wave force by whatever her speed may be. A big race boat running under spinnaker in 35-knot winds may well be achieving 20 knots boat speed. The chaps on deck can almost light a cigarette without having to cup their hands, but if she broaches and loses way, their smokes will be blown clean out of their mouths. The difference is less dramatic on a cruising boat, but it remains a benefit not to be ignored.

The secret of running safely is to maintain a sensible speed. As the wind rises, the boat will be reefed progressively and the time will come when a decision must be made about dropping all but one sail. It's easy to assume that the last sail left up would be the storm jib, but in some cases, a boat will run more stably with a triple-reefed mainsail so long as the boom is heavily vanged and a preventer employed to keep it steady. A trysail might also be considered, but as with the jib, since it lacks a boom, it may gybe involuntarily from time to time, which is heartily to be avoided in gale or storm-force winds. Only experimenting can decide what is best for each boat.

Extreme running

Bare poles As the wind rises and the boat runs faster and faster under steadily reducing canvas, sooner or later all sail will be taken in and she will continue to run under nothing more than the windage of her mast. This proposition can sound far-fetched to sailors who have not experienced it, but in fact a typical modern cruiser will steer downwind under bare poles with as little wind as force 6. In a whole gale, many heavier boats will have joined her.

There are well-documented instances of boats surviving storms in huge seas by running free under bare poles. Two exponents of the technique were Bernard Moitessier in *Joshua*, and Conor O'Brien in *Saoirse*. Both were Southern Ocean circumnavigators, their boats were of comparatively heavy displacement, both had long keels and both were short-handed. Exhaustion was an issue but they survived.

One problem with running free under bare poles is that most yachts will only retain proper steerage so long as the wind is well abaft the beam. If the boat broaches, or momentary inattention at the helm allows her to fall beam-on, she may be some time before she pays off and gets going again. Until she does, she will be at risk, leaving the skipper with the choice of either starting her engine to regain control, or unrolling a few square feet of jib. Neither is desirable, so if this begins happening, further steps must be taken to keep her stern up to the weather. An added complication is that as the boat runs faster with increasing wind she may exceed the desirable speed and start surfing. If this is not what you want – and many would agree that it isn't – you'll have to consider trailing warps or a drogue to take off way. Should pitchpoling appear to be a growing possibility, different tactics must be tried, as there is no known cure for this spectacular dénouement.

Trailing warps The classic solution to the dilemma of too much speed downwind is to stream heavy warps from the stern. The drag takes off considerable way, while the pull from aft keeps the stern up to the weather, assisting the helm or even rendering it wholly or partially redundant. The warps are generally best streamed in a bight from either quarter. The pull is substantial, so make appropriate arrangements not only for securing them, but also for retrieval. This technique has been promoted by no less a seaman than Sir Robin Knox-Johnston in *Suhaili*, another circumnavigator with a boat of heavy displacement.

Trailing warps

The fact that these authorities have reached different conclusions delivers a clear message: a seaman must be aware of and prepared for all options, then find out what is best for the actual boat on the real day.

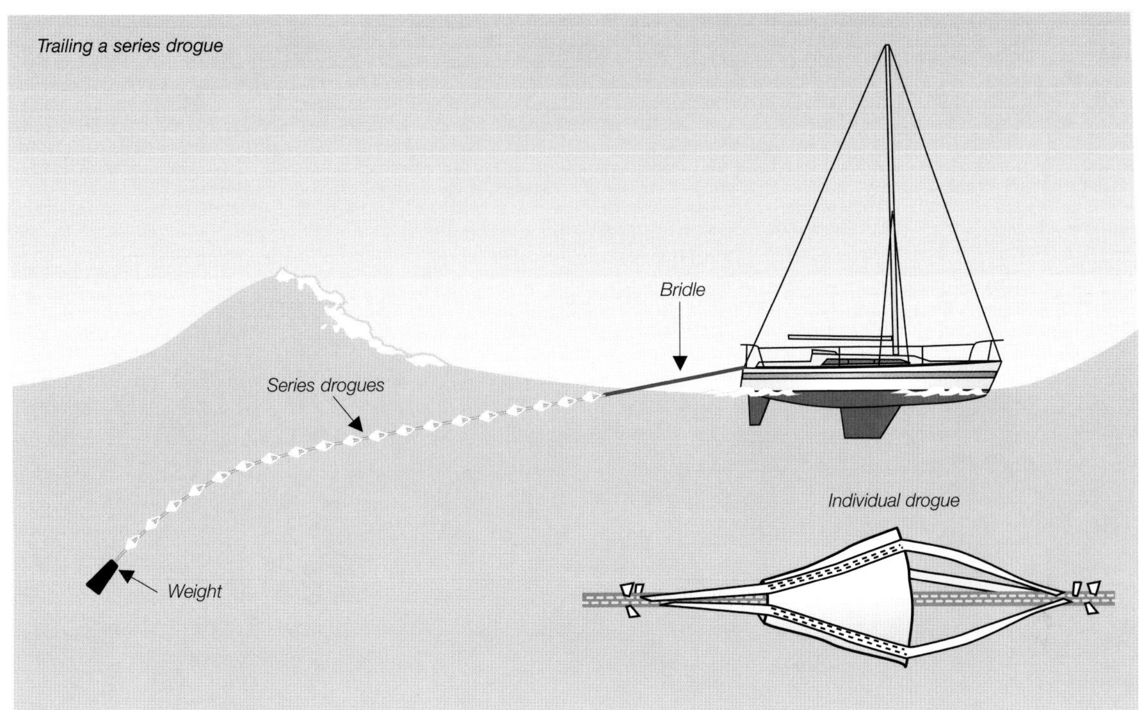

Drogues Even more drag can be achieved by streaming a drogue. A number of designs for drogues are commercially available, but it must be understood that the effect on a sailing boat can be dramatic. Drag is very considerable, loads are correspondingly high, and chafe is a real danger. Some users note that while the drogue certainly reduces way and holds the stern up to the waves, it is so effective that the boat is pooped (swept end-to-end) far more regularly than was otherwise the case. This was the experience of Charles Watson in *Saecwen*, a 35ft long-keeled yacht in a North Atlantic storm using an Attenborough drogue after broaching and being knocked down under bare poles. So severe was the punishment that Watson gave up on the drogue and lay a'hull. A series drogue (see below) may well have proved a safer option, although it was not generally available in 1990 when *Saecwen* had her experience.

The series drogue is a development of the single drogue that is favoured by some experienced multihull skippers. It has also been successfully deployed by many monohulls. It is built up from a large number of 5-inch cones set around 20 inches apart on a long nylon line. Size depends on the boat's displacement, but a typical example would be 100 cones on 16mm line for a 5 or 6-ton boat. The extreme end carries a weight which is often a bight of chain, but can be a conventional anchor of around 25lb (11 kilos). The whole drogue is streamed from a bridle to the stern(s) of the boat, with about 70 - 100ft (22-31 metres) of line between the bridle and the first cone.

This type of drogue is said to be easy to set and can be retrieved without a winch or trip line. It also delivers a surprisingly steady pull because the length over which the cones are spread means that at least some of them are always loaded up despite the pulsing of the waves.

If a drogue holds the boat back too hard, there is no law against using one with a storm jib set. The strains will rise substantially, but it may still be worth trying.

Motor sailing to windward

Motorsailing to windward

Another method for keeping a boat more end-on than beam-on to the waves is to sail to windward. This was a conclusion drawn by the SNAME/USYRU committee considering lessons from the great storm of the 1979 Fastnet Race. Clearly, this option will depend on weatherliness, but it can certainly work for powerful craft in a moderate gale.

However, many of today's cruisers do not have a storm jib or perform erratically under main and deep-reefed headsail because of their hull characteristics. Boats with poorly balanced hull lines may experience sudden weather helm problems as they heel. This sorry state of affairs is usually dealt with by easing the mainsheet or allowing the mainsheet traveller car to slide to leeward, but once the seas build, steering to windward is a different matter altogether. In something less than storm-force heavy weather, given a blow not expected to last beyond the range of fuel in the tank, a better survival option for any of these craft can be to motorsail very slowly upwind with no headsail set. The main is deep-reefed, sheeted hard in and generally flattened as much as possible; a mizzen may prove even better where available. The technique is more or less the same as 'dodging', (page 89).

The trick is to adjust speed so as to maintain steerage way and no more, because the last thing you want is to go leaping off wave-tops and tumbling into the trough behind at speed. Motorsailing may be useless for yachts in colossal seas on prolonged passages, but for coastal craft caught out beyond their normal comfort zone, it can literally be a life-saver.

Heaving to

Heaving to is a traditional method for taking off way and leaving a boat lying well up towards the wind. It has fallen out of general use with the arrival of yachts with a cutaway forefoot. A traditional gaff cutter heaves to phenomenally well because of her deep forefoot and her rig, whose centre of effort moves forward very little as she reefs. She is able to use this ability to survive any gale in which it is possible for her to carry canvas. Traditional Bermudan yachts can heave to after a fashion, but for yachts with flat underbodies and salient keels this old save-all is not a survival option. It does, nonetheless, have its uses for them in easier conditions, allowing them to lie-to at sea without having to steer.

The theory of heaving to A boat is hove to by arranging her sails so that one fights the other. The rudder takes up the slack and a state of equilibrium is reached. In theory, this is how it happens:

- Back the jib — this forces the bow off the wind.
- Sheet the main well in — this pushes the bow back upwind again by shoving the stern to leeward as the boat swivels around her pivot point.
- The net effect is that the boat tends to fall away beam-on and gather way.
- Lashing the helm to steer upwind (tiller hard to leeward) take cares of this. A well-balanced boat ends up lying between 35° and 55° from the wind.
- A hove-to boat does not in fact stop; she drifts under control. A late nineteenth century pilot cutter of around 50ft drifted square across the wind in force 8, making no leeway at all. A modern yacht will drift anything up to 45° to leeward of square.
- Drift can be checked with GPS, but if this is unavailable, sight along the slick you are leaving with the handbearing compass. A typical drift speed for a 40-footer in a whole gale would be around 2.5 knots. Armed with this information, you can at least make a stab at maintaining the navigation plot.

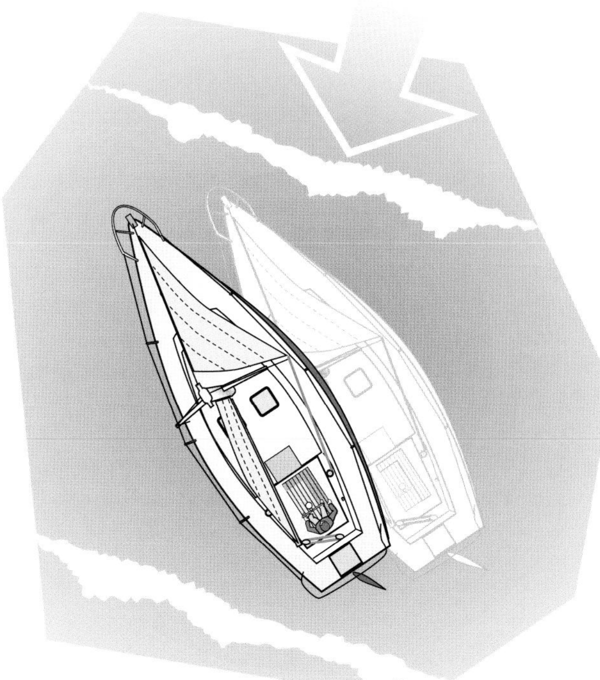

Heaving to in practice While it is perfectly possible to heave a yacht to by hauling the jib across to weather and waiting for her to slow down, less energy will be consumed by simply tacking and leaving the old working headsail sheet made up 'closehauled' instead of letting it fly. The boat will lurch nastily as she comes about onto the backed headsail, but she'll soon settle down. Steer high to help her lose way, then when she finally stops answering the helm, lash it 'down' and put the kettle on. If you've contrived to lay-to on the starboard tack, the whole world will be obliged to give way to you into the bargain.

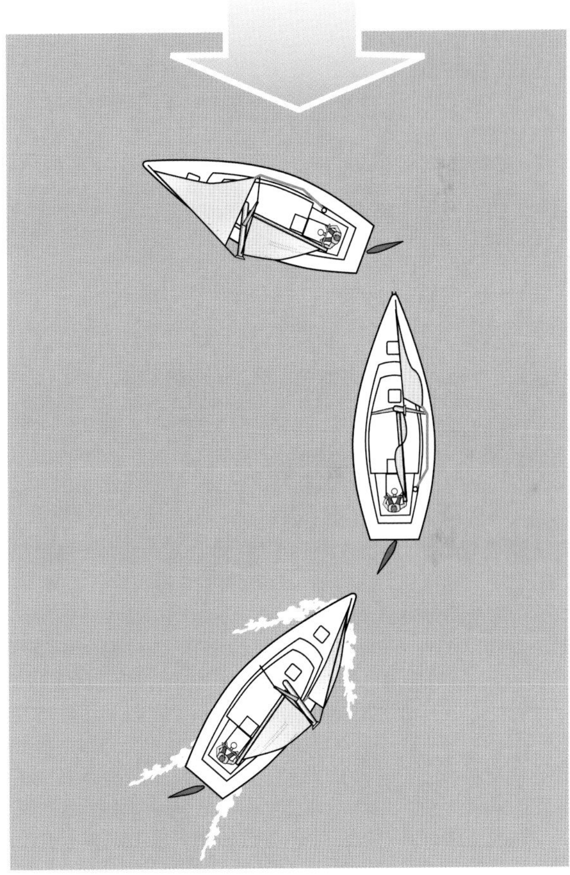

The easiest way to heave to is to tack, leaving the headsail sheet made fast so that it falls aback as the boat comes through the wind. Now carefully steer to windward on the new tack until the boat loses way.

The para anchor

The desirability of being able to heave to in a storm is obvious to all who have done it but, as we have seen, modern yachts are to a greater or lesser extent compromised in their ability to do so. The main problem is the lack of forefoot which allows their bows to blow off the wind, a situation exacerbated by the way the Bermudan mainsail and headsail move their centres of effort forward as they are reefed. Smaller yachts that may have inherently more suitable characteristics suffer from having their bows knocked to leeward by each successive sea, but any of these yachts can be persuaded to point up as high as the skipper wishes by deploying a para anchor.

The para anchor is in effect a large parachute that works like a drogue, except that it is generally streamed from the bow. Unassisted, it will leave the boat lying head to wind, which may be what you want. However, by attaching a spring line led from the quarter to the warp via a snatch block, the angle at which the boat is lying can be adjusted to find the optimum. Although she can lie thus with sail set as though hove to, she may well be better off under bare poles. Boats vary, and only experiment will reveal what suits best.

The slick left by the para anchor is said to assist in calming the worst of the seas. Lin and Larry Pardy, short-handed sailors of vast experience in small yachts, have written extensively in praise of this technique which goes a long way towards making up the shortfall in the modern yacht's options. It should pass without saying that attention to chafe is a vital consideration.

Lying to a para anchor

When lying to a parachute anchor, adjust the rode length so that the boat and parachute lie in approximately the same part of their respective waves. This is because the movement of water on the surface of each wave varies from place to place, and not to have them synchronised may cause the rode to snatch or slacken suddenly.

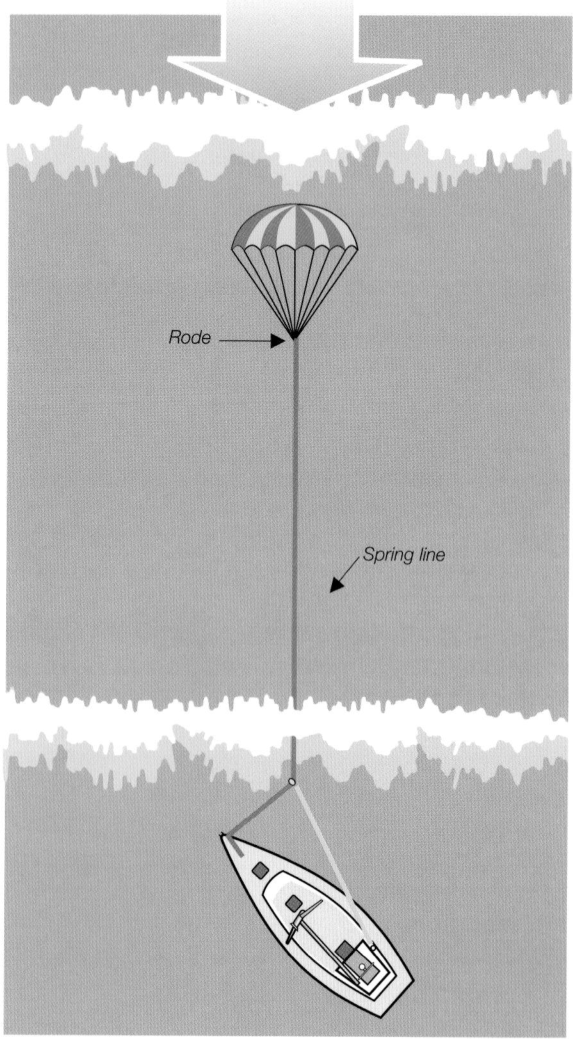

Lying a'hull

Before considering lying a'hull, it is vital to understand the boat's stability and capsize resistance characteristics. These are not necessarily the same things (pages 101-103).

A boat left completely to her own devices will usually end up around beam-on or with the weather some way abaft the beam. If she doesn't have excellent natural ability to look after herself, therefore, a prudent skipper should not even contemplate it. However, suitable craft can lie a'hull with reasonable safety as long as the waves are not so steep and high that capsize is inevitable for any vessel at all. Many have done this successfully, including the writer, whose 32ft gaff cutter of the heavy Norwegian pilot-boat type survived two protracted storms of at least force 10 in the North Atlantic with appropriate open-ocean seas. Given enough wind on the mast to steady the boat, things are less uncomfortable than you might imagine. For a long-keeled yacht of substantial displacement and moderate beam, leeway may not prove so shocking either.

Although lying a'hull can provide a viable answer for the right vessels in wind that is too strong for them to heave to, the inevitable beam-on aspect renders them more vulnerable than other techniques. As soon as the weather moderates enough for alternative action to bring the boat away from beam-on, it should be taken.

Helm position When lying a'hull, It is tempting to lash the helm to leeward (wheel to weather) in order to encourage the boat to lie with her head closer to the wind, but unless the steering arrangements are completely invulnerable this is not necessarily a good idea. The author can testify that when a boat's head is knocked away to leeward by a wave, she begins sailing under bare poles and, as she gathers way, rounds up on the face of the next wave. She now stalls near the top almost head-to-wind, to be thrown backwards onto her steering gear. At best, this may break linkages and tillers. Risk to the rudder must be weighed against spending rather more time beam-on, but securing the helm amidships with the lashings close to the rudder post to minimise leverage may be considered a safer option.

Emergencies

Distress – Safety issue or genuine emergency?

It has been shrewdly observed by a senior lifeboat cox'n who is also an RYA examiner that the definition of distress (the state of affairs beyond which point you need rescuing) is entirely subjective. His actual words were, 'If you think you need rescuing, you probably do need rescuing. That's the time to call for help.'

If things seem to be getting out of control, take a cool look at the situation with this always in mind and consider which of the following categories you are in:

- A thoroughly nasty turn of events which, on reflection, you are confident you can handle within your on-board resources.

Action – Get on with sorting things out.

- Circumstances similar to the above – still short of a direct emergency – but which differ in degree, leaving you less than certain that you can cope without assistance or advice. A deteriorating medical condition is a common example.

Action – Broadcast a PAN-PAN message indicating the nature of your problem and what you are doing about it. Typically, you will ask the coastguard to await further signals. In due course, you can either 'stand down' the call, or up-grade it to a Mayday.

- Dire emergency demanding immediate assistance. If you're in any doubt about the lifeboatman's definition, here's the official one: 'When a vessel or person is in grave and imminent danger and requires immediate assistance.' Typical examples might be fire, flooding, driving up on a lee shore, man overboard and life-threatening illness.

Action – Activate GMDSS procedure if the boat is suitably equipped. When a response is received, or if no GMDSS is available, broadcast a MAYDAY on VHF Ch16. Deploy distress flares. Consider abandoning ship. Details of the options for this are set out on page 122.

Safety and emergency equipment

Some of the kit generally categorised as 'safety gear' is used on a regular basis. Other items are only brought into action when all else has failed. As such, they are better thought of as 'emergency equipment', and the good seaman is relentlessly pre-empting emergencies. Just as he develops an instinctive respect for a lee shore, so he must constantly cast his eye around for danger that may be lurking on board. With regular attention, this capacity becomes as natural as breathing. Classic examples are encouraging good safety practice in the galley such as shutting down the gas supply whenever it is out of use, while regular inspection of fuel-burning systems and ensuring all electrical wiring is well insulated should render fire extinguishers virtually redundant. Requiring crew to clip on before going on deck in bad weather – even just reminding them that if they fall in, it will be a long swim home – reduces the risk of a man overboard casualty and means the 'overboard package' hanging on the pushpit will remain unused year after year. Careful attention to ropes around the deck can save a bight being inadvertently washed over the side to foul the propeller and perhaps initiating a Mayday. The list is without end, but you'll take the point.

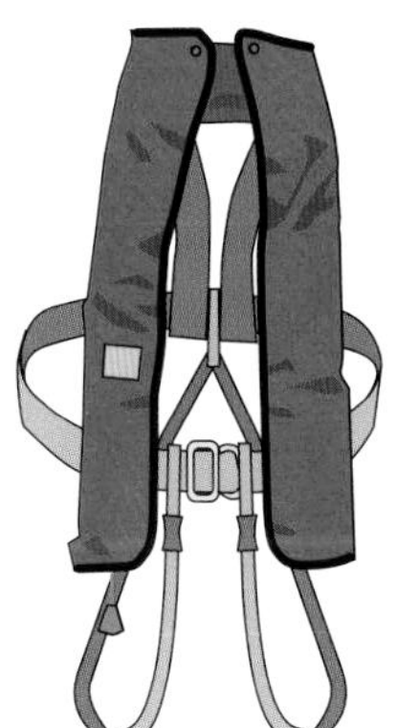

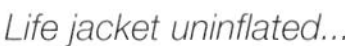

Life jacket uninflated...

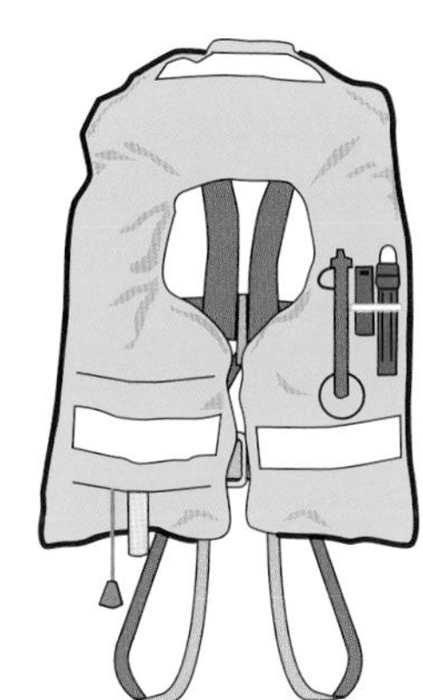

...and inflated

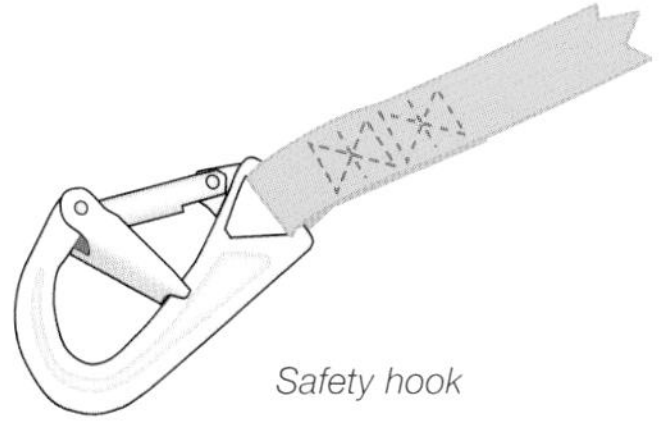

Safety hook

Safety equipment

- ***Life jackets*** – Some countries have laws about who wears a life jacket, how and when. At the time of writing, the UK authorities still prefer to leave this to the common sense of its citizens. Not so many years ago, the wearing of life jackets was only contemplated when the ship was going down. Solid or pre-inflated jackets were so unwieldy that donning them compromised freedom of movement and sometimes made a situation less safe. Today, leisure jackets (known as Personal Floatation Devices – PFDs in North America) are worn uninflated. They are so neat that they cause no inconvenience at all unless the user is wearing nothing but a bathing suit. Such jackets often incorporate harness attachment points and are as easy to put on as a waistcoat. Many feature a self-inflating bottle, some of which activate automatically on being immersed, giving an unconscious casualty a chance of survival. All have retro-reflective tape for night visibility, a lot carry lights as well, while a hood confers even greater chances of surviving prolonged immersion in a seaway. Life jackets must be stowed where they can quickly be reached, and each crew member should have one allotted, already adjusted for size.

Times to consider wearing life jackets – Depending on boat, crew and circumstances it is up to individuals to decide on a policy in accordance with their own experience and conscience, but once in place, this must be complied with. Some skippers insist on life jackets being worn by all hands on deck at all times; many demand them only in heavy weather or fog; others ask for them when a harness is appropriate (see page 112). Clearly, any non-swimmer on deck should wear a life jacket at all times and should pay the closest attention to using a harness.

The wearing of life jackets in yacht tenders is considered by a number of authorities as an essential, as it sensibly is in most dinghy racing clubs. However, while always accepting that many lives are lost from tenders in rough weather, after dark, and especially after taking on a full cargo of alcohol, there are other times when the mature seaman may feel the requirement to be redundant.

Perhaps the best answer is always to look to the worst-case scenario, then to use one's own judgment.

- ***Safety harnesses*** – These are now almost universally incorporated into the life jacket as described on page 111. Most offshore sailing craft are fitted with jackstays to which the harness may conveniently be attached. The tether is best made of non-tangling webbing and the snap-hooks must be of a safety type. This latter feature is extremely important as studies (including the SNAME USYRU post-1979 Fastnet Race enquiry) have found that ordinary clips can and do flip open. The Offshore Racing Council (ORC) rule for tethers requires a stress indicator to assess overload. It reads, 'A safety line purchased in 1/2000 or later shall have a coloured flag embedded in the stitching to indicate an overload. A line which has been overloaded shall be replaced as a matter of urgency.'

As to when they should be worn, a sensible rule of thumb is that harnesses, like life jackets, make sense on sailing craft whenever somebody feels safer by wearing one, or according to ship's standing orders. Typical policy might be to clip on before leaving the cockpit in weather when the mainsail would normally carry a reef, and in any conditions after dark. Watch keepers in the cockpit, especially alone at night, may be well advised to clip on in some circumstances; in heavy weather, anyone exiting the companionway should probably reach out and clip on while still below decks.

Emergency Equipment

This encompasses the gear that must be at hand when all safety measures and good seamanship have failed – whether by bad luck or bad judgment is immaterial. Fire extinguishers are dealt with in the section (see page 113) on handling a conflagration. The liferaft and its attendant kit, including flares and 'Emergency Position Indicating Radio Beacons' (EPIRBs), are described in the advice on abandoning ship, while the humble softwood bungs find their lifesaving place in 'Flooding'.

Specific Emergencies

Flooding

When a boat starts taking on catastrophic amounts of water, you either know why straight away or you don't. If you have just run into something, the first task after starting the pumps is obviously to investigate the damage. Where the source of the leak is a mystery, then you must activate a pre-planned series of actions to determine the root of your trouble. When the bilge is filling steadily, begin by tasting the contents, no matter how unpalatable, to see if the water is fresh or salt. If it's fresh, you have a damaged water tank or water line. You may end up thirsty, but you aren't going to drown. If it's salty, find the leak.

Bilge pumping

With an emergency-grade leak, a couple of big electric pumps will free up your crew to help source the problem, but because electricity cannot always be relied upon, all small craft should have at least one hand bilge pump. Any pump should have its bilge suction pipe protected from debris with strum boxes. An extra boost to the outflow may be to disconnect the main engine cooling pump from the sea cock (after first closing it) and allow the engine to draw cooling water from the bilge. Every little can help when your back is to the bulkhead. At the last ditch, there's an old saying with a lot of truth in it that the most reliable pump is a frightened person with a bucket!

Finding the leak

Skin fittings and stern gland – Whatever the material of hull construction, the greatest probability is either that a skin fitting has failed or that the stern gland is giving up on you. A glance is enough to decide about the shaft (pages 34-35) because there won't be more than two, but there

- ***Tapered wooden bungs*** *are ideal for hammering into failed skin fittings. Ideally, these should be hung from the fitting, but they must at least be stowed accessibly in a dedicated place. They aren't needed often, but when they are, there is not a moment to be lost.*

may be many skin fittings. Perhaps a pipe has let go that can be cured simply by shutting off a seacock. If the boat has been properly constructed these outlets will be accessible. They should all have been visited long before a problem develops and the skipper should know where they are. The engine is a good place to start. If it proves impossible to close the aperture with a seacock, drive in a softwood bung with a big hammer. Ideally, one of these should be hung from the fitting. As a second best, a selection must be stowed accessibly in a dedicated place. They aren't needed often, but when they are, there is not a moment to be lost.

An extreme case of skin-fitting failure occurs when a spade rudder is lost. The open gland aperture may lie on or just below the surface and be too large to bung. As always, this possibility should be considered early, ensuring that the kit necessary to shore up some sort of cover inside the hole is on board to save the ship. The result might not be watertight, but it can bring the leak within the capacity of the pumps.

Hull failure - If the watertight integrity of the hull itself is breached then, no matter what material the boat is built of, you have a major problem. With the hole anywhere near the waterline, the first job is to trim the boat to keep the damage as close to the surface as possible. This is easily arranged for a sailing boat with damage around amidships by 'tacking' the hole onto the windward side. More initiative will be required on a motor vessel, perhaps involving moving heavy weights all to one side - to windward if this can be contrived.

A number of proprietary products exist on the market to cope with such a contingency, and at least some of these can be taken seriously. The old sailing ship method of 'fothering' a leak by passing a spare sail under the boat and covering the hole has been known to work well enough to see a yacht home. If, however, the boat has been constructed so that the whole hull is accessible from within (as it should be), then there is precedent for contriving a bung by stuffing bedding wrapped in plastic into the gap, or shoring things up with plywood and wedges. Ingenuity and a cool head must be assisted by a plentiful supply of mastics, old pieces of plywood and, in particular, fast-acting underwater epoxy or putty.

Fire

In 2004, the RNLI statistics showed that of 1,711 launches to sailing craft, only a dozen were for fire. Motor boats have a higher level of call-outs, but even so, the danger lies low down the list. The statistics do not tell the whole story, however, because boats also suffer fire damage or total loss from fire in harbour. Whatever the figures, however, fire at sea is a terrible experience which debilitates the mind. This is therefore a case where training, or at least a planned series of actions, can give a crew their best chance of surviving and perhaps saving their vessel as well.

Guidelines when fire is discovered

- Advise all crew of the situation and get them on deck in life jackets. On larger vessels it may be necessary to shout, 'Fire!', but raised voices are best avoided in small craft as it winds up stress levels unnecessarily.

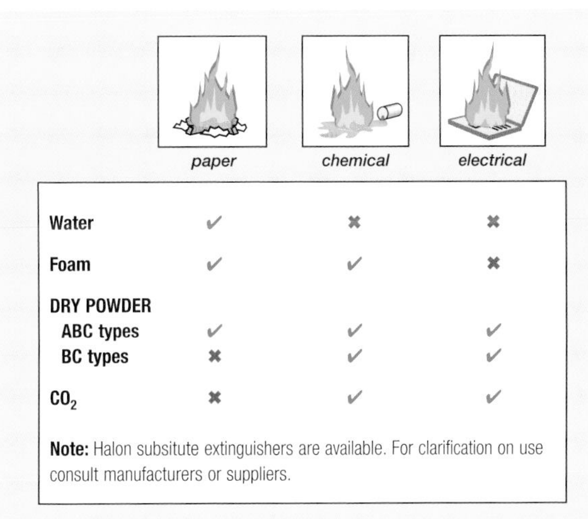

	paper	chemical	electrical
Water	✔	✖	✖
Foam	✔	✔	✖
DRY POWDER			
ABC types	✔	✔	✔
BC types	✖	✔	✔
CO_2	✖	✔	✔

Note: Halon subsitute extinguishers are available. For clarification on use consult manufacturers or suppliers.

The exception is where excessive outside noise dictates the need to be heard.

- As you leave, grab the handheld VHF and/or the EPIRB. Also take the fire extinguishers from the companionways. At least one of the larger extinguishers should be stowed in a cockpit locker or elsewhere on deck. If the source of the fire is known and accessible, shut it down as you go; for example, an electrical fire may be controllable by switching off the batteries, and a cooker or engine fire by shutting off the fuel supply. If the flare pack seems in danger, get it well out of the way or even dangle it over the side.
- On a large vessel with a big crew, detail someone to count heads.
- Regardless of the above, without wasting a second, try to fight your way back in. If it's possible to site the chief fire fighter between the fire and the exit point, he or she should commence work straight away while the rest of the crew are evacuating. Common sense must prevail, but do not let anyone become cut off from an exit by the fire. Be especially aware of someone being in aft cabins.
- The fire fighter should beware of inhaling fumes. Even cushions may be toxic when on fire.
- If possible, turn downwind to minimise the 'bellows' effect of the boat's progress through the air, and try to avoid spreading fire by blowing it all over the place with an ill-aimed bucket of water or a fire extinguisher.
- Send out a PAN-PAN or MAYDAY call as soon as possible. If it is safe to use the main radio, do so with caution. Don't worry about the possibility of having to stand down the rescue services if you douse the fire. They'd rather you did than find the boat burned to the waterline.
- If things look out of control, don't hesitate to launch the liferaft early, balancing the risk of it being damaged alongside the boat against the unacceptable event of it being burned in its chocks by a sudden downturn in your fortunes.

Fire extinguishers

All vessels carrying inflammable material such as fuel or gas must be equipped with suitable fire extinguishers. More is better, but the following minimum guidelines may prove useful.

Decked vessels over 6m and under 15m

- Some sort of fire pump should be readily available. A deckwash pump is ideal.
- A dedicated engine-space extinguishing system. At worst this can be a hole in the engine box granting access for one of the boat's extinguishers. Ideally it will be an extinguisher permanently sited in the engine space and activated by heat.
- A multi-purpose fire extinguisher of the dry powder type of at least 4Kg.
- At least two multi-purpose dry powder fire extinguishers of 1Kg or more sited at the exits from the accommodation.
- Two buckets with lanyards.
- A fire blanket for galley and clothing fires. Fire blankets can sometimes quickly smother a small fire.

Decked vessels over 15m are recommended similar specification, but at least one extra extinguisher of 4Kg or more should be carried.

Steering failure

This takes one of two forms. The first is that the rudder has ceased to work, because either its bearings have been compromised or the unit itself has parted company with the ship. The second is failure of the mechanism for controlling it (the tiller or wheel system). Steering failure is more common in sailing yachts than power craft because of the forces imposed by the rig – indeed, it is five times more likely to occur than fire. On long passages far from help it has delivered some crushing blows, yet there is often much that can be done to mitigate its effects.

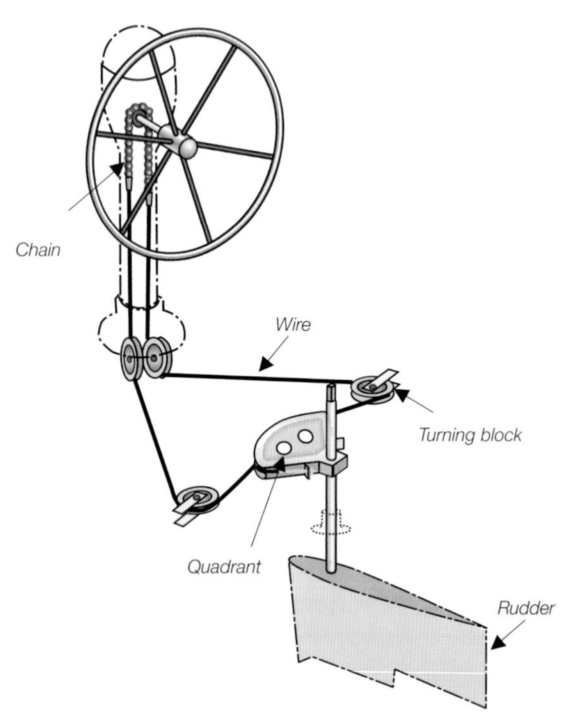

Rudder failure or loss

Short of major surgery or diving under the boat, there is little that can be done to repair this without hauling the boat. However, when rigging a jury steering system it will help to know that the absence of the rudder will have a bad effect on directional stability. Even a motor boat will suffer, and a fin-and-spade sailing boat will be in dire straits. Similarly, if a bearing fails with the rudder set at any other angle than straight fore-and-aft, it will be extremely hard to control the boat, so the first job will be somehow to lever the rudder back into line.

Tiller failure

This is easily rectified. Unless a tiller is of unassailable strength, such as a hefty iron example in a traditional yacht, a spare must be carried. It won't take up much space and may never be needed, but if it is you'll be sorry if you left it in the garage.

Wheel steering failure

Far more regular than other forms of steering mishap, the usual problem here is that a rod or wire has come adrift or jumped the sheave of a turning block. It behoves every skipper to have investigated how the steering mechanism works, and to have confidence that if one of its parts malfunctions, it can be accessed then fixed within the limits of the ship's tools and spares kit. Meanwhile, the emergency tiller will have been installed. This must also have had a 'dry run' before it is needed. Don't assume the one supplied by the builder will work. Some distressed mariners have been disappointed.

Loss of rudder – Powerboats

With twin screws, losing a rudder is an inconvenience not a problem. Single-screw motor boats are similarly placed to sailing craft, although they have an easier time because their propulsion is more or less shoving them straight ahead, while the sailboat's rig is tugging her every which way and back again. Some single-screw powerboats with dual trim tabs can actually steer in a rudimentary manner by using one tab at a time. They might not be able to manoeuvre into a tight berth, but they are in with a chance of reaching the safety of an anchorage to 'take it from there'. Try it with the rudders amidships and see what you can achieve. In other cases, the best answer is usually to rig a simple jury rudder (see page 116). Most sailing boats can contrive this from existing gear. Power craft may have to ship something in anticipation if it is felt the risk is real enough.

Loss of rudder – Sail

A sailing boat that loses her rudder has two choices, although she generally ends up with a combination. She can either steer by means of her sails, or she can contrive some form of jury rudder.

Steering with sails

To a greater or lesser extent, all sailing craft can be steered by their sails. In a large square-rigger the rudder supplies little more than the final trim, while boats such as cruising dinghies that are able to control their angle of heel by trimming weight can be sailed entirely rudderless. Fore-and-aft rigged ballasted yachts rely heavily on their rudders.

Choosing the right speed – It's well known that a boat can be induced to turn by using the inherent qualities of her sails. Unfortunately, unless she has a finely balanced hull, as soon as she heels beyond a certain point, she develops too much weather helm for the sails alone to counterbalance. The answer is to reef down, especially the mainsail, because this is exacerbating the weather helm.

Learning to balance the sails

- ***Headsail*** – Start with a boat not making way, beam-on to the wind with the helm lashed amidships. Hoist and sheet the headsail alone. She will bear away and may well continue to do so. Some boats will come back into line as they gather way, but by no means all. Only experimenting will tell.
- ***Main and/or mizzen*** – Do the same thing with the main, or better still, the mizzen if you have one. The boat will round up towards the wind. Try easing the sheet to arrest the process or, if you are moving slowly enough, perhaps even to bear away a little.

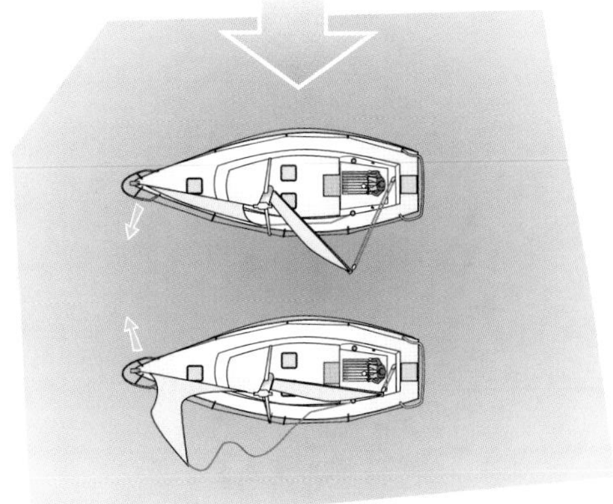

Steering with sails.

- ***Going for it*** – Now get under way with both sails. Ease the jib or roll some in to luff up to the wind, heaving in the mainsheet to help if need be. Next, bear away by letting off the main and hauling in the jib. Try different combinations of reef and sheet until the boat is more or less stable. She may not want to go in the direction of your choice, especially if this places the wind abaft the beam, but she'll probably manage to limp into a safe anchorage.

Spinnaker pole jury rudder

Locker lid lashed to spinnaker pole

Rigging a jury rudder

Given a little help from the sails, and reefing as required, many boats have made it to safety using some sort of jury rudder, so a contingency plan for rudder loss or jamming is well worth the trouble. If at all possible, this should be tried and tested to make sure all necessary gear is to hand and that it does actually work. The methods considered below are by no means exhaustive, but they have all succeeded and will serve to indicate the sort of thing that can be contrived.

The self-steering paddle – Many long-distance sailing yachts have windvane self-steering arrangements. Some of these work by auxiliary rudders which supply an obvious backup. Others have servo paddles that can be modified. Although far less powerful than the main rudder any of these may deliver enough punch to do the job so long as the boat is going slow enough and the sails are balanced.

The spinnaker pole – The spinnaker pole or some other spar is lashed to the pushpit so as to allow free movement. A cabin-sole board, a locker lid, or perhaps a dinghy oar is somehow secured to it to create a paddle blade. This 'steering oar' is lowered into the water, perhaps helped by the weight of a spare anchor attached to the end to keep it down, and off you go. It's not a joy to steer with one of these, but it does work. If it gets too heavy, take lines from the inboard end to the winches, or rig tackles. This will be far and away the most realistic method for a motor boat, which should carry some suitable spar.

Rig an offset drogue – Since a yacht is usually trying to turn one way most often to windward a drogue can be set up to turn the tendency to advantage. Rig a pole out on the lee beam with a fore guy, after guy and topping lift. Attach a block at the outboard end. Reeve a line through this and hitch a light drogue to its bight between the boat and the block on a moderately short length of line. The drogue can be made up of anything that will provide water resistance – a stout bucket with a large hole knocked into the bottom, perhaps – anything that will raise the resistance of the trailing rope. By heaving the drogue in or out, the degree of offset pull it is delivering can be fine-tuned until the boat can be steered with her sails. More sophisticated systems can be contrived using poles on both sides.

Jury steering with a drogue

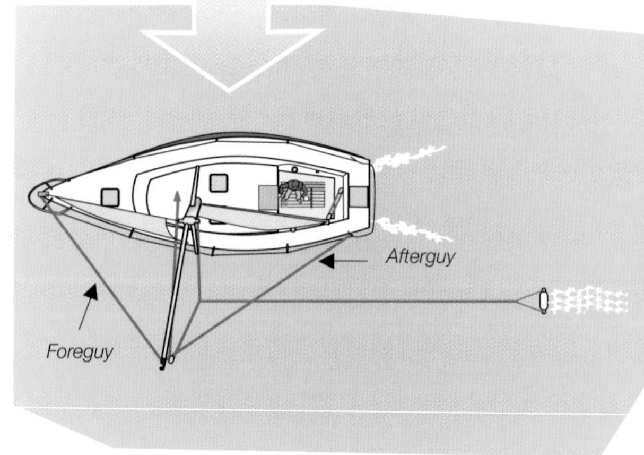

Engine Failure

Power craft

Where a vessel is propelled by a single power unit, that unit must be rigorously maintained, especially its fuel supply and electrical requirements. Despite all precautions, however, things can still go wrong. When they do, the seamanlike reaction is not immediately to call for assistance, unless either the boat or her crew are in immediate serious danger. A few miles out to sea on a calm day, for example, the crew should be trying to sort out their own problems, not troubling the SAR people. Even if the boat were close up-tide of a shoal, the first and automatic action in fair weather should be to anchor securely, then consider what has gone wrong. If the anchor will not hold and all efforts to restart the machinery have failed, it would then be prudent to call for help. Clearly, in storm conditions there should be no hesitation about at least a PAN-PAN, nor would the SAR people want you to have any.

Fuel and cooling problems – A surprising number of lifeboat call-outs are to vessels with empty tanks which, bluntly, is an abuse of the rescue services. Fuel supplies must be actively managed and emergency supplies carried, although these will be of little value if nobody on board knows how to bleed a diesel system. This process is described in general terms on (page 33), but the on-board engineer must have checked up on the whereabouts of all taps and bleed points, and be sure that the relevant tools are to hand. The same knowledge will be required if the fuel filters clog. It is not enough to carry spare units or to understand in theory how to clean them. The process must at least have had a dry run.

The other common cause of engine failure during operation is overheating, usually resulting from a blockage in the sea water circulation. As with fuel, this is often readily cured, but only by those with the necessary spares on board and the ability to use them. The methodology for engine trouble-shooting is on pages 31-32.

Sailing craft engine failure

Unless it is absolutely calm and the boat is in dire danger of stranding without the option to anchor, it is hard to imagine the circumstances in which a sailing boat can be in distress through engine failure. She has ground tackle and a suit of sails which are, after all, her main source of propulsion. Yet almost one out of five UK lifeboat call-outs are to sailing yachts that have suffered machinery failure of some sort. The indications are that in the USA things are even worse. It is worth bearing in mind that until World War II most yachts did not have engines at all and many of them then were far more unwieldy than today's comparatively athletic craft. Even if you don't fancy sailing the boat into a marina berth when power is lost, it is usually possible to change your destination to sail into a safe anchorage. From there, all sorts of options may be available, including easy access to the shore and an engineer via no more hi-tech means than the yacht's dinghy.

Typical engine spares:

Oil for engine and gearbox

Oil filter

Fuel filter elements

Air intake filter, if appropriate

Crankcase breather element, if fitted

Drive belts

Impeller & gasket for water pump

Water pump face plate screws

Thermostat

Antifreeze

Engine anodes

Gasket materials and sealant

PTFE tape

Grease

Rig failure

If a main component of the standing rigging such as a forestay or backstay fails in rough weather with the boat driving hard, a deck-stepped mast will usually go over the side. If the spar is stepped on the keel through the deck, there is some chance that it can be saved. Loss of lesser components such as a shroud or baby stay is often 'survivable' given the right action, while more traditional rigs which are less highly loaded may also offer a second chance.

Whatever gives way in a rig, the first action must be to take the load off the damaged component. This is usually best done with the helm. If a forestay breaks, or is seen beginning to strand, run the boat off the wind straight away. When a shroud looks like letting go on the weather side, tack immediately so that it goes comparatively slack, then deal with it. These actions should be as instinctive as going for the brake in a car. If you think about them often enough, they can become so.

Running repairs – Repairing standing rigging at sea from within a yacht's own resources is a tough call. Spare shackles, lengths of wire and bulldog grips are essential for long-distance ventures, but today the availability of rope such as Spectra® which is as strong as wire and stretches even less make jury-rigging far more viable than it was. To create a backstay, for instance, a length of Spectra® core could be run between some fitting at the masthead to a spare rigging screw at the deck, or even a tackle winched up hard. The job would see you across an ocean if need be.

Action on dismasting

- Do not start the engine immediately. You will almost certainly have ropes over the side. A locked-up propeller is the last thing you want now.
- Make a head count. Have you lost anyone? Check for personal injury and prioritise casualties. Bear in mind that without the roll inertia of the mast, the motion of the boat will be very much worse. Remind crew of this and make sure everyone hangs on bearing in mind as the guardrails may have also been damaged.
- Unless you are in immediate dire danger, make a PAN-PAN call. Advise the coastguard of your situation and what you are proposing to do. A positive approach from you will reassure them. If you don't need rescuing, say so.
- Assess the damage. Is the hull in danger from pounding spars still attached by rigging?
  Yes? Cut the wreckage free as quickly as possible, saving only what you sensibly can. You should have on board a pair of hefty bolt-croppers for this wretched contingency, as well as a generous supply of hacksaw blades. You will also be pleased now if you have opened your split pins only as far as shown on (page 23) and resisted the temptation to bend them round so they can never be moved again.
  No? Is a safe haven within range of your fuel tanks? If it is, you can afford to free yourself of the wreckage. Nonetheless, if conditions are not so tough that motoring home with spars on deck or lashed alongside could create further damage, bear in mind that your insurers may take a more positive view of your efforts if you have hung onto the mast. If motoring to safety is not an option, sort out the wreckage and salvage everything you can for a jury rig. You never know what may prove useful, and there are no chandlers in mid-ocean.
- Only when all ropes have been cleared and stowed so that they cannot be kicked or washed back over the side should the engine be started. Getting under way often eases the extreme motion and does wonders for morale.

- Do what you can to contrive a jury rig if this is appropriate. The possibilities are too varied to list here, but now is when the prudent seaman draws on the boxes of old junk, the bits and pieces, the U-bolts, the hanks of small line, the pop-rivets, the rolls of duct tape, the epoxy and the fibreglass kit he has squirrelled away, pending the unforeseeable day when they might just be needed. Unhappy is the man whose tool kit falls short at a time like this.

Suggested rigging spares:

Bosun's chair

Spare hanks and sail slides

Polyester thread, palm and needles

Replacement sheet

Spare halyard

Length of wire

Coil of Spectra® rope

Spare winch handle

Whipping twine and small cordage for lashings

Selection of spare shackles and split pins

Bulldog clips

Adhesive sail repair material

Crew Overboard

Search patterns

Text-books and training schemes abound with sound advice on how to manoeuvre a boat under power, or sail back to a casualty who has fallen overboard. This will therefore not be reiterated here, but the technique of instituting a search is generally less well covered. A number of tried and tested patterns of search exist. The one illustrated is the 'expanding box search'. 'D' is the range at which you will be able to see a casualty from the boat. If in doubt about this, sacrifice some floating object that won't blow away. Start from where you think the casualty should have been, toss the mark overboard and steer north until you are still within sight of it. Then turn to starboard and start looking. The other courses are East, South and West. You won't forget those.

In a tideway or current, if you are ten minutes between losing the crew and beginning the search, any GPS 'Man Overboard' position generated at the time of loss may be so far out of date as to be virtually irrelevant. You can either calculate the set and drift, plot a new position for the casualty and start looking from there, or accept that so long as you haven't been careering all over the ocean, the boat and the lost person will have been drifting at the same rate and in the same direction. The search pattern will now drift with you both, and your chances are as good as they can be under the circumstances.

Expanding box search

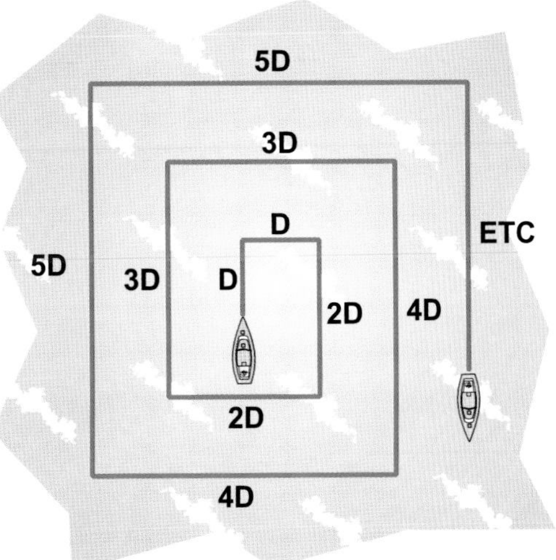

Recovering a casualty from the water

Bringing the boat within reach of the person in the water is only the first part of the job. Equally important tasks are getting the victim back on deck and attending to the trauma.

Casualties capable of helping themselves

Ladder or stern platform In the first instance, look at using the boat's natural resources to assist the person back on board. If there is a 'sugar scoop' bathing platform aft, or even a boarding ladder, try using it, but beware of injuries caused by the boat pitching. All helpers should be clipped on, because it is easy to take a tumble when leaning over in a seaway, and one person in the water is already more than enough.

The dinghy If you haven't the strength to heave the swimmer up over the rail, launch an inflatable if there's time. Even a tired person can usually roll into one of these. Once aboard the dinghy, they can either scramble up themselves, or a fitter shipmate can join them and assist. Only in absolute emergencies, perhaps if the victim is unconscious, should a second crew member enter the water to assist the first.

The bight and winch method for sailing boats Here, a line is led from forward to a snatch block on the quarter or an aft fairlead, thence inboard to a cockpit winch. A reasonably fit casualty is assisted to grab the toerail. He then manoeuvres his feet onto the bight of the line in the water. As the boat rolls, his weight will float upwards, relieving some of the weight from the line. The slack is rattled up on the winch. In surprisingly short order, the casualty will be high enough to get a leg over the rail and back to safety. Lest a cynical reader might imagine that this method is pure fantasy, the writer can reassure that it was used to lift him back aboard a yacht in mid-Atlantic by his only shipmate, a woman of half his weight. It has the advantage of being very rapid to rig.

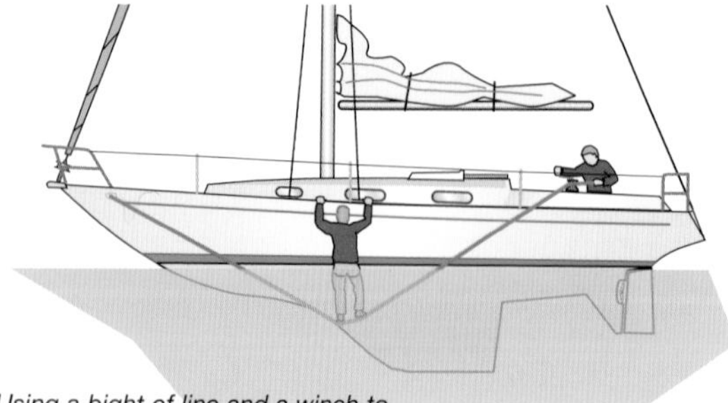

Using a bight of line and a winch to recover a conscious casualty.

The grunt If freeboard is modest and enough muscle is left on board, it is well worth trying literally to heave the casualty up over the side. Perhaps because of the extra adrenalin in everybody's system this often works, especially in a sailing boat where the lee side is lower. It may help to slash the lashings on the guardrails, since these can get in the way, especially if the casualty is fully clothed and wearing a life jacket. If the guardrails are shackled on with bottle screws, think again next time you rig them and use lanyards instead.

Casualties compromised by exhaustion

The straight lift

Attaching a line Where manhandling or scrambling aboard is not possible, a straight lift must be organised. First, a line must be attached to the casualty. If he is wearing a harness of some sort ideally a modern life-jacket-harness this is easy, because he already has a ring at chest height. If he is not kitted up with a harness, try to get one on him. If this is not going to work, hand him down a line and ask him to tie a bowline under his shoulders. Best of all, use a helicopter-style sling passed underneath the arms and attach the rope to this. Such slings are available commercially and should be shipped by all yachts not otherwise equipped. Many also feature a length of floating line as part of a proprietary rescue sling. If the boat is steered around the casualty, this line is bound to make contact, enabling him to haul in the sling, shrug it on for hoisting and become attached to the ship as well.

Dangers of the vertical lift If you're obliged to lift someone out of the water it's reasonable to assume that supporting them with a strop of some sort under the arms would be the best way to attach a lifting line. While this has the advantage of being quick and easy, it lifts the casualty vertically and so introduces an increased risk of hypothermic aftershock. This can induce side effects as serious as heart attack in a cold, exhausted person, especially one in poor general condition in the first place. While the danger is most significant for high lifts into helicopters, even the short hike up to a yacht's deck is potentially dangerous. Skippers should be aware of this when considering what method to apply. If no means of horizontal lifting is available, however, don't hesitate. Better a sick survivor than a healthy total loss.

Horizontal lifting arrangements Unless you have a tiny sail handy and have practised rigging it as a parbuckle support, a horizontal lift can usually only be arranged using a patent device dedicated to this purpose. A number are available, a good example being the 'Tribuckle'.

The traditional parbuckle

The tribuckle

The Tribuckle uses the ancient technique of 'parbuckling' to raise the casualty. Originally used for lifting barrels up ships' sides, the parbuckle works by attaching two ropes to the ship's rail, passing their bights under the barrel from inboard outwards and thence back aboard from outside the barrel. By heaving on both ropes at once, the barrel can be rolled up the side with surprising ease. As used in the Tribuckle, the lines are substituted by a triangle of sailcloth. This is secured to the toerail and passed beneath the casualty so that its pointed end can be bent onto a spare halyard. As this is hauled, the casualty is rolled upwards securely in the bag formed by the cloth with remarkable efficiency. Failing a dedicated piece of gear, you might be able to use a small jib with its luff secured along the rail, the clew attached to a halyard and the casualty in the bight of the sail. Few boats carry such a sail nowadays and even those that do may find theirs to be the wrong size. Only by trying it on a calm day will you ever know for sure, so if you imagine this to be your safety net, make sure it functions before you need it.

Power for the lift This can be achieved in numerous ways depending on the available gear. Typically, a power boat will use a davit of some description. A sailing yacht of sufficient size to have powerful halyard winches may manage the lift using one of these, but smaller boats' winches will not be adequate on their own. A dedicated tackle hoisted aloft on a spare halyard with its fall led to a primary sheet winch may do the trick. If no tackle is carried, it may be necessary to contrive one from a reversed mainsheet or kicking strap, but to organise this at sea on a rough, dark night is no joke at all, especially if it has not been practised. Such ideas are by no means guaranteed to succeed in the stress of real life.

The best way of all is to use the anchor windlass, if one is fitted. Lead the halyard to the warping drum via a snatch block and heave away. An electric windlass of any substance will lift a surprisingly heavy individual.

Whatever method is chosen, it cannot be overstressed that it must be tried first in easy weather. Find a volunteer one summer day and, when you're securely anchored, shove him over the side in his life jacket. Make sure it's slack water, or that may be the last you see of him! See how your plans work out, then imagine the same job with the boat standing on her ends and everyone thoroughly alarmed. It's the only way to face the most awful of realities with any degree of confidence.

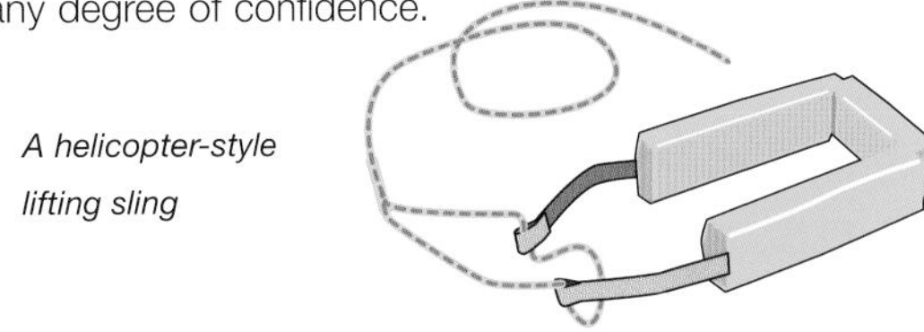

A helicopter-style lifting sling

Lifting a casualty with a windlass

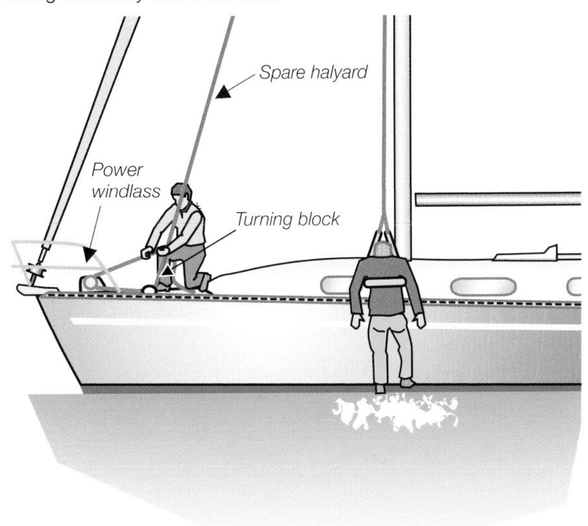

Abandoning Ship

When the yacht herself is in dire danger and all else has failed, the time may come when the only remaining possibility seems to be to abandon ship. However, it is well established that if she is still afloat in open water and not terminally burning, her crew is generally better off staying with her than climbing into a liferaft. Things may be desperate on board, but many lives have been lost by abandoning ship too soon. A good rule is only to step off when the boat sinks under you.

The options for the business of abandoning ship are listed below, but whichever you adopt, do all in your power to ensure that the rescue services know about your plight and where you are to be found. Broadcast a MAYDAY before leaving the ship, make every effort to wait for a response, and begin the informed use of your distress flares.

Options for abandoning

- ***Scramble ashore*** This can be a useful choice close to the coast, but it is a judgement call that depends on conditions and the nature of the terrain. Under the right circumstances it is far better to power a sinking boat up a beach and scramble ashore in life jackets than it is to launch a raft a few miles to seaward. Piling her onto a rocky plateau with an onshore gale blowing is going to be folly, but grounding on a shelving foreshore with an offshore wind may be the most seamanlike action.
- ***Take to the dinghy*** A fair-weather option for craft with no liferaft. If the ship's boat is an inflatable normally stowed below, it makes sense to keep it semi-inflated on deck during offshore passages just in case.
- ***Liferaft*** For full details on abandoning to a liferaft, consult a specialist manual. However, in the absence of further assistance, the following guidelines may help.

Boarding

- Kit up all the crew in appropriate foul-weather gear and life jackets. If harnesses are available, use them.
- Make sure the raft's painter is secured to the boat.
- Launch the raft to leeward – you may be surprised at how heavy it is – pull the painter and keep on pulling until the raft inflates.
- Try to bring the raft close enough to board it 'dry'. In any event, whether swimming or scrambling, the strongest, fittest person climbs in first to assist weaker shipmates.
- If it is necessary to enter the water, clip onto the painter so as not to be washed away.

On board the raft - 'Cut, stream, secure'

- With all hands settled evenly around the perimeter of the raft to encourage stability, cut the painter. Most rafts have a dedicated knife in a pocket near the access point for this job. All sailors should carry a personal knife, so if the raft's knife cannot be found there will be no problem. Beware of puncturing the raft with non-specialised blades.
- Next, stream the drogue that is part of the liferaft pack.

This minimises drift but more importantly, it confers additional stability.

- Finally, secure the entry port, bail out any water; activate the Emergency Position Indicating Radio Beacon (EPIRB) if you have one and it is not already operating.
- For techniques of survival in liferafts an approved sea survival course is strongly recommended, but it cannot be overstressed that doing all you can to maintain the comfort and morale of your crew is of paramount importance.

Gear to be taken aboard

- An offshore raft contains fresh water, provisions, First Aid material and general survival equipment. However, if you are voyaging far from potential assistance, it is recommended that a grab bag is kept to hand containing additional items appropriate to the crew, the probable conditions and the reasonably anticipated duration of the ordeal. Typically, these might include an extra torch, high-energy food such as chocolate, water, seasickness remedies (the motion in a raft can only be described as wicked), further First Aid kit and the medical manual, plus any additional comforts you may require. Whether your list ends with the Bible and Shakespeare remains a matter of priorities.
- The EPIRB, once activated, sends out distress messages which automatically give your GPS position. It is best carried in the raft rather than left floating at the scene of the ship's foundering.
- The ship's flare pack.
- A hand-held GPS, batteries and some sort of chart.
- Whatever else you take, don't forget a fully charged hand-held VHF radio.
- If you've time, cast your eye around the boat for any other items that could conceivably be of use. It's impossible to second-guess all eventualities.

Flares

All craft venturing out to sea should carry flares suitable to their needs. Flares carry a 'use-by date' that tells you when to replace them, but in practice they generally work long after this has expired. Decked vessels with stowage capacity may feel it worth stowing the previous flare pack in addition to the up-to-date one for double protection. It is easy for a ship to miss a flare, and if your VHF fails, they may be critically important. More is better than fewer. Flares are available as follows:

Red parachute rocket flares are used for attracting attention.
Red hand-held flares for pinpointing your position with a rescuer in sight.
White parachute rocket flares are for illuminating a scene in the darkness. They are not a distress signal.
Orange smoke flares indicate the position of a distressed vessel in daylight.
White hand-held flares are for identifying the boat and her position to a vessel which may not have seen her. They also are not a distress signal. Any white flares should be stowed ready for instant firing.

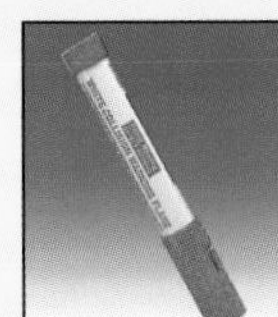
White hand held flare (not available worldwide)

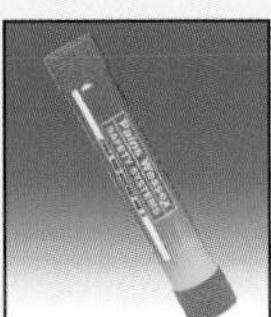
Red parachute flare

Red hand held flare

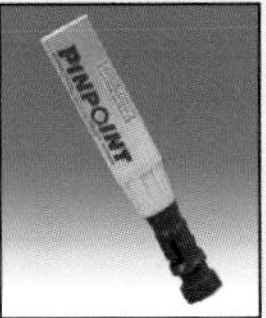

Hand held orange smoke

Buoyant smoke

		White hand held flare (not available worldwide)	Red parachute flare	Red hand held flare	Hand held orange smoke	Buoyant smoke
Category A	**Ocean**	4	12	6		2
Category B	**Offshore**	4	4	2		2
Category C	**Inshore**	4	2	4	2	
Category D	**Sheltered Waters**			2	2	

Crew care and watchkeeping

Seasickness

Seasickness is a truly debilitating infirmity which affects most people to some extent. Numerous proprietary remedies are available, most of which help somebody some of the time, but none is universally efficacious. Commenting on these lies beyond the scope of this manual, except to say that whatever is chosen, it is vital to read the instructions. The tablets preferred by the writer's crew seem to work very well indeed, but only if the 'course' begins 24 hours before hitting the first rough water. The fact sheet supplied with the medication recommends this, yet many of those for whom it does not seem to be successful wait until they feel queasy before opening the pillbox.

Regardless of medicines, patches and the like, certain well-tried measures can be counted upon, if not to cure the malady, at least to help the patient to carry on living.

Staying in the fresh air or going below In the face of things it would appear self-evident that going below to deal with some task is not a good idea if you are feeling 'on the edge'. Many a skipper has managed well enough until attending to the chart-table chores; volunteer cooks have fared even worse. Staying on deck or at least in the cockpit is therefore a sound plan, but only up to a point. The trouble is, exposure to the weather ultimately adds to the seasickness and creates a nasty combination. Listlessness follows and a point can be reached when victims seem hardly to care whether they are alive or dead. Sending sufferers to their bunks with a large bucket before this state is reached is a primary duty of any skipper. Once their head is down, most people recover to a limited extent and sleep is a great healer. There is no need to undress for we are not at home. Better a bunk made damp by wet oilskins than a sailor pushed over the brink by trying to get ready for bed. It's 'down the hatch and straight to the horizontal mode' for seasick sailors off watch.

Other contributory factors On a longer passage, most people recover from seasickness within three or four days, sometimes less. Knowing this can help one to muscle through the dismal period, but while you are seasick, it's vital to pace yourself, avoid tasks you know will set you off, and spend as much time as possible in the bunk. You'll feel better for a while after being sick, this is the time to

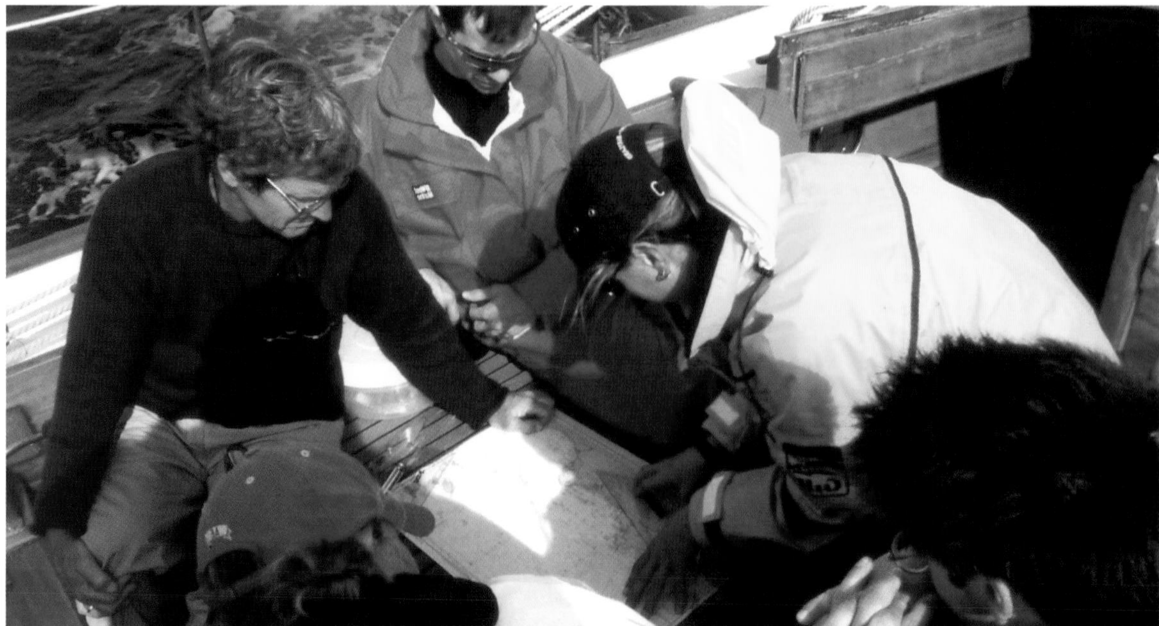

Keep the crew well briefed.

deal with navigation. Avoid evocative smells such as diesel, and keep to windward of your messmate's lunch if it comes back to haunt him. A whiff of that is the worst of all.

Whatever happens, you must take liquid, because dehydration is the real enemy. Eat if you can, but make it simple. Maintain a supply of dry water biscuits on board. They don't taste great, but they might keep someone going until he can fancy your curries again.

Meals on time

On a long passage, it's impossible to overstress the importance of meals being served up regularly and on time. Appetising food coming on the dot does wonders for making a crew feel secure. Oddly enough, hungry people are just as likely to feel seasick as well-fed ones and they will be less able to cope if they start actually vomiting.

Food is critical on shorter passages as well, and here seasickness is more often a factor because potential cooks are less likely to fancy their chances at a spell in the galley. Pre-planning is helpful, with hot drinks in flasks, sandwiches ready cut, and maybe a pre-cooked, one-pot dish clamped in the pressure cooker on the stove which can be served in mugs with a spoon to help it on its way.

Cooking on board can be the most daunting of tasks. If you're only half up to the job, think through everything you intend to do before you go below or get out of your bunk. That way you won't waste time with your head stuck in a smelly locker searching for something you could have managed without. Stick to single-pan meals wherever possible. There's no need to be ambitious. A hungry watch on deck will be delighted if they get a can of stew with a can of spuds and another of peas chucked in with it. A quick twist of the pepper pot, a hunk of bread, and they'll be happy mariners. If you feel rough afterwards, just dump the washing up in the sink or a bucket and deal with it when you arrive. And if there's any food left over, save it and serve it in an omelette for breakfast. No waste, and by that time most people will be a lot better, especially if it's day three of the trip.

Watch systems

Short daytime passages

By far the majority of trips in small craft are accomplished in daylight. Assuming everyone has had a reasonable sleep the night before, there is no obvious demand for a watch system, even on a passage of twelve hours or more. However, this doesn't mean that the skipper should spend every available second on deck. Tiredness can creep up unnoticed and he or she needs to be on top form as the destination approaches. More mistakes occur entering and leaving harbour than ever befall at sea, so it's important to husband one's resources and take a turn in the bunk at some stage. Read a good book if you can't sleep, but whatever you do, take your mind away from the stresses of skippering the boat. If you're worried about feeling sick, just dive below and get your head down, after making sure the watch on deck know their duties and will call you in good time.

Single-night passages

For all practical purposes, any passage that takes place over a single night can be thought of as having a 24-hour duration. Staying up all night is a gruelling option for most of us. Our body clocks will be firmly set to shorebased rhythms, so if we don't get any rest we'll be struggling to stay awake by around 0200.

Short-handed The typical small-boat scenario is for two watch-keepers, often with the mate less experienced than the skipper. Some people like to set up a full 24-hour watch system under these circumstances, but many prefer to take things a little more casually. The critical time is the dark hours. During the daylight, things can usually be managed on an informal basis according to need and conscience, but it makes sense to introduce some form of regulation to cope with the sleepy period. Most folks can manage to stay interested in life on their own for three hours in good weather. As the going cuts up, two is often enough. With a couple of watchkeepers, a three-on, three-off system running for the twelve hours between dinner and breakfast works very well. Even if you have to shorten the spells to two hours you'll still find yourself adequately rested, though you may feel as though you never really got to sleep at all.

Three or more watchkeepers Three watch-keepers makes luxury out of a single night at sea. Stick with one person on deck at a time and go for two-hour watches. That makes it 'two-on, four-off' cycled twice. The night's over before it's hardly begun. If there are more than three crew it's unlikely that on a typical yacht or power cruiser they all will be equally experienced, so beginners can be doubled up with old hands. The shellback will enjoy having a watch-mate to help pass the time, while the apprentice will learn what ships' lights look like in the best possible way — real life alongside somebody who knows.

A 3-hour night watch cycle for a crew of four

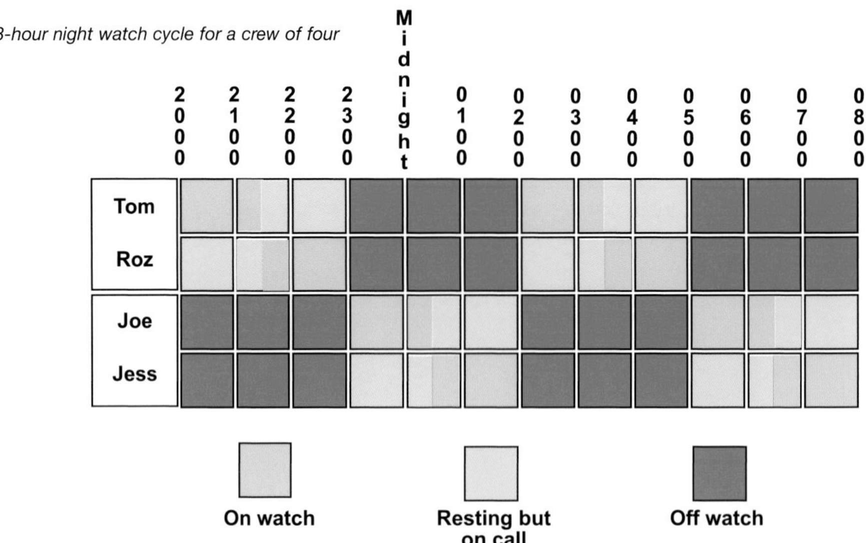

Longer passages

A formal watch pattern becomes essential when a boat is to be at sea for two nights or more. 24-hour systems come into favour on long voyages, but short-handed crews may prefer to stick with the two and three-keeper options described above. The advantages are that anyone who has had a bad night of it can be given a longer stretch below the following day, and rotating the system is easily done if that is what you want. The writer and his wife have crossed many an ocean on 'three-on, three-off' for the dark hours, and catch-as-catch-can in the daylight.

If you're unhappy about such easy-going arrangements and prefer to keep things on the straight and narrow around the clock, four hours is not too much for a daylight watch alone. You can either run three of these, which rotates the night watches perfectly, or if you all like the watches you have and find your body adapts better to a fixed system, run two and a pair of dog-watches (see below) to keep things as they are.

Rolling watches Four crew means you can have two on watch easily, but on a small vessel out of shipping lanes, there is really no need to have two people on deck unless a task demands it. This means that if Joe and Jess are scheduled for the watch from 2300 - 0200, only one or other need actually turn out at first. So long as the second watch partner is 'on call' and someone on deck is doing the job conscientiously, the watch can organise their own timetable so far as I'm concerned. If they opt to split their time into halves, one way or another they are going to get $4^1/_2$ hours in the sack followed by a quick ninety minutes doing the business. And very nice too!

Some skippers choose to formalise such arrangements. On other boats the watch contrives to change in such a way that you start your trick with one person, end with another and never have the same watch mate two nights running. There seems no reason to quarrel with this or any other system which can be made to work, but many will prefer to keep it simple.

The classical four-hour watch-on-watch system

No description of watches would be complete without the ancient four-hour arrangement still used on commercial and naval vessels. I have employed this successfully on fully crewed ocean crossings. Given enough hands, the skipper and cook can even stay outside the cycle so the galley staff can rest up for the day's work ahead, while the skipper is permanently on standby. Such luxury is rare, but so long as flexibility is allowed in the area of how many are actually required on deck at a given time, watch-on-watch can be highly successful, even with modest crew numbers. Here's how it goes:

0800 - 1200 — Forenoon watch
1200 - 1600 — Afternoon watch
1600 - 1800 — First dog watch
1800 - 2000 — Second dog watch
2000 - 0000 — First watch
0000 - 0400 — Middle watch
0400 - 0800 — Morning watch

Living with watches

A good watch system leaves all hands thoroughly rested. However, it takes time for the body to adjust to the way of life. One or two tricks of the trade can make the most of the watch below and help time pass on those long nights alone.

Go with the flow Don't try to fight your body's natural inclinations, always excepting the natural one to want to sleep all night long. Find how yours functions best and help it to do just that. For example, some skippers take the first watch below after dinner because it panders to the metabolic 'low' that follows a big meal. Other sailors love to see the night turn grey followed by the sunrise. If that's what turns them on and the remainder aren't clamouring to get up early, give them the dawn watch, and so on.

Don't mess around As with seasickness, the trick to achieving maximum hours in the sack is to get on with it when you go below. You may only have three hours in total. Of course it's agreeable to clean your teeth and change into clean pyjamas when you go off watch, but you may find it's better to hit the hay straight off and worry about such niceties in the morning. In heavy weather, turning in 'all standing' is not slovenly, it makes good sense, because you might be needed on deck in short order, and in the meantime you need all the shut-eye you can get.

Keeping awake Many modern small craft have autopilots of some description. If this is so, keeping awake should be easy because you are free to move about. Take a really good look round the horizon and if all is clear, hop below and brew up. Take your coffee on deck and enjoy it under the stars, if there are any. If it's blowing a hooley, hide under the dodgers and feel the rhythm of the boat as she rides the waves. Note down the weather forecast and, if it helps, read a good book in between regular scans of the surroundings. Better to be alert every two minutes than half asleep after an hour struggling with boredom. Take the opportunity to familiarise yourself with the navigation instruments, and fill in the log book creatively so that the next watch has something worth reading in addition to the data that you are correctly noting down for the skipper. There really is lots to do.

If you are obliged to steer, don't peer permanently into the compass. This is the road to the 'mesmerized zombie' effect. Try picking out a star that's sitting above your bow when you're on course, then steering by it; or use the run of the sea, or the wind. Recall snatches of poetry or consider what your speech might include at your daughter's wedding. I once sailed with a West Indian skipper who could recite huge tracts of Shakespeare he'd learned while sailing a trading schooner as a young man. There is no excuse for an active mind to fall asleep on watch. Indeed, many experienced people actively look forward to having this time to themselves in fair weather to sort out their heads.

The change of watch

It's a good idea to establish a process for handing over the watch, even on a family boat, because tired people can otherwise miss out vital data. The log book should be filled in by the watch going below, and rather than waiting for alarm clocks to wake their successors, it's generally better for them to call the new watch. A cup of tea all ready for them goes down well, because it puts the new watch in a more amenable frame of mind while using up the last quarter-hour for the old one. When the sleepers come out into the cockpit or wheelhouse, the retiring watch should brief them on weather and sails, or any engine peculiarities they are monitoring. Switching sails is best kept for the change of watch if it can humanly be managed — more people on deck, and nobody is dragged from his bunk. Next, ships in the vicinity are pointed out, with comments as to their aspect and relative movement. Finally, any night orders are reiterated.

Night Orders

All crew should be absolutely clear about what is expected of them when left in charge of the ship. These 'night orders' are often best written down so there is no doubt, because crew of only modest experience may otherwise find themselves in a dilemma about whether to waken the skipper or not.

Orders can be many or few, but a typical set of requirements might be as follows. These are examples only. Skippers will set their own limits to suit operational needs:

- Monitor oil pressure and engine temperature.
- Log standard navigational data every hour on the hour.
- Check the bilge.
- Note voltage on the domestic batteries and call the skipper if it drops below 12.0.
- Call the skipper if any vessel comes within an agreed distance as defined by radar.
- Call the skipper if any vessel is on a collision bearing, even if it is still four miles off.
- Call the skipper or mate if the mean wind increases or falls more than five knots, or changes in direction sufficiently to affect the tactical course.

Fog and poor visibility

Open any useful navigation manual and you'll find a well-reasoned section on piloting in reduced visibility. The related sound signals are also well covered in any course text book. In addition to these obviously vital elements, however, there is a substantial slice of seamanship involved in handling yourself and your vessel when you can't see where you're going. Most experienced sailors prefer to face a gale in open water than fog. Even when far enough from land to make stranding no issue there still remains the spectre of collision but, leaving such rational elements aside, fog strikes dread into the heart in a more elemental way.

The majority who go to sea enjoy vision of at least a reasonable standard. Sight, for most of us, is the most important sense of all. To be effectively robbed of it leaves us feeling extraordinarily vulnerable. Like all situations where fear or anxiety are clouding our judgement, the best policy is systematic action. We need to know in advance how to handle it, and the most effective way is training.

Interpreting fog forecasts

The ideal answer to fog is not to get involved with it at all, so when it is forecast, don't allow having a GPS and a chart plotter to encourage complacency. These wonderful tools can make a huge difference if you're caught out, especially backed up by radar, but it's far better not to be there at all. Interpreting forecasts to avoid fog is very much more effective when you understand how it forms and what its performance is likely to be on the day.

Land fog This appears in rivers and estuaries on chilly nights when the ground dumps heat faster than the moisture in the air can handle. This condenses out as that friendly mist you sometimes see on fields. Cows stroll around knee-deep in it and you know it won't last. The rising sun will 'burn it off' as soon as it brings the temperature up a few degrees.

Land fog can drift out beyond its home country and be found a short distance offshore. In this form, it generally rises ten or twenty feet above the comparatively warm sea surface. The further out you go, the less likely it is, and you can be confident that it won't last.

Land fog can fill valleys – and often the mouths of rivers.

Land fog

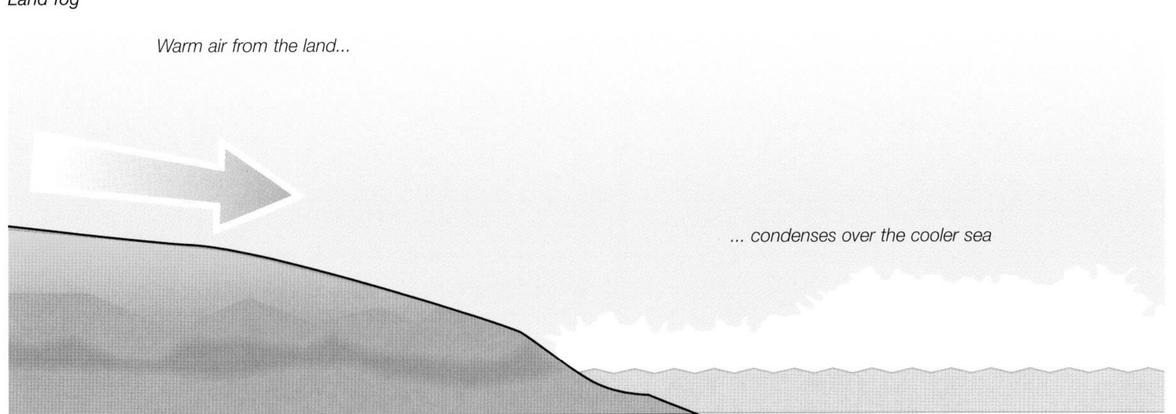
Warm air from the land...
... condenses over the cooler sea

Sea fog – Sea fog is a nastier proposition than its land-based cousin. Like all fog, it develops when moisture in the air condenses on contact with a cooler substrate – in this case the sea. Because the air mass generating it is often huge, and the water temperature setting it off may be widespread, it can cover large areas and last a long time. This is the case with a forecast for 'fog banks', or 'extensive fog'. 'Fog patches' means that the difference between the sea temperature and the 'dew point' of the air mass (the temperature at which it will condense its moisture into fog) is near the critical level, so fog is less certain in density and location.

The classic scenario for sea fog formation occurs up the eastern seaboard of North America, from New England to Newfoundland, where a 'smoky sou'wester' blows all the way up from the Caribbean to meet the icy Labrador current. Such fogs can last for weeks. Similar, less dramatic combinations occur in European waters.

Because sea fog relies on the water to cool the air below its dew point, a sort of 'fog shadow' can show up in a moisture-laden airstream blowing across the lee of a point of land or an island. Typical English Channel examples are to find the Solent clear behind the Isle of Wight in a damp southwesterly, or a substantial area of moderate visibility to the east of Guernsey or Jersey when a southwest wind is filling the western Channel with fog. Being aware of this likelihood can give you the confidence to make a landfall when you might otherwise be losing hope.

Single-station forecasting

As with most hazards, it helps to be forewarned. Even if fog is not forecast, you can often spot it coming. Look out for signs of an impending dew point dump:

A halo round navigation lights This is a sure sign of bad news at night.

Dew in your eyebrows Another indicator you don't want.

Sails inexplicably damp Sails suddenly get damp on what seems a nice day? Look out for fog around the corner!

Conduct on deck in fog

Life jackets and harnesses The question of when life jackets are to be worn is better left to the common sense of a skipper than laid down as a set of rules in a seamanship manual. However, there is accepted wisdom in the recommendation that all hands should wear their life jackets in thick fog. The reason for this is less about what happens to them if they fall overboard than their dire peril in the event of being run down. Collision risk is obviously much increased and, if the boat is hit, she may go down faster than people can find their 'lifers' and put them on. If they are already around their necks, there will be no unseemly rush for the locker.

The ever-present horror of losing a crew overboard is also exacerbated in fog, because the likelihood of finding a casualty is heavily reduced. It makes sense therefore to treat going on deck as one might after dark. If a harness is considered necessary then, perhaps it ought to be worn in fog also.

Be seen and heard Do all you can to increase your boat's visibility. Run your navigation lights in daylight; if you're a sailing boat, hoist your main even if motoring and, above all, remember to exhibit a radar reflector if yours isn't permanently rigged. Sound your signal every two minutes as laid down in the Collision Regulations (COLREGS).

The Lookout It may be sufficient to leave a solitary helmsman to look out alone in good conditions in a small yacht, but in fog this will not do. Unless there is no choice but to maintain a one-person watch, an extra lookout is undoubtedly worth the trouble. If conditions permit, he or she should be stationed on the foredeck. In fifty yards visibility, even thirty feet can make the difference between collision and safety.

Radar The COLREGS state that the lookout must be kept by all available means, which includes radar. This is especially the case in fog. If you have radar you are obliged to use it when necessary.

Listen Under power, a foredeck lookout is better placed to hear sound signals, engines, or bow waves than someone aft near the machinery. In any case, the boat should be slowed down periodically in order to hear better. Noises from ashore can be useful when piloting close in. The writer recalls working up the coast of Norfolk using depth soundings and the regular reports of the shotguns from wildfowlers. Dogs barking on beaches can also supply handy input to the overall picture.

Interpreting sound signals Try to note the relative bearing of sound signals from another vessel. It is notoriously difficult to be accurate about this because the mist often seems to distort the direction, but do your best. Expect some discrepancies, but try to determine at least whether it is moving forward, aft or, worse, maintaining a steady bearing.

Collision regulations in fog

It is not enough for a skipper to say, 'I needn't remember all the sound signals – I can look them up if I have to.'

In fog, there may not be time to do this before you have proceeded between a tug and her tow and brought your ship to ruin.

Safe speed The rules state that in restricted visibility every vessel must proceed at 'a safe speed'. For a small sailing yacht, this may be rather an academic requirement, but for a power yacht or larger sailing boat it means what it says. The rules are non-specific as to what this speed may be. In the case of a small boat it seems reasonable that a skipper should be able to stop her or manoeuvre her realistically within the limits of the ambient visibility. Add to this the contingency of another vessel looming up ahead on a reciprocal course, and you'll realise that cracking on is not an option.

Action by vessels not in sight of one another It's easy to assume that the normal collision rules apply at all times, but in Rule 19, special regulations are laid down for vessels not in sight of one another in or near an area of restricted visibility.

Subsection 'd' of this rule deals with collision avoidance using radar alone. Its advice is priceless and ignoring it exceedingly unwise. We cannot do better than reiterate it here:

('A vessel which detects by radar alone the presence of another vessel shall determine whether a close-quarters situation is developing and/or risk of collision exists. If so, she shall take avoiding action in ample time, provided that when such action consists of an alteration in course, so far as possible the following shall be avoided:

(i) An alteration of course to port for a vessel forward of the beam, other than a vessel being overtaken;

(ii) An alteration of course towards a vessel abeam or abaft the beam.')

Subsection 'e' lays down that unless it has been decided that there is no danger of collision, if you hear another vessel's fog signal forward of the beam you are to reduce speed to the minimum requirements of steerage and, if necessary, take off all way. In any event, extreme caution is to be the watchword until danger of collision is over.

The practicalities of radar on small craft in fog

The only truly satisfactory way of using radar to monitor collision situations is to have a hand permanently stationed at the screen. An occasional glance does not give the continuity that proper assessment of a variety of targets demands. The facts of life are such that in a typical small vessel there may only be one person qualified or experienced enough to use the equipment. This individual is more often than not the skipper, whose place is better on deck taking an overview and standing by should the need for instant action arise. The only answer is for owners of short-handed yachts and power boats to arrange for at least two people on board to be able to handle the radar effectively.

Strategies for fog

The most seamanlike of all fog strategies is not to be caught out in it, especially at night. Fog in daylight is horrid. At night it seems doubly so, especially in tight waters and in the proximity of traffic – and not without cause. After dark, nothing whatever can be seen in dense fog. Therefore, if you are at sea when fog descends and there is any chance of making a safe haven rather than pressing on, this should receive full consideration. Whether by night or day, the essential options for smaller craft are as follows:

- Abort and stay in harbour. A forecast for fog banks

should be enough to settle this as the right action, unless your passage is short, under the lee of land, and protected by a reliable navigational contingency plan.

- Proceed into water that is shoal enough to be non-navigable for commercial traffic. Either anchor or stand 'off and on' pending an improvement. This has the advantage of not demanding certainty of position if your electronic navigation systems have failed.
- Use all available means to navigate to a safe haven. Choose a harbour or anchorage with a minimum of traffic, because the risk of collision usually outweighs that of stranding for a vessel navigated by a competent person aided by GPS.
- Continue the passage with extra lookouts, using radar where possible, and noting all the precautions mentioned above. It may prove prudent to modify the passage plan to avoid areas of dense shipping or tricky pilotage. If the coast is close enough for alternative options to be realistic, the decision may also depend on an assessment of how long the fog is likely to last, especially if this includes the hours of darkness.

Log Book

Although the ship's log book may appear more to do with keeping a navigational record than pure seamanship, it is in fact an area of genuine overlap between the two disciplines. Almost everyone navigates using GPS as the basic fixing system, which has the inestimable advantage over all previous arrangements in that it matters not a jot whether you can see the horizon or not. The fix is there just the same. However, if that fix is not recorded on a regular basis, together with the associated data of time, log reading and course steered, the ship's position will be in serious doubt should the GPS fail in poor visibility for any reason, expected or unexpected. Given a recent fix and an up-to-date log book, it will take only minutes to work up a dead reckoning plot. This is the only method anyone had until the 1990s. It didn't make folks feel as confident as GPS, but it kept generations of seafarers safe. Log all positions and any passing buoys or other recognisable features too. If the electronics go awry, all will not be lost.

Time	Log	Course steered	COG/SOG	Position	Bar.	Eng.	Remarks
							HARWICH TOWARDS THE SCHELDT 15/06/2006
							Skipper - Horatio, Crew - Emma & Brendan
							Out of the lock at Shotley. Heading out towards
				'P' Various	1018	ON	Cork Sand under power. Main up. Dawn mist clearing.
0500 BST	0	'P' Pilotage	Various 6.8 kn	Eyeball			Wind SW3 Sun coming up. Vis good.
				Cork Sand	1018	OFF	
0605	5.5	110C	105T/5.8	N. Cardinal			Wind SW4. Sea slight. Lovely morning.
				Roughs Tower	1019	OFF	
0628	8.1	110C	107T/5.7	1.2m. Abeam to Stbd.			
				S Shipwash	1019	OFF	Sunk light float broad on stbd bow. Bacon sandwich in hand. Breeze and sea picking up. 1 reef.
0715	11.3	115C	110T/5.5	S. Cardinal			
				51 50.2N			Breeze steadied out at SW15 Knots. Cirrus in West.
0800	17	115C	120T/6.2	01 41.8E	1018 falling	OFF	

Manners and customs of the sea

Years ago, all who went to sea served some sort of apprenticeship, whether formal or casual, and a lad's elders and betters instilled in him a respect for 'the way things were done'. Failure to uphold these forms of behaviour invited ridicule and perhaps a clip around the weather ear. Thus, the established *modus operandi* passed on through the generations. It is only now that the maritime community has widened that such issues need to be written down. The spread of yachting and power boating has brought its own conventions. Some are inherited from commercial seafarers, others apply to us alone but, whichever is the case, to ignore them renders us liable to that uncomfortable feeling that we are 'not doing things right'. Nobody wants to stand out for this reason, so a number of the more important questions are highlighted here.

National ensigns

All yachts must wear the ensign of their country of registry. International law requires any vessel that 'goes foreign' to be on a national register. This is not an option. It is a legal requirement. However, a British yacht may fly the Red Ensign without troubling the UK Shipping Registrar if it is intended that she stay in home waters.

Types of Ensign
Some countries do not use their national flag for a sea ensign. Among these is the United Kingdom. Here, a plethora of ensigns of special design may be found in a typical yacht harbour. However, they all stem from three basic forms:

Red Ensign – The National Maritime Ensign of the UK Shipping Register. Worn by all commercial craft and yachts unless they fall into the categories below.

Blue Ensign – An undefaced Blue Ensign is a privileged ensign and may never be worn without its associated club burgee.

White Ensign – The only yachts entitled to fly the white are those whose owners are members of the Royal Yacht Squadron.

Defaced ensigns
A defaced Red Ensign and a defaced Blue Ensign are all called 'privileged' ensigns. Defaced means that the ensign has a badge on it. Certain yacht clubs are authorised by warrant to wear a specific one of these or, in certain cases, an undefaced blue ensign. A privileged ensign may never be worn without its associated club burgee.

Illegal ensigns – It is illegal to fly anything that is not the recognised ensign of the vessel's country of registration. A European flag with a national ensign in one corner falls clearly into the illegal category and is NOT an alternative national maritime ensign.

Under no circumstances is a Union Flag to be worn as a seafaring ensign by British craft. Nor is it an appropriate courtesy ensign for foreign visitors. It will only be seen flying from time to time on naval vessels, right forward as a 'jack'.

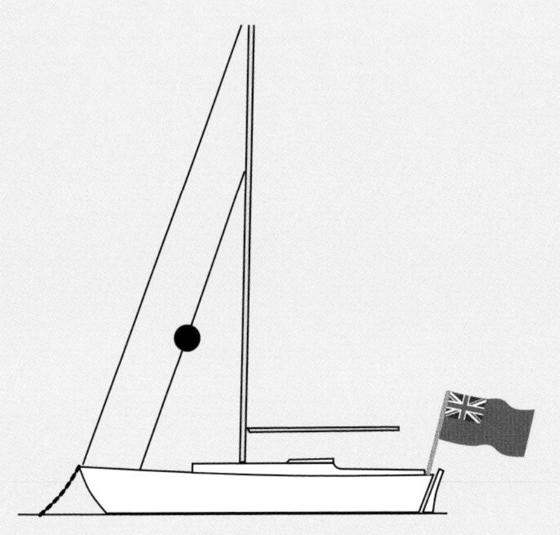

- In harbour, from a dedicated staff mounted right aft on the taffrail. If this is unworkable, the ensign may be carried on the backstay.

- Ditto at sea for Bermudan sloop-rigged sailing yachts.
- Power craft at sea may wear the ensign from a suitable dedicated staff as far aft as convenient, but in harbour this should be on the taffrail.

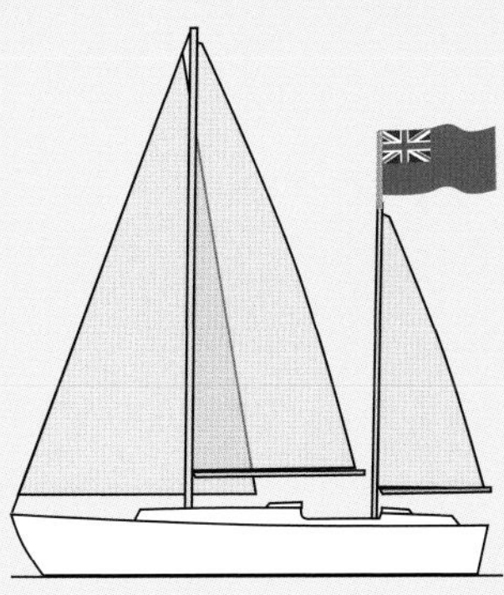

- Ketches or yawls at sea may wear the ensign at the mizzen masthead, but in harbour it should be transferred to the taffrail.

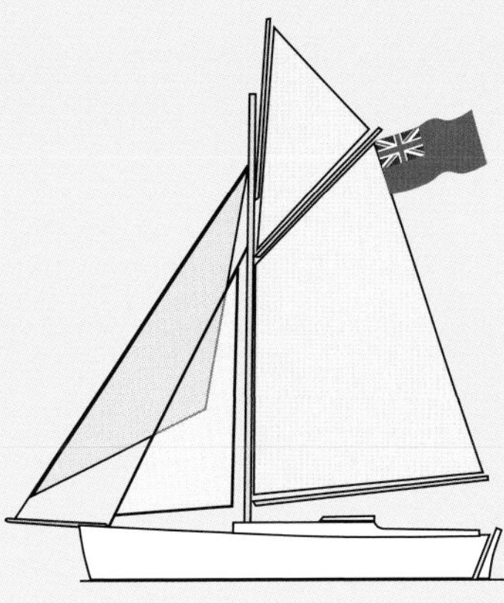

- Gaff-rigged craft at sea are at liberty to fly the ensign from the peak of the gaff. Technically, this is 'from the leech of the sail', but in practice it is flown from a halyard block at the peak. In harbour, the ensign is moved to a staff on the taffrail.

Signals and courtesy ensigns

The only signal flag flown regularly by most yachts today is the 'Q' flag which indicates arrival from outside the EU. It is a 'request for pratique' or, to use more modern language, a statement that the yacht has not yet cleared customs and immigration. Like all signals, this one is flown from the starboard cross-trees on a sailing yacht or from the starboard halyard on a motor yacht's mast. Also on this halyard is any courtesy ensign. Yachts visiting foreign ports have traditionally worn a small version of the country's ensign as a courtesy to their host. This should be flown superior to any other signals. It is not technically a legal requirement, but to omit to display a courtesy ensign is, as you might expect, blatantly discourteous. The officials of certain countries have been known to harass those who fail in this duty of politeness.

Signal flags and courtesy ensigns

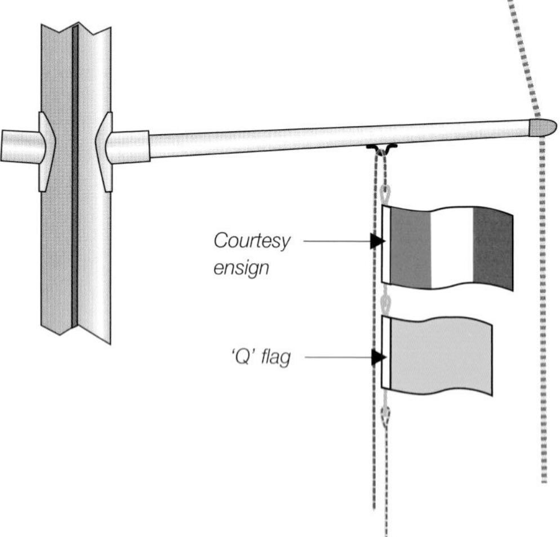

When not to fly the ensign

There are those who 'nail their ensigns to the backstay and leave them there until they rot'. This is not unlawful, but it is uneconomic. In the seventeenth century, an official in the Royal Navy noticed that the bill for bunting was extortionate. He therefore directed all captains to bring in their colours at sunset and to set them at sunrise. The cost halved in a year and the institution passed into common usage. All properly run professional yachts still adhere to it, as do many others whose owners care about the traditions of the sea. Here are the 'rules' for any who, like the writer, may choose to follow them:

- Ensigns are worn entering or leaving harbour, and at sea at any time they may be observed from another vessel or the shore of any country. When out of sight of land or shipping, displaying the ensign is at the skipper's discretion.
- In harbour, the ensign is hoisted at 0800 local time, or at 0900 in the winter months (between 1st November and 14th February inclusive). It is lowered at sunset or 2100 if this is earlier. If a Naval vessel is present, follow her lead.

Club burgees and associated ensign duties

All yacht and sailing clubs have their own burgees. A burgee is a triangular pennant worn at the masthead on a 'burgee stick' that allows it to swivel with the wind. With the proliferation of wind instruments the practice of mastheading the burgee has fallen away somewhat, but certain senior clubs such as the Royal Cruising Club insist. Their members seem to manage perfectly well. The idea that a burgee can just as well be flown from a halyard below the port spreaders is not really the answer. If it proves the only option, a rectangular house flag should be used here instead.

Any boat flying a defaced ensign (red or blue), or an undefaced blue, MUST wear the associated club burgee, the warrant holder should be on board or in the immediate vicinity, and the 'permit to fly' must be carried. The privilege goes with the person, not the boat.

Privileged ensign and associated burgee

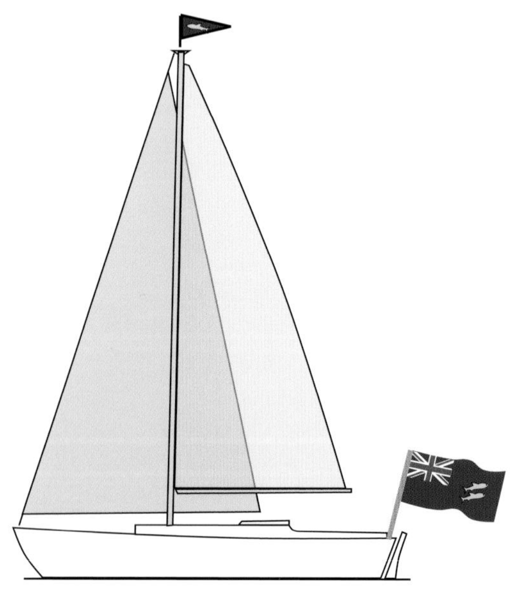

Setting up a burgee with a modern masthead

- Secure a light cheek block to one side of the mast immediately below the top and pass a light halyard through this. The halyard can be belayed at any convenient point around the deck, the lower shrouds or on the mast itself.
- Prepare the burgee stick. This should be as long as necessary to carry the pennant well clear of the masthead paraphernalia. Burgee sticks, or 'pig sticks', are available via the Internet. They can also readily be constructed from a length of dowelling, some stiff stainless wire, a few washers and a round-headed screw.
- Tie the two ends of the halyard together to make it endless. Now attach the halyard to the stick with a pair of clove hitches as shown. To make each hitch, simply flip two half-turns of the bight over the end of the stick and snug them down together.
- Hoist the stick, bringing it upright to clear the instruments once mastheaded.

The burgee stick

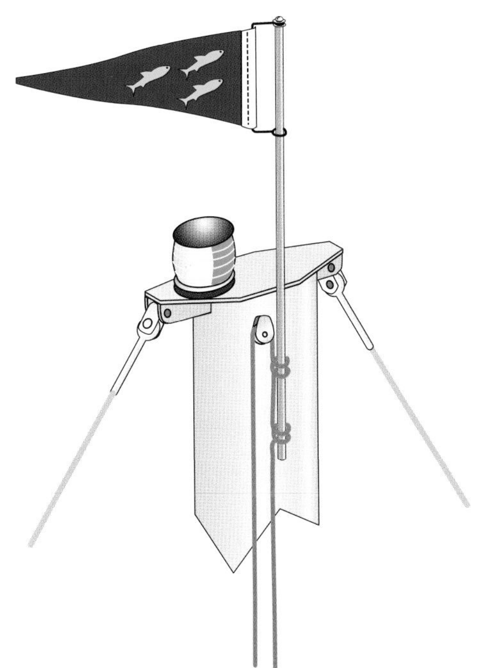

Wash

Wash in harbours and where moored or anchored boats may be found is antisocial and unacceptable. Almost any powered boat, including most modern sailing craft, is capable of creating enough wash to be a nuisance, and every skipper is responsible for making sure it doesn't happen in the wrong places.

CAUTION
YOU ARE RESPONSIBLE
FOR YOUR WAKE

A boat travelling well within her hull speed (see page 12) is unlikely to disturb the water much but, as this critical velocity is approached, wave making increases dramatically. Typically, if speed through the water is kept below $\sqrt{LWL}$ (around 5 knots for an average 32ft sailing boat), all will be well. Some planing hulls have serious wake problems at sub-planing speeds. RIBs are a classic example. The only answer here is to be sensitive to others. If you're motoring up a waterway at well within a posted speed limit but dragging half the river behind you, slow down if you see people on moored boats or fishermen on the bank. Whatever you're driving, always look astern and assess your level of wash.

Harbour speed limits Note that a speed limit is based on water speed not ground speed. In other words, your GPS might be reading 6 knots if you're logging 8 through the water against a 2-knot stream. You'll be piling up 8 knots worth of wash though, and will richly deserve the black looks. Posted speed limits in America are often backed up by the further constraint, 'No Wash'. What a good idea!

Wash at sea Sailboat wash is not an issue at sea. Occasionally, a heavy powerboat can cause major upsets if she is steered too close to others. This is especially true in calm weather where a sailing boat may be trying to coax some progress out of an unpromising breeze. A big wash will shake her canvas into lifelessness and the resulting loss of way can take several minutes to make good.

Children and outboards A child let loose in the right circumstances with a rowing dinghy is a happy person who is learning. The input is not only about how a boat really manoeuvres, it's also about the limits of human strength when confronted with tide and wind. A grand package, to be contrasted with a small boy (it always seems to be boys) given free reign with the family's outboard tender. He will inevitably drone around an anchorage creating noise and wash as he rapidly becomes bored, and doing neither himself nor anyone else any good at all.

Sailing boats' abuse of searoom

It's easy for a sailing skipper to forget that while his opposite number in a power boat could well be a perfectly good seaman, he may not fully understand the nuances of manoeuvres under canvas. The timing of a tack, for example, might be anything but obvious to the master of a semi-planing cruiser making 16 knots in a seaway. To tack into the path of an oncoming motorboat can be as antisocial as for her to shake the wind out of a yacht's sails. Courtesy here is all about trying to think yourself into the next person's head. Not easy, but more than worth the effort.

Noise

The same could be said for noise pollution. So long as we keep thinking about the neighbours and remember that noise carries surprisingly long distances over still water, we won't go far wrong.

Parties When you're in harbour and you feel a really good bash coming on, take a look round, see who it's going to disturb, then try to find a way of mitigating the pain. A civilised guideline is to make sure all the revellers are below by the hour more enlightened times than our own set down for pub closing (around 2230), but if there are young children rafted up to you on the next yacht, it might be kind to do so considerably earlier. If in doubt, one golden rule is always to invite anyone who might be upset to come over for a drink. Given the opportunity, they may turn out to be the rowdiest funsters of all.

Running engines and generators In harbour among other craft, a neighbour's engine droning away and pushing out fumes is a major source of disharmony. If you must charge your batteries, try to do it between sunrise and sunset. Even a generator can be surprisingly antisocial to those not on board. Some boats must start a generator to boil a kettle. Their crews should be aware that by doing so in a quiet harbour or anchorage outside 'working hours' they are committing an act that might offend. They should keep the irritant to an absolute minimum.

Boarding other boats

In landsmen's terms, a boat's deck is as private as your garden or back yard; her accommodation is the equivalent of your house or apartment. Therefore, always ask before boarding someone else's boat. A hail with her name ('Ahoy, Saucy Sue') should be enough to attract attention. Even if you are approaching with intent to raft up, don't put a foot over the rail until someone has said it's OK, unless you have been directed there by the harbourmaster and are convinced that nobody is on board.

The exception to this is when you are in an established raft-up. Stepping across other boats, if someone is on deck, catch their eye and look for a nod. Otherwise, just move quietly across.

The rules for crossing boats are as follows:

- If nobody is out and about, don't disturb them below, just cross softly and positively.
- Always walk forward of the mast.
- Never cross someone's cockpit without being asked.
- When stepping aboard late at night, be careful not to twang rigging and wake everyone up. Also, watch out for booming-out poles and the like stowed on deck. Kicking one of those inadvertently can produce enough noise to raise the dead.
- Never jump down onto someone else's deck. Always try to lower your weight gently. Walk on the sides of your feet and try not to put your heels down first. In other words, creep like mouse, don't stride like a buffalo!

The environment

Oil

Bilge pumping For some reason, boats seem to generate oil. Most cannot pump their bilges without at least some degree of oil pollution, yet to pump out any sort of oily matter into coastal or tidal waters up to three miles offshore without consent of the Environment Agency is an offence punishable by unlimited fines or imprisonment. This applies even if the discharge is by accident. In one or two specific areas these regulations are policed to the extent that yachts must pump out into containers for disposal in approved sites.

All this can be a major inconvenience, but enforcement is difficult, often impractical, and sometimes less than just. The best solution in practical terms is to try to keep the main bilge as clean as possible by isolating it from the engine bilge or drip tray. The latter must be cleared in some way that prevents its contents getting into the environment, typically by hand-pumping into a can to carry ashore to an approved oil dump. If the main bilge is contaminated, one workable solution is to use oil-absorbing or 'bio' soak-up pads. These hold onto oil and other pollutants, allowing relatively clean water to be pumped over the side.

Ecology in the engine bay

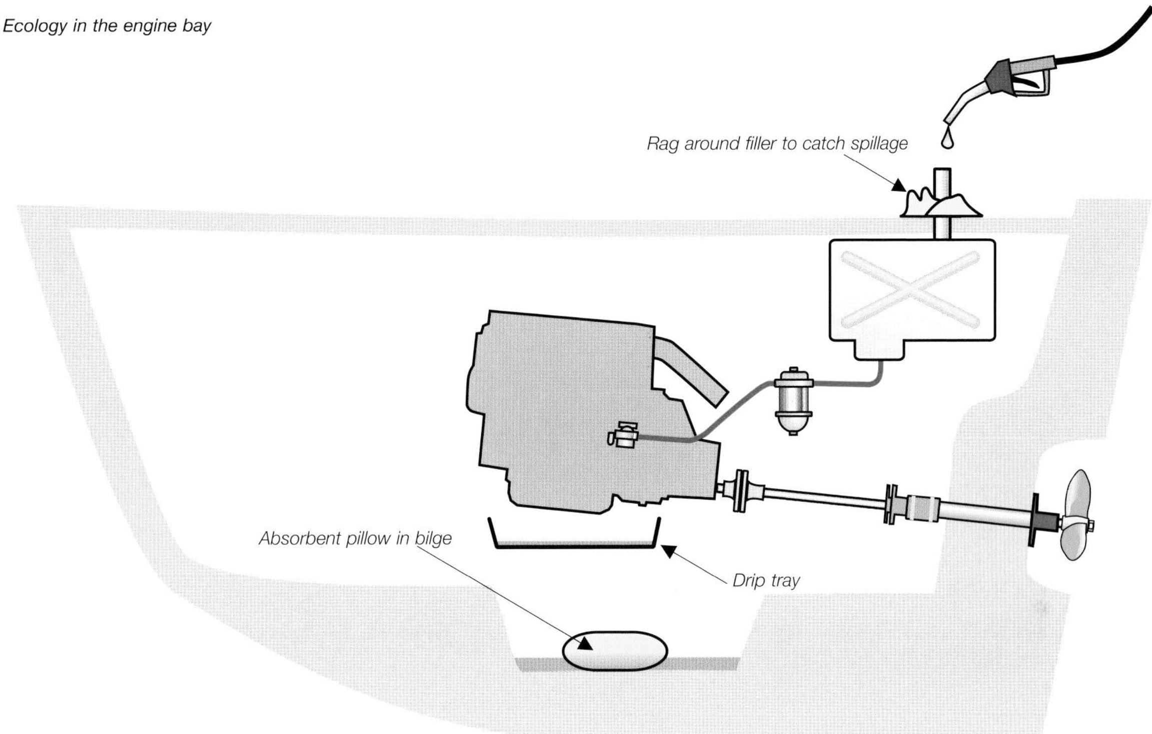

Fuelling up When fuelling up, be careful about allowing oil spills on the rationale that they can readily be neutralised by a quick shake of the detergent bottle. Some detergents do more harm than the oil. A supply of soak pads or baby's nappies (diapers) laid around the filler hole is the best answer. Power craft taking on larger quantities of fuel at high pumping rates should consider fitting 'splash stops' in the line.

Detergents There seems little doubt at the time of writing (2006) that regulation may come into force concerning the use of non-bio detergents. In any event, there is no question about the fact that biological chemicals are injurious to the marine environment. Fortunately, ecologically sound detergents are available, and should be used on the water.

Holding tanks

In an ideal word, all sailors would use holding tanks anywhere near the coast, only pumping heads straight out when far at sea. For this to happen, plentiful convenient pump-out facilities must be supplied. Sadly, they are not, so unless navigating in an area governed by clear regulation to the contrary such as parts of the Eastern Mediterranean, we are left to our own consciences and certain guidelines.

Basic Principle:

- Do not discharge a sea toilet where it will affect water quality or harm the amenity value of the local waters.

Good practice suggestions:

- Use shore facilities wherever possible – tell the harbour authority or marina operator if these are inadequate.
- Do not discharge a sea toilet into non tidal, or weak tidal waters in an area where local sewage is adequately treated before sea dispersal.
- Do not discharge into crowded anchorages, near amenity beaches or close to commercial shell-fish beds.
- If you regularly use your boat in such inshore areas, fit a holding tank.
- Do not empty a chemical toilet into the sea.

Discharge of holding tanks

It is lawful to do this via a proper shorebased pump-out facility, or directly when more than three miles offshore.

Dinghy Work

All yachts and power boats intending to cruise beyond their immediate home waters need a tender for emergencies and to ferry crew to and from shores too shallow to approach with the main vessel. Dinghies are expensive to buy, and choosing the right one can make a big difference to the success of a cruise.

Let's look at a few different types of dinghy.

Simple inflatable

Soft-floored inflatable dinghies are used in many yachts and power craft with no davits aft and a stowage-space issue on deck. These boats stow into bags similar in size to a genoa headsail. They can be inflated by hand. Rowable after a fashion, they can also take a modest outboard, but they are limited in range and endurance. Although their inherent buoyancy makes them surprisingly safe, they can be extremely wet. They remain the only realistic tender for many boats.

Small RIB

In many ways, the RIB (Rigid Inflatable Boat) is the ideal yacht tender unless you intend to row seriously. Easily driven under power, a RIB can travel fast without a huge, thirsty outboard. RIBs are extremely seaworthy and, because of the way they plane, they are drier than regular inflatables except in strong winds. A RIB cannot be collapsed beyond deflating its tubes, so in all but the largest yachts it requires either deck stowage or davits.

Hard dinghy

A hard dinghy, with either a pram (blunt) bow or a pointed stem, makes the ideal tender for anyone who wishes to row ashore. It can also generally carry a useful small outboard, but is unlikely to reach planing speeds. It is by far the driest form of shoregoing transport for the discerning sailor, but sadly it requires more space on deck than any of its rivals. For many production yachts it is simply a non-starter, although it is still preferred by most traditional sailors.

Propulsion

Most tenders have outboards, but oars must be carried against breakdown or fuel mismanagement, and they must be known to work reasonably effectively. It is perfectly possible to cruise around the world in peace without an outboard, and many have done so. The cost is low, theft and pilfering are reduced and the health-promoting exercise is nothing but good, but the dinghy must row well. Sadly, most inflatables do not.

Rowing an inflatable When rowing an inflatable, don't try to make long sweeps. Typical inflatable oars are really little more than paddles, so make short, deep strokes. With any type of dinghy it helps to angle the blades so that they bite into the water on the power stroke rather than trying to feather their way out.

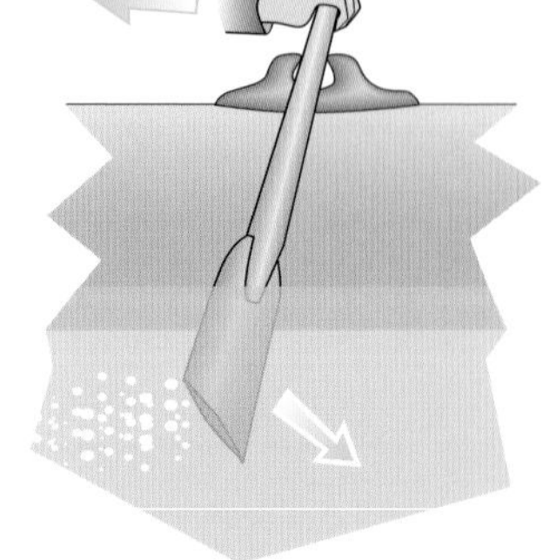

Angle paddle blades so they 'dig-in' to the rowlocks.

Loading

In calm conditions a good dinghy can accommodate a surprising weight of bodies and general cargo. When the going cuts up it can be a different story. Many manufacturers issue loading recommendations, which we do well to note. However, in the end it is down to the common sense of the skipper. Many a crew has rowed ashore in a heavily loaded tender on a calm evening only to find half a gale blowing when they return. At such times it is better to make two trips, however inconvenient, rather than risk the highly dangerous overcrowded alternative.

Boarding

Board a dinghy carefully, with due regard to the effect an individual's weight will have on trim. By far the safest place to board from the yacht is amidships if freeboard permits. Even if the deck is too high above the water to make this a one-stop proposition, it may be better to use a solidly constructed ladder than to take your chances on the stern platform. The reason is that if there is any current or a strong wind, the dinghy will lie sweetly alongside, while under the stern she will be trying to blow or stream off continually unless securely tied up. It's easier to board from a stern platform if the tender is brought up beam-on across it, but this is exactly where the dinghy does not want to be in anything other than calm conditions. If you're stuck with having to board in this way, make sure the small boat cannot flip out as you step in.

Life jackets

Some countries insist that life jackets are worn in dinghies at all times. This catch-all policy is, of course, as safe as you can get. Without being gratuitously macho, others would say that they only wear life jackets in the dinghy occasionally, perhaps when they expect to be returning late in a strong tide. The decision is a personal one, but before making it, everyone should bear in mind that a large number of sailors are lost between ship and shore every year. A sensible attitude is based on the assumption that some unforeseen circumstance will upend the dinghy. The question then is, 'Am I confident that in the ambient conditions all aboard can save themselves without life jackets?' Interestingly, the US Coast Guard do not insist that life jackets are worn by adults, but that one must be carried for every soul in the dinghy. This is not necessarily a policy recommended by this manual. It is included because no regulations are in place in British waters at the time of writing (2006), and it may offer a guideline for those who feel they need one.

Anchor and cable

A small anchor can be useful, not only to maintain position if the outboard fails and you can't row for any reason, it can also be handy for holding off when the dinghy is left on a lee shore. Lay out the anchor as you come in, wait until everyone is ashore, then haul off a few feet, setting the hook as you do so. Now pull in hard on the painter and stretch the warp out, hop off and with luck the boat will hang just out of reach of danger until you return. If it's warm weather, you can haul off properly, then wade ashore with the long painter.

Painter

A short dinghy painter is a waste of time. On a tight dinghy dock it's also antisocial. To tow successfully a painter should be long enough to let the boat hang back to the next wave at least. To leave the dinghy alongside a tidal wall of even modest significance, you need a good 25ft, while to secure it on a busy pontoon with a short line stops anyone else using the berth. If everyone's dinghy hangs off a few boat's lengths, all can manage with ease.

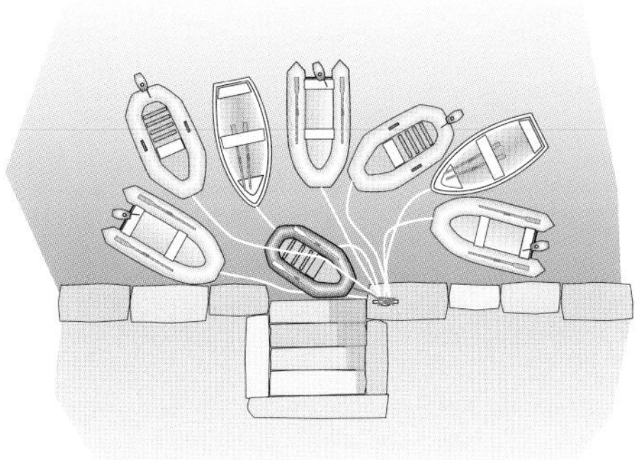

One dinghy on a short painter spoils everybody's day.

River seamanship

Since many rivers are tidal and are regularly navigated by vessels coming from the sea, the title of this section is not, in fact, a contradiction. Rivers carry their own challenges, and specific techniques are required for their ready negotiation. Some rivers are fully charted, but the fact that many are not is no reason for refusing to explore them. If navigable within the limits of most users, a pilot book will generally offer enough data to proceed.

Collision regulations

Tidal rivers are often subject to local byelaws, particularly speed limits. If you are in doubt as to what these may be, proceed at a sensible speed – slower rather than faster – leaving no unnecessary wash. Generally, speaking, the International Regulations for Prevention of Collision at Sea (COLREGS) apply in rivers as far as their connection with tidal waters remains uninterrupted. For example, they cease at the first lock gate, if there is one. Thereafter, the regulations may still be adopted, but local, national or continental byelaws could well modify or augment them, such as the European CEVNI regulations for inland waterways.

Tidal considerations

Height If in doubt, enter a tidal river around half-flood, then proceed with caution knowing that, should you run aground, the rising tide will lift you off. Navigating a strange river on a falling tide is strongly discouraged.

Springs/Neaps While arriving at High Water, Springs appears to have much to recommend it, to run aground on top of a big tide can be disastrous. If the next High Water is lower and you have failed to get off, you are condemned to wait for the next spring tide, which may be a fortnight or much more away. This unhappy state of affairs is called being 'neaped'.

Controlling depth When entering a river whose depths are uncertain, note your exact track and keep an eye on the sounder. Record the shoalest point. Once inside, you can reduce this controlling depth to soundings and be sure that on that line at least you know what the depth will be as you return to the sea.

A typical tidal river

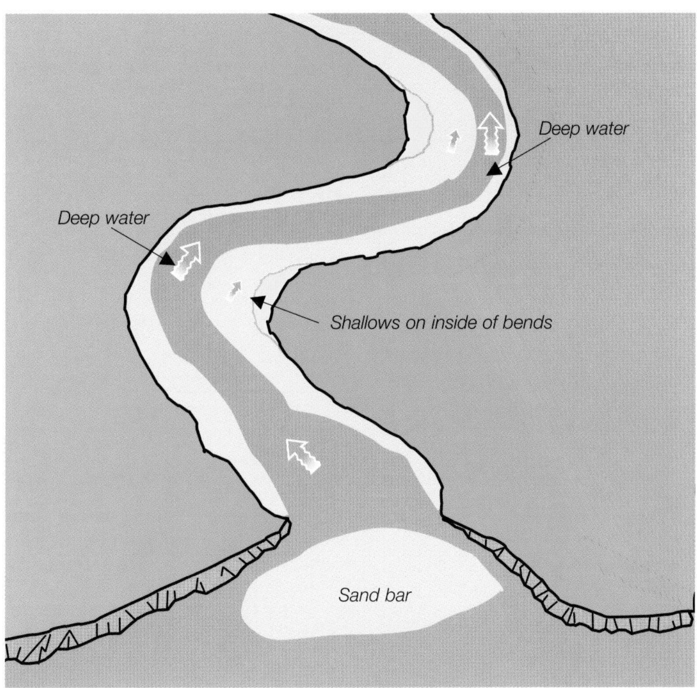

Bars

Many rivers deposit debris and silt in the sea either at or immediately to seaward of their mouths. Be ready for shoaling and take special care approaching any river bar in strong onshore weather, especially when the tide is ebbing to windward.

Navigating an uncharted or marginally charted river

Generally speaking, rivers run deepest in the middle. Rounding bends, they tend to shoal on the inside of the corner as the current is thrown straight ahead by centrifugal force to scour away the outside. Given these basic premises, the rest is down to observation and common sense. Watch the bank carefully. A rocky cliff may indicate a steep-to foreshore. A gently shelving meadow probably continues in the same vein below the water, and so on. Watch out for bars off the mouths of tributaries, especially in areas where flash floods may be expected. Here, boulders and other rubbish may be carried down and deposited in the midstream area of the main river. If in doubt, favour the opposite bank.

Expect currents to be strongest in deep water. This effect is sometimes marked by noticeable wavelets where the water is running faster and oily calm in the slack areas. Careful observation can reveal much.

Echo-sounder alarms In rivers, one is often as keen to know how rapidly the water is shoaling as to be told the precise moment at which a predetermined depth is reached. Without forward-looking sonar, a depth alarm can only show the latter so, while it has its uses, relying on an alarm may be less beneficial than at first appears.

Power craft

No special considerations apply to sailing craft operating in rivers under engine. Power vessels with exposed propellers must take additional care to avoid grounding.

Sailing yachts

COLREGS – Rule 9(b) of the Collision Regulations states "that a sailing vessel shall not impede the passage of any other vessel navigating within a narrow channel or fairway". Subsection (a) of the same rule requires all vessels to keep to starboard as far as is safe and practicable. These provisions to some extent compromise the sailor's rights of 'power giving way to sail', and a sailing boat making full use of the opportunities offered by a shifting wind will sometimes find herself on the 'wrong' side of the river. If no other boats are around, this presents no difficulties. Where traffic is dense, especially with power craft whose skippers may not have experienced sailing issues, you are left with a judgement call. If in doubt – and in any case where confronted with larger vessels who may be inconvenienced by your actions – you must drop to leeward and accept the inconvenience. Don't forget though that if you are obliged to stand on for reasons of safety, the other skipper still has a duty to keep clear under Rule 17a(ii), even though you are technically the give-way vessel. Communicate if you can. Most people will help out if they fully understand what is going on.

Keep well to windward – Sailing free in a river, keep up to windward as far as you can within the COLREGS because of the possibility that the wind will head you. If you've sagged away to leeward, you'll be faced with an unnecessary tack. After extended practice, this policy becomes second nature and is one of the classic signs of a good seaman.

Take no chances with the lee shore

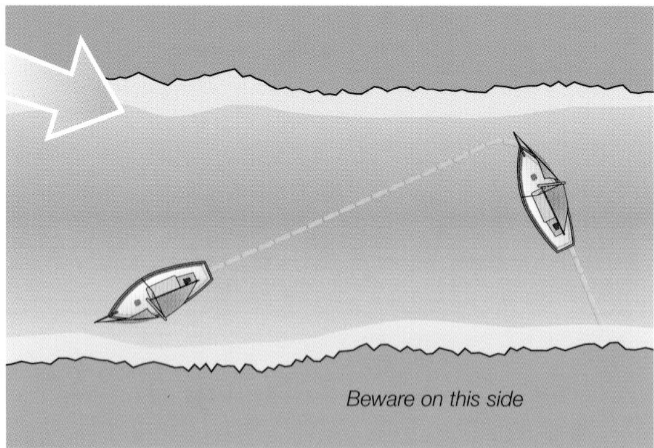

Sailing to windward in close quarters, the favoured tack – the one that makes most progress – is the one which ends up on the lee shore. Special care must be taken at the end of this tack because if you touch and lose way you cannot sail off. You'll be reduced to starting the engine or launching the dinghy, laying out a kedge and winching yourself off.

Touch and go

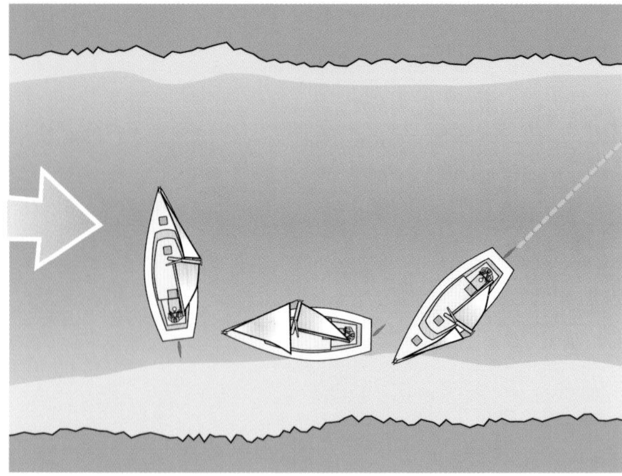

If you touch bottom on a tack just before you intend to come about, steer hard to weather immediately and don't let go the headsail sheet. With luck, you'll carry enough residual way for the yacht's bow to come through the wind. The jib will then 'back', shoving the head around with enthusiasm as the boat begins heeling the right way. Once you reach this point, there is a fair possibility she will sail straight off into deep water. Miss your chance by hesitation and you're stuck!

Keep way on

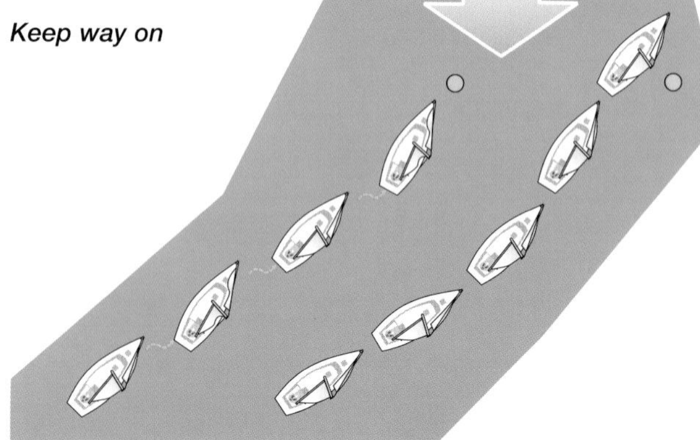

It takes confidence to steer downwind of something you really need to lay when you're closehauled, and it's a natural reaction to try to win an extra yard or two by pinching high of a proper course. Pinching, however, must be avoided at nearly all times. As soon as a boat comes above closehauled she begins sliding sideways as her speed drops below 2 or 3 knots, so although you appear to be pointing to where you want to go, you're actually slipping to leeward of it. The only answer is to bite the bullet and steer full. Once the boat is sailing positively, luff her gently but persistently and you'll be amazed how high she'll point.

Huffling

In flat water with plenty of way on you can often shoot head to wind for several boat's lengths as you come about. The technique can also work when you aren't quite making a corner beyond which you'll be sailing free. This 'huffling' gains valuable distance, especially amongst moorings and other awkward obstructions. If the boat develops lee helm when she fills on the new tack, you've allowed her to shed too much way, so learn for next time. Huffling doesn't normally work at sea because of the waves.

Lee-bowing

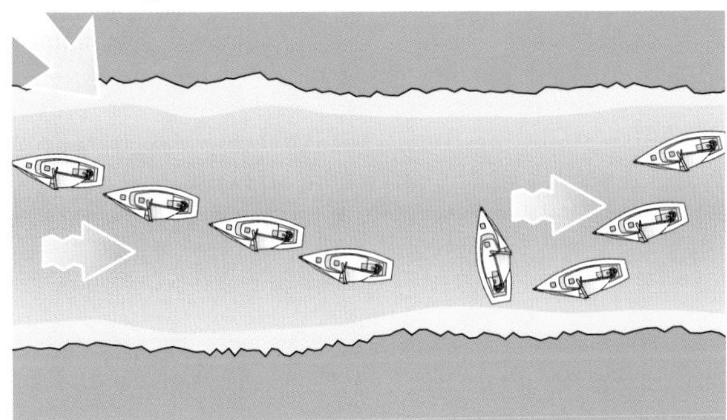

Closehauled and facing a foul stream, huge advantages can accrue if you can steer to place the tide on your lee bow. The boat will be magically set upwind, while the apparent wind will be freed by a geometrical mystery. Lee-bowing can save whole tacks. Once in a while it even excuses pinching.

Use of transits Wherever a tide or current is running, the boat will not be going where she is pointing. This holds good for power craft also, but the sailing-boat skipper who is tacking must be especially observant about where the boat will end up. The only real answer is to use the transits of two objects in line whenever you want to arrive at a specific place. If your interest is more in not hitting something, note whether the appropriate transits are changing. If it's a moored boat, make sure both of her ends are moving in the same direction. If the stern's gobbling up the background and the bow is spewing it out, you're passing clear ahead, but if both stern and bow are progressively obscuring background, alter course or wait for the crunch.

Keep an eye on your masthead Tacking up a river full of moored boats on a windy day with your boat heeled well over, it's frighteningly easy to forget your masthead. Watching transits at eye level does not guarantee immunity from fouling other boat's rigs with your wind instruments. Always look aloft.

Think ahead Make a point of thinking ahead in a river. Beating, try to plan a tack ahead – preferably two. Don't be over-ambitious with your tactics, and you won't end up at the bitter end of a blind alley.

Exit strategy Sailing in tight waters, things can slip out of your control quite suddenly. One moment you are enjoying the ambience, the next you've run out of space. Especially when sailing alongside or into a tight berth, an exit strategy is axiomatic so that if things go horribly wrong, you know before you start what the alternative is. Given this, the only decision is when to activate 'Plan B'.

Grounding

It has been said that if you never run aground, you aren't trying hard enough. Whilst there may be some comfort in this, most shipwrecks result from a stranding of one sort or another, so running aground is obviously to be avoided. However, some groundings are worse than others. For a boat with no vulnerable under-water appendages, to slide gently onto soft mud on a quiet weather shore with the tide rising should be a cause of no concern whatever. For the same craft to strike a rocky shoal with the wind blowing onto it from the open sea would be very bad news indeed, even if the tide were making. For this to occur on a falling tide could prove catastrophic. A sailing yacht short-tacking up a muddy river on a flood tide might safely take some calculated risks with the weather shore. A power boat with vulnerable propellers navigating close to rocks in a big swell would be irresponsible to proceed without the utmost caution. In short, groundings must be considered in a seamanlike context, and the duty of care exercised to avoid them will vary in degree with circumstances.

The echo sounder

In conjunction with a chart and an awareness of the vessel's position, the front-line guardian against grounding is the echo sounder. These instruments are generally highly reliable, but the readout is only as good as the skipper's knowledge of how it has been calibrated, if indeed it has been at all.

Depth below transducer Left to itself, an uncalibrated sounder reads depth below its own transducer. To know the depth, it is only necessary to be aware of how far this is below the boat's waterline and add the two values together.

Water depth Many sounders can be calibrated to read depth of water. The best way of verifying this readout is first to sound a depth with the backup leadline all vessels should carry, then calibrate the instrument to read the same. Anything else involves numbers and some degree of guesswork. This choice of calibration datum is a good one because it does away with any extra number-crunching when reducing to soundings. So long as the boat's draught is in no doubt, you'll know when she is about to run aground.

Echo sounder variables

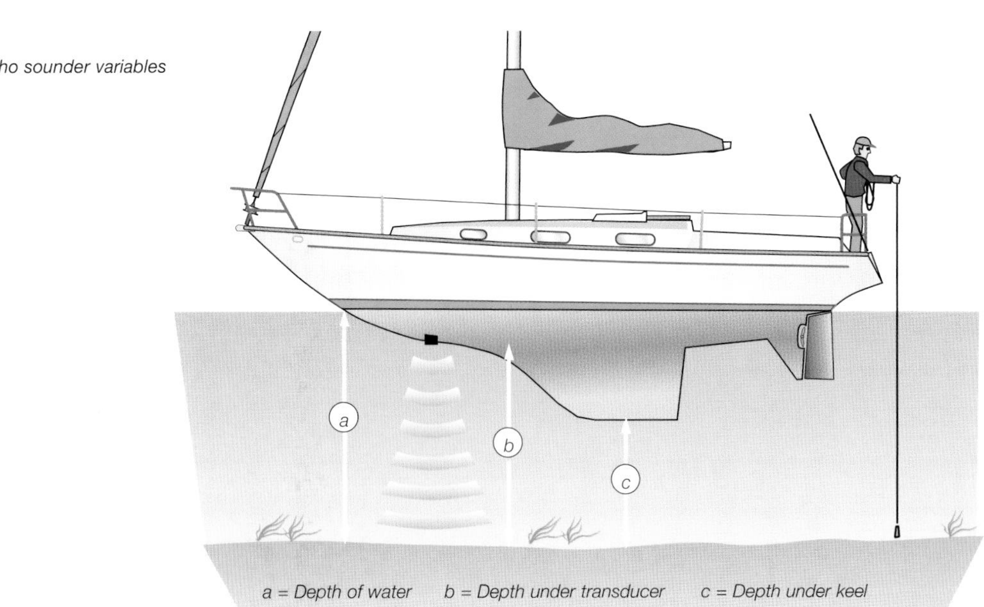

Depth below the keel Many people calibrate the sounder to read depth below keel so that they can see at a glance how much shoaling is needed to ground the vessel. There is much to be said for this, but it must be done accurately. Some charter operators 'add a bit for safety', thus rendering any seamanlike depth calculation – in fog perhaps – null and void. It is in any case necessary to add the boat's draught to the reading when such a depth is being used for navigation.

Action to be taken on grounding

'Safe' groundings If the grounding is in a non-threatening situation, perhaps with nothing more to do than wait for the tide to rise, a good skipper would invite the cook to put the kettle on as the crew settle down calmly to await re-floating.

Dangerous groundings If a stranding seems even remotely likely to be serious, action must be taken as quickly as possible. As to the specifics, (see page 146), but in general the first concern must be the crew's security. Their best chance may well lie in saving the ship, but if the likelihood of this seems in doubt, assistance should be called promptly. The SAR team can always be stood down later if the boat saves herself.

Checking for damage

If the boat has literally glided to a standstill on mud, harm is highly unlikely. On the other hand, when she has banged to a sudden halt and is bouncing on rocks, her continued integrity will be in grave doubt. If she is making water faster than it can be pumped out, the best place for her – or at least her crew – may even be to stay where she is because at least she won't sink any further.

Bilge Lift the cabin sole and see if she is making water. If not, well and good for the moment. If she is, start pumping and monitor progress. So long as you are winning, move on to the next checks. If you aren't, call for assistance, then see if you can improve things.

Rudder It is common for a rudder to be damaged in a heavy grounding. Check to see if the tiller or wheel moves freely. If it does, either the rudder has gone or all is probably well. Most likely the latter. If it is heavy or jammed, be prepared for the additional challenge of steering problems when you come off.

Keel bolts A sailing boat which grounds hard is likely to have strained her keel, which is evidenced by leaking around the keel bolts. If water is coming in fast, try to check these, because if this proves to be the source of the water you may have to look no further; there will be little that can be done about it in the short term without hauling out or beaching the boat.

Propellers This is the nightmare scenario for the power boat. Propellers that stand proud, unprotected by skegs, are very vulnerable. If they touch the bottom it's highly possible that the screw itself or its shaft and bearings may be injured. This can result in leaking, or an inability to power away once the boat has been re-floated. Be prepared.

Getting off under power

Come off as you went on If you can contrive to reverse out on a reciprocal course to the one that put you aground, you know for sure that sooner or later you will float. Unless a different route seems viable or you have no choice, going out as you went in is the preferred option.

Ahead or astern? Having made the point that 'back is often better', bear in mind that many propellers and gearboxes deliver more grunt going ahead than in astern. If yours is known to be like this and you can't get off astern, try applying full helm and trying to spin the boat off ahead. The extra power may just do the trick.

Sound around When circumstances militate against 'Option 1', either eyeball a better route if the water is clear enough, or use the backup leadline to sound around for deeper water.

Haul off It's not uncommon for a boat's engines to lack the power needed to pull her off a shoal. In the absence of outside assistance, so long as a line can be secured somewhere off the boat in the direction you wish to go, it can be led to your most powerful winch and hove in as you gun the engine. The extra pull often makes the difference. Attach the line to a shore object or even a well-anchored mooring. If nothing is available, lay out your own anchor or kedge (secondary anchor) from the dinghy and use this. In the days of sail, the choice was often 'kedge or nothing'.

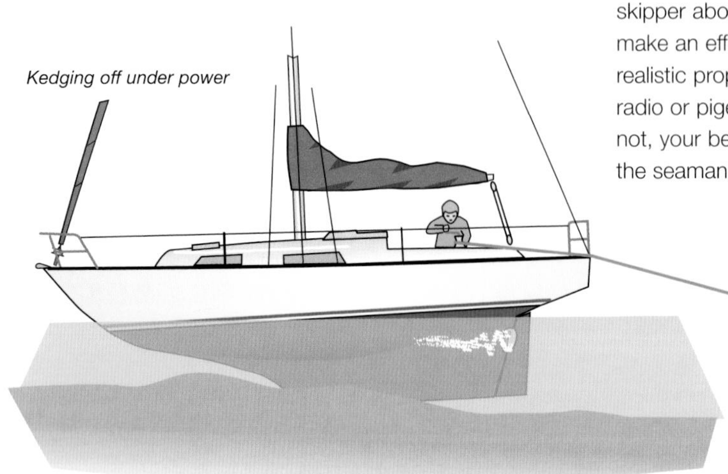

Kedging off under power

Shift weight

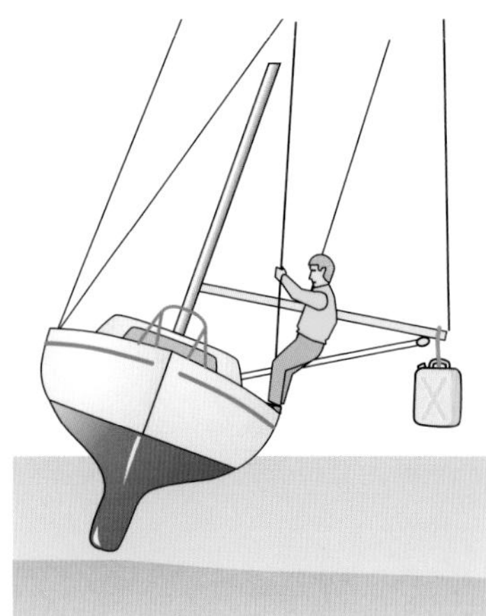

When a boat has her maximum draught on her fore-and-aft midline, it's sometimes possible to reduce this a little by shifting weight. This is comparatively easy for sailing boats to achieve. As well as having all hands hang over the 'low' side, weights such as a full water can or an anchor can be attached to the end of the main boom then swung outboard. Adjusting fore-and-aft trim may also help. Gathering the crew right forward occasionally raises a power boat's propellers clear of the bottom. On a sailing vessel this can lift the heel of the keel off. The difference may not be much, but a lot may not be required.

Dump weight If you're well and truly stuck, draught can be reduced by pumping the water tanks over the side, humping inside ballast ashore (traditional craft often have moveable ballast), and generally lightening ship.

The 'pluck off' By all means accept an offer of a pull off from another boat, but be ready for heavy loadings and make sure you secure the towline to a very strong point, especially if the other boat has power to spare. Try to remain in control, because you don't know how well your rescuer understands the task. Speak with the other skipper about any salvage claims he may have in mind and make an effort to contact your insurer. This is a more realistic proposition by mobile phone than ever it was by radio or pigeon. If in doubt, strike a deal. More often than not, your benefactor will be helping out in a friendly way on the seamanlike basis that it might be him next time.

Getting off under sail

Grounding when heeled well over

Conventional fin keels When beating up a narrow channel that shoals near its edges it's important to remember that a yacht with a conventional fin keel draws less water when heeled over. If she grounds near the end of a tack, her plight is exacerbated as she comes upright.

Other keel configurations Rather than decreasing their draught, some keel configurations actually draw more water in the heeled condition than they do upright. These, notably, are wing keels and bilge keels, both of which are used in significant numbers of yachts. If one of these grounds in the heeled condition, she has every chance of floating off again if she spills wind or drops her sails.

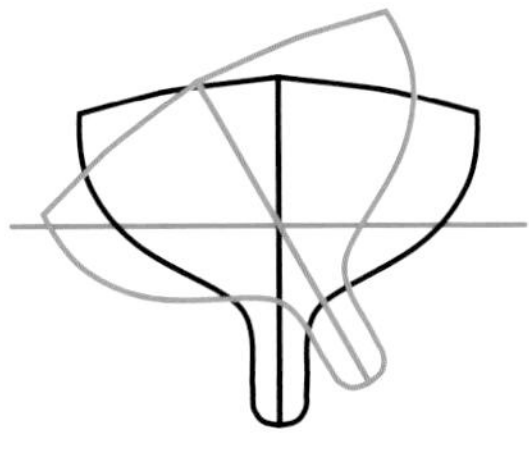

Extreme measures to reduce draught

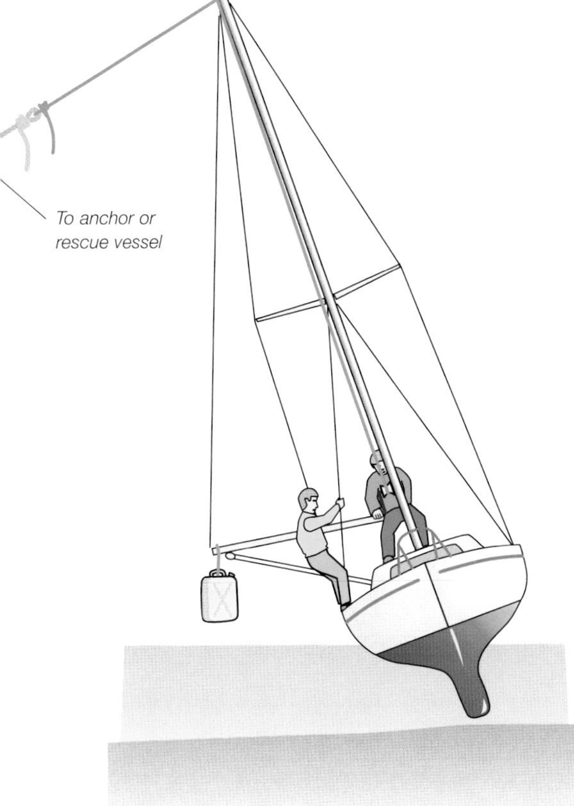

Lee and weather shores

Lee shore To ground on a lee shore is among the worst-case scenarios for any sailing vessel. It was the biggest cause of total loss in the days of commercial sail. Unless the wind is well abaft the beam, any boat propelled by canvas slides to leeward as she gathers enough way to steer from a standstill. For a boat on a lee shore, any attempt to sail off is therefore doomed to failure. It may be possible to shove a very light craft far enough off to surmount this rule, but once the grip of the mud on the keel is added to the equation, sailing out of the dilemma becomes a non-starter. Aground on a lee shore, the first action is to drop the sails and start the engine if one is fitted. If not, the only answer is to haul off, either by laying out a kedge or by some alternative ruse for pulling the boat into deep water.

Weather shore Because the wind is blowing off the weather shore, a grounded sailing yacht sliding to leeward as she tries to gather way is doing herself nothing but good. Any leeway will take her into deeper water, which opens up various courses of action:

Increasing heel Dropping sail should not be the first reaction to grounding on a weather shore. Sometimes a conventional monohull can literally be 'heeled off' by pulling the sheets in hard to increase the effect of the wind. Adding the movement of body weight, etc, may just give a vital final inch or two of reduced draught.

Extreme heel In severe cases, a boat can be made to heel to a dramatic degree by laying out a kedge (or securing to a fixed object well away from the boat), then leading the warp to a spare halyard. A spinnaker halyard is favoured because it is rigged from a swivel and can accept pull from any direction, but if all you have is an extra jib halyard, use this. Lay the kedge as far to seaward as you are able, set the anchor with a good heave from deck level, then attach the halyard and start winching the boat down. Not only does this substantially reduce the draught of a simple deep-keeled yacht, it also encourages the keel to 'skip' along the bottom rather than drudge through the seabed as it does when the pull is from nearer deck level. It's not pretty and it can be downright alarming, but it's as near to being a sure-fire winner as you'll get. The technique can be equally useful on a lee shore, but it's unlikely to work with a bilge keeler or a yacht with any sort of 'plate' at the bottom of the keel.

Wind and wave

It could be argued that the material in this chapter does not fall within the brief of a manual of seamanship. The seaman's art, however, is all about helping the ship to live with the conditions she finds, so it sits comfortably as a final section. Assessing the likely effect of waves is a vital part of every skipper's portfolio of skills, and they are better placed to make judgments if in possession of the facts about what the waves are likely to do. Although a full exposition of weather at sea rightly belongs in a volume of its own, certain areas of practical interest to the seaman on passage or in harbour are sometimes not covered in general texts. Such questions as how quickly the sea may build in rising winds, what sort of fetch will produce seas big enough to trouble the boat, and whether an approaching squall cloud is likely to generate crushing wind forces are important ones. They and certain others are therefore dealt with below.

For strong winds, a surprisingly large fetch is required before full wave height is achieved. A 20-knot wind, for example, requires 150 miles of fetch before the last of the 'lee' offered by land finally disappears. The waves created by a force 8 gale are to some extent impeded as far to seaward as 450 miles, but in such winds, or stronger, it takes a good deal less fetch than this to render the seas dangerous to small craft, especially when affected by currents or shoaling water.

Time factor Waves do not appear by magic as soon as the wind kicks up. They develop with time. Quantifying this is not easy because of numerous extraneous factors, but it can vary significantly. In the storm which wrought havoc on the Fastnet Race in 1979, the waves rose from 2m to 8m in 9 hours. In a more typical late Autumn storm in the Western Approaches to the English Channel, heights might take a day to grow from 3m to 11m.

Waves

Anatomy of a wave

Length and height Waves are defined in terms of height and length. The length is measured from crest to crest, while the height is noted from the bottom of the trough to the top of the crest – not from some mean sea level.

Fetch Waves that are of interest to seamen are largely generated by wind. If this is blowing off a weather shore, the water immediately under the land will have no significant waves. As the distance to leeward increases, wave height grows until it reaches the maximum that can be generated by that wind speed. The distance the wind is blowing uninterrupted across water is called the 'fetch'.

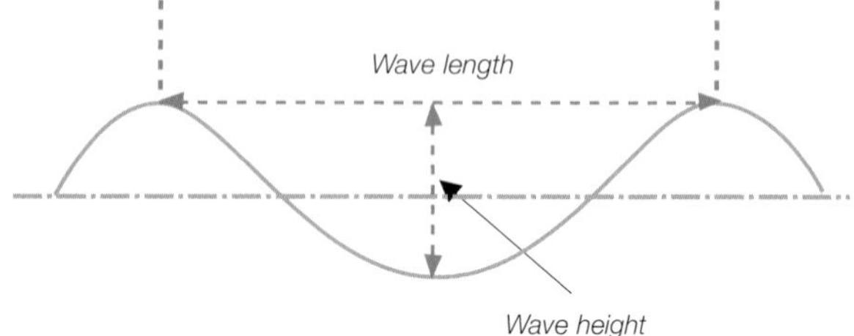

Wave height increases with fetch

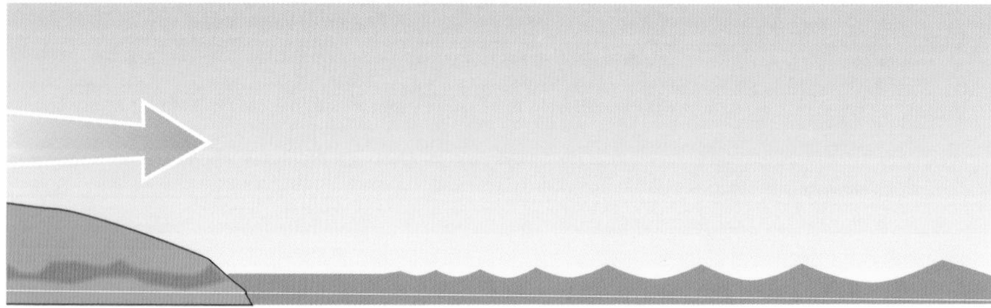

Composite waves At sea, waves do not conform accurately to theoretical models. For all sorts of reasons, a particular wave may catch up the one in front of it. When it does, the two form a single heap of water that may be half as big again as the mean wave height. This is predictable and is tabulated in Beaufort scales as the 'probable maximum wave height' for a given wind speed. Other disturbances usually affect the wave pattern produced by the wind. Cross-seas left over from a previous wind, or swells running in from far away, can combine with the main wave pattern to kick up much larger seas from time to time. Such seas may be unusually steep and more likely to break dangerously than the undisturbed deep-water wave.

Tides and races A tidal stream or any other current running hard to windward heaps the waves up, causing them to break more readily. This is exaggerated in charted tide rips off certain headlands and over shoals in otherwise open water. Such places are to be avoided assiduously in heavy weather, especially on a weather-going stream. Certain ocean currents are equally notorious, notably the Gulf Stream as it runs up the Eastern Seaboard of the United States.

Shoaling water In anything other than extreme conditions, wave height and length in water over 40m deep is unlikely to be affected by the bottom. As the water shoals, waves become less high as the length diminishes. Further shoaling makes the waves shorter and steeper until, at a depth of between one-and-a-half and twice their height, they break. Navigation is now impossible, and no boat should be anywhere near water so shallow with a heavy sea running. Note that offshore shoals have an identical effect to coastlines, making areas far from the nearest land like parts of the North Sea and the Coral Sea dangerous, where the chart indicates depths that would otherwise be safe for navigation.

Waves breaking on a bar or shoal

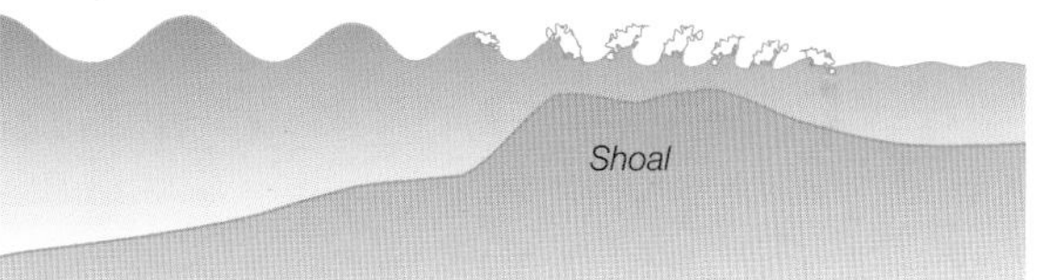

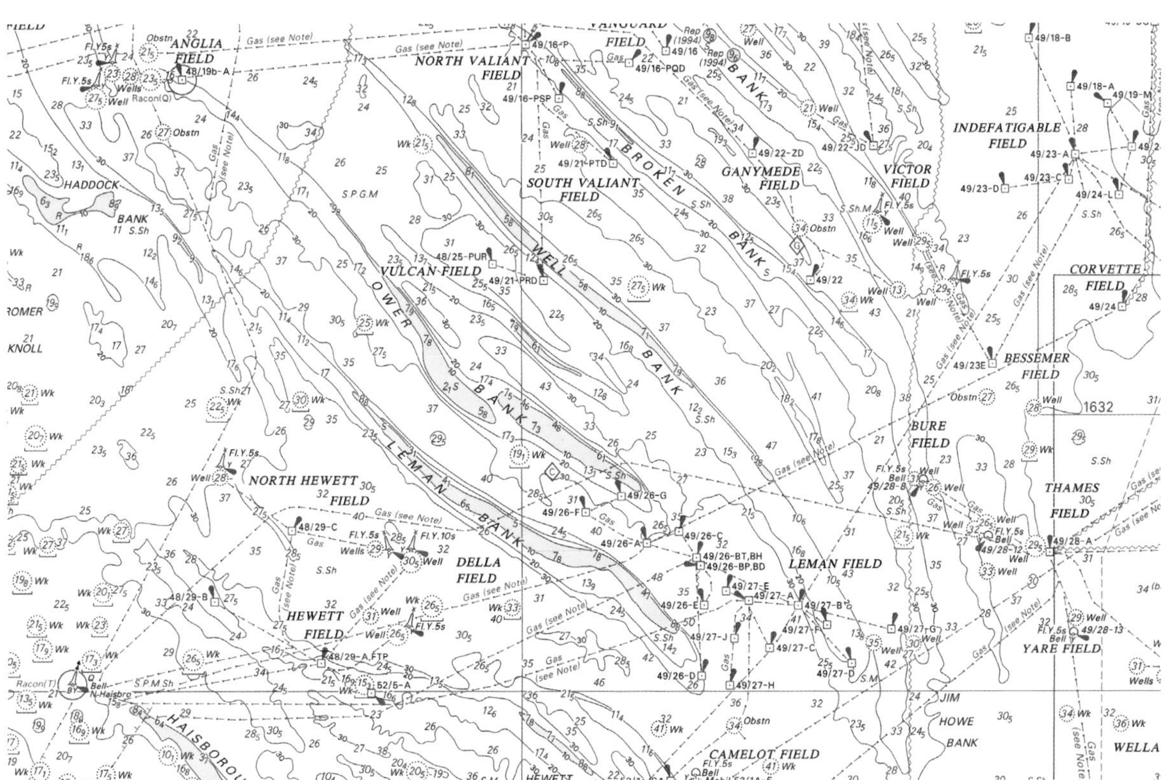

Shoaling areas are extremely dangerous in heavy weather. This area off England's East Coast has been a graveyard for vessels for centuries.
© Crown Copyright. Not to be used for navigation. Courtesy of UK Hydrographic Office.

Land-based obstructions Waves running in onto a lee shore may be perfectly harmless until they run into a cliff face or perhaps a breakwater or sea wall. They then bounce back out to sea, meeting those following them in a diametrically opposed wave train. The results can be perilously akin to the inside of a washing machine.

Inside the wave

Anyone who has helmed a boat – sail or power – in a following sea has experienced the feeling that she is carried forward as a wave comes up astern and held back in the trough. It is a subliminal attention to these unseen forces which enables a good helmsman to 'catch the wave' and surf with the upper part of its leading face. The reason is the motion of the water particles within the wave. As the wave travels, the water circulates as shown in the diagram, giving rise to higher speeds at the crest than in the trough.

Breaking in open water

We have seen above how a wave has no choice but to break as it approaches water too shallow to support it. This 'plunging break' is somewhat different from the 'spilling break' that occurs when a wave in deep water is piled up too steeply by the action of other waves, current, or extreme wind to support itself. Any wave that becomes steeper than around 1 in 7 is at risk from breaking. It is the breaking wave that represents the greatest threat to craft caught out in extreme weather.

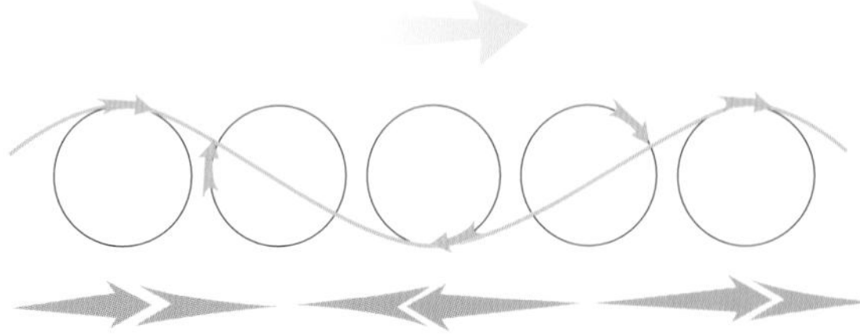

Waves have a rotational action within them which means that the surface water moves in different directions depending upon its position on the wave. Note how, if travelling downwind, the surface flow will propel you over the crest then rush up to meet you in the trough – a powerful rolling action if you are caught beam-on.

Wind phenomena

The barometer

The barometer is the bedrock of single-station forecasting. At sea its readings should be logged every hour, even in the tropics where its movements may be small. At best, a forecast comes from someone who is not where you are, predicting what is expected to happen, but you can tell better than they can what's happening now by poking your head out of the hatch. You can also see with your own eyes what the barometric pressure is doing. Interpreting this is not necessarily high science. Even if you don't understand the full implications of the saturated adiabatic lapse rate, you can reckon that a rapidly falling 'glass' in mid-latitudes foretells strong winds. These may well back (shift anti-clockwise) in the northern hemisphere or veer clockwise in the southern before the barometer levels out with the approaching weather front. Similarly, if you have been suffering a spell of heavy westerly wind with persistent rain, a sharp rise in the barometer accompanied by a breaking of the cloud is a likely sign that a cold front is arriving, bringing relief, although perhaps not before the breeze has piped up even more for a short time.

Diurnal variation A sailor crossing the ocean in tropical latitudes can expect an essentially steady glass which will probably shift up and down a little in a predictable manner as the day progresses. This 'diurnal variation' is tabulated in pilot books and should be watched carefully. 'Highs' are generally around 1000 and 2200 local time, with 'lows' at 0600 and 1800. Any deviation from its regular progress, even by as little as 2mb, can foretell a disturbance which may develop into a full-blown tropical revolving storm.

Predictable gale-force winds In higher latitudes where the temperate depression rules, certain rates of barometric movement are virtual guarantees of wind strength. If the breeze starts out fairly light, a fall of 8mb in 3 hours is a promise that winds of force 8 will arrive within the next 3 hours or so. A 5mb fall in the same period indicates that force 6 is likely to be your lot. Similar predictions can confidently be made with a rapidly rising barometer.

Single-station predictions based on barometric movement are usually associated with moving weather systems. However, strong winds are possible in stable conditions where the isobars are squeezed between two systems. In such cases, the wind may blow a whole gale for days with the glass not moving at all. A classic example occurs regularly off Cape Finisterre in Northwest Spain where low pressure over the Iberian Peninsula in opposition to the North Atlantic High results in strong to gale-force northeasterlies. In such places, a sailor would actually look for a steady change in pressure for relief.

The sea breeze

Sea and land breezes are local winds driven by temperature differences. They are noticeable around shorelines worldwide and have an important effect on coastal sailing. Once familiarity with a given area is established, they are to a large extent predictable.

The mechanism of a sea breeze The process starts slowly, building steadily according to conditions. Land takes on heat from the sun more readily than water. Warm air is less dense than colder air, so on a hot day the heated air floats upwards. The lower pressure left at ground level is in effect a partial vacuum promptly filled by cooler, denser air from over the sea. As the wind blows in off the water, its place to seaward must be taken by air that has drifted offshore after rising from the surface. This subsides into the area left behind by the breeze blowing towards the shore. The sea-breeze engine is thus a circulation of air rising over the land, drifting out over the water, sinking down and blowing back onshore again.

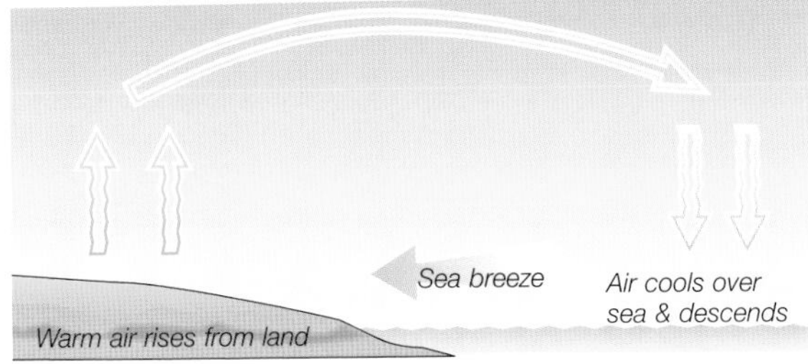

Facts about sea breezes -

- The temperature difference required to work the sea-breeze mechanism can be as little as 2°C. In Britain, the right conditions are often found in late spring when the sea is still cool after winter, although sea breezes can occur all summer long.
- It's unusual for a sea breeze to start up much before noon, but thereafter it may blow until a short while after sunset. Large flat land masses are ideal, but rising ground can do the trick as well, so that even such coasts as West Norway enjoy a strong 'sun wind' in season.
- An undisturbed sea breeze begins by blowing directly onshore, but as the afternoon wears on it may well be veered (backed in the Southern Hemisphere) by Coriolis forces.
- Left to itself in still air, it can blow at force 4, or even 5 close in where it is usually at its strongest.
- The strength of a sea breeze is profoundly affected by any underlying wind due to larger pressure systems. Most winds are created by global air movements resulting from differences in pressure. A moderate overall wind drifting offshore does not, as you might expect, knock out the sea breeze. Instead, it picks up the air at medium altitude and accelerates its progress seawards. This makes room for more air rising off the land which in turn pipes up the sea breeze blowing in to fill the gap. Any sea-level offshore wind can soon be overcome by this effect, and the resulting sea breeze can blow as strongly as force 6. Perhaps surprisingly, by the same mechanism working in reverse, a moderate onshore wind can play down the tendency for sea breezes to develop.
- The sea breeze effect can be felt as much as 20 miles offshore in ideal conditions with essentially offshore airflow. In the evening, it fails first along the beach and cliff tops, being last felt offshore as its decaying remnants are carried out on the re-establishing general wind.

Land breezes

Just as land absorbs heat more rapidly than the sea, it also sheds warmth quicker when the sun goes down. At night, this leaves a low-pressure area over the water that is filled by colder, heavier air draining down from higher land inshore. No mini-system like the sea-breeze engine is established, so the resulting air movements are often less dramatic than their sun-whipped opposite numbers, but in specific areas they are reliable and can make a useful contribution to a coastal passage.

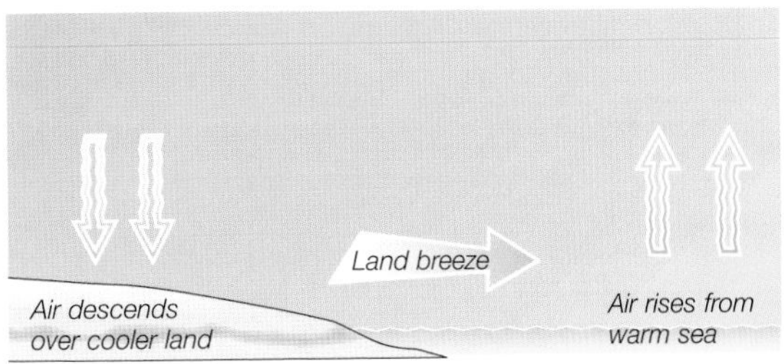

Katabatic winds

These can best be thought of as supercharged land breezes. The same mechanism occurs, but much more powerfully as a parcel of cool, heavy air comes tumbling off a high mountain or down a steep valley, often into a harbour or sound below. Such winds are regularly experienced in areas where conditions suit their formation. Look to the study of a good pilot book to keep you informed.

Disturbance to leeward of an obstruction

A vessel passing through the lee of a vertical obstruction such as a large vessel or a cliff is likely to suffer major disturbance in the wind for up to 7 times the height of the object. Close in, a 100% reversal of the wind direction may be experienced. Interference will also be felt to windward of the barrier as the air stream rises to pass over it, but only out as far as two or three times its height. A high cliff or mountainous island can produce a 'falling wind' in its lee that blows vertically downwards. These are notoriously dangerous because a sailing boat cannot ease her stress by spilling wind. Normally, the further a yacht heels over, the more she spills air naturally from the top of her sails, especially if they are over-sheeted. In a falling wind, her crew's only redress is literally to drag the canvas down before it lays the yacht flat. Watch the foot of any high cliff with the wind blowing over it for disturbed water. It may be your only indication of impending mayhem.

Gusts in the lee of high ground

Less dramatic but still very noticeable effects occur much further to leeward of certain obstructions, particularly where the interference takes the form of an extended cliff or a flank of high ground. Here, an offshore wind can establish a series of waves not unlike the standing waves or the 'stoppers' used by canoeists down-stream of rocks in a rapidly flowing river. As the lower extremities of these waves approach the sea surface, the breeze gusts up, only to drop again further out as the wave swirls upwards, and so on. The outer limits of this type of unrest in the weather can be as much as four miles offshore. Inshore, they can be felt in certain expansive anchorages.

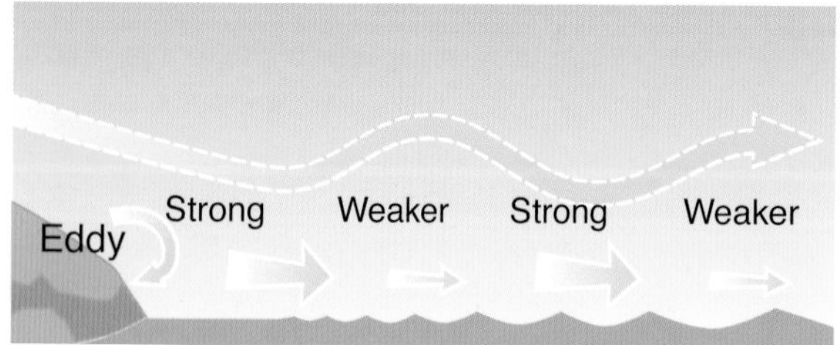

An open-sea squall

Squalls

Squalls are isolated disturbances recognisable by a significant cloud. They produce rain, wind or both, and may affect the wind direction as well. They are, however, comparatively short-lived, with half an hour as a useful reckoning for the likely duration.

In different latitudes and zones squalls behave in various ways. Some areas have local specialities. The white squalls of the Caribbean and the Great Lakes can generate very high winds indeed for brief periods, while some of the villainous-looking black clouds that prowl the Inter-tropical Convergence Zone produce nothing more dangerous than heavy rain. Anyone who has made a trade-wind ocean crossing knows that otherwise pleasant weather can be interrupted regularly by squalls which raise the wind speed by up to 100%. These are a serious nuisance, but fortunately they can be seen clearly as they approach from windward. By day, the cloud simply cannot be missed. Even on a moonless night, the general aura of looming darkness is enough to advise the watch on deck to shorten sail.

Types of squall and action to take

- ***The line squall*** - This is usually associated with a cold front or the passing of a trough. A line of cloud spreads across the sky to windward, sometimes in the form of a shallow arch. Cumulonimbus clouds may tower above it. These squalls can prove violent, with lashing rain or hail and a strong, gusty, veering wind (backing in southern hemisphere). Be prepared for this in terms of sail combination. If caught 'napping' by a squall from forward of the beam, heave to until the squall passes if your boat can do this properly; otherwise, run off in order to lessen the apparent wind. This tactic might increase the time you are under the squall's influence, but unless you are in a super-fast craft the loss will be more than offset by the reduction in general unpleasantness. In certain specific areas, line squalls can be lethally powerful, such as the isolated cold front that can run up the Eastern Seaboard of the US generating 60-knot winds out of a calm afternoon. It therefore behoves all skippers to make enquiries when cruising strange waters, either by consulting sailing directions or local knowledge.

- ***The thunderstorm*** - A thunderstorm not directly associated with a travelling front behaves much like a squall, although it may last somewhat longer. Along the coast, these are commonest late in the afternoon when the land has heated up. Offshore, they are more prevalent at night. Try to avoid them if convenient by steering so that the bearing of the closest edge alters. If you're caught, thunder and lightning are alarming at sea, especially as the mast of a sailing yacht (particularly a metal one) is likely to be a focal point for a lightning strike. Disconnect antennae and other masthead equipment to protect your electrics, and keep your crew well away from the mast and shrouds. Strikes are mercifully rare, but if you are unlucky enough to take one, this offers your best chance of keeping them from harm. The worst winds under thunderstorms are best avoided by steering to leave the big cloud to port (starboard in the southern hemisphere).
- ***Isolated squalls*** - These can occur anywhere in generally windy weather with a comparatively clear sky. Assess an approaching squall by noting whether or not you can see the horizon underneath it. If the cloud has a complete 'skirt' of rain, it is more likely to produce wind than not. If you can see rain underneath the cloud but the horizon remains visible, you may be fortunate. In any case, prepare for the worst and steer to avoid passing under it if you can.
- ***Waterspouts*** - A waterspout is the aquatic equivalent of a tornado, or 'twister' seen mostly in the tropics, but it can also venture into higher latitudes. In the right conditions it will appear at first as a funnel descending from a heavy squall cloud. The water beneath the finger becomes disturbed and finally the whole column joins with the sea. Assess the direction of its motion and steam as hard as you can at right-angles to this. Except over open ocean, the greatest danger appears to come from flying debris, so if a hit seems unavoidable, either go below and hold on or, if things look really desperate, attach yourself to the boat with a long line and jump overboard until the danger is past. Although one US authority suggests swimming underwater for as long as you are able, this manual is more inclined to recommend wearing a good-quality lifejacket.

D.662

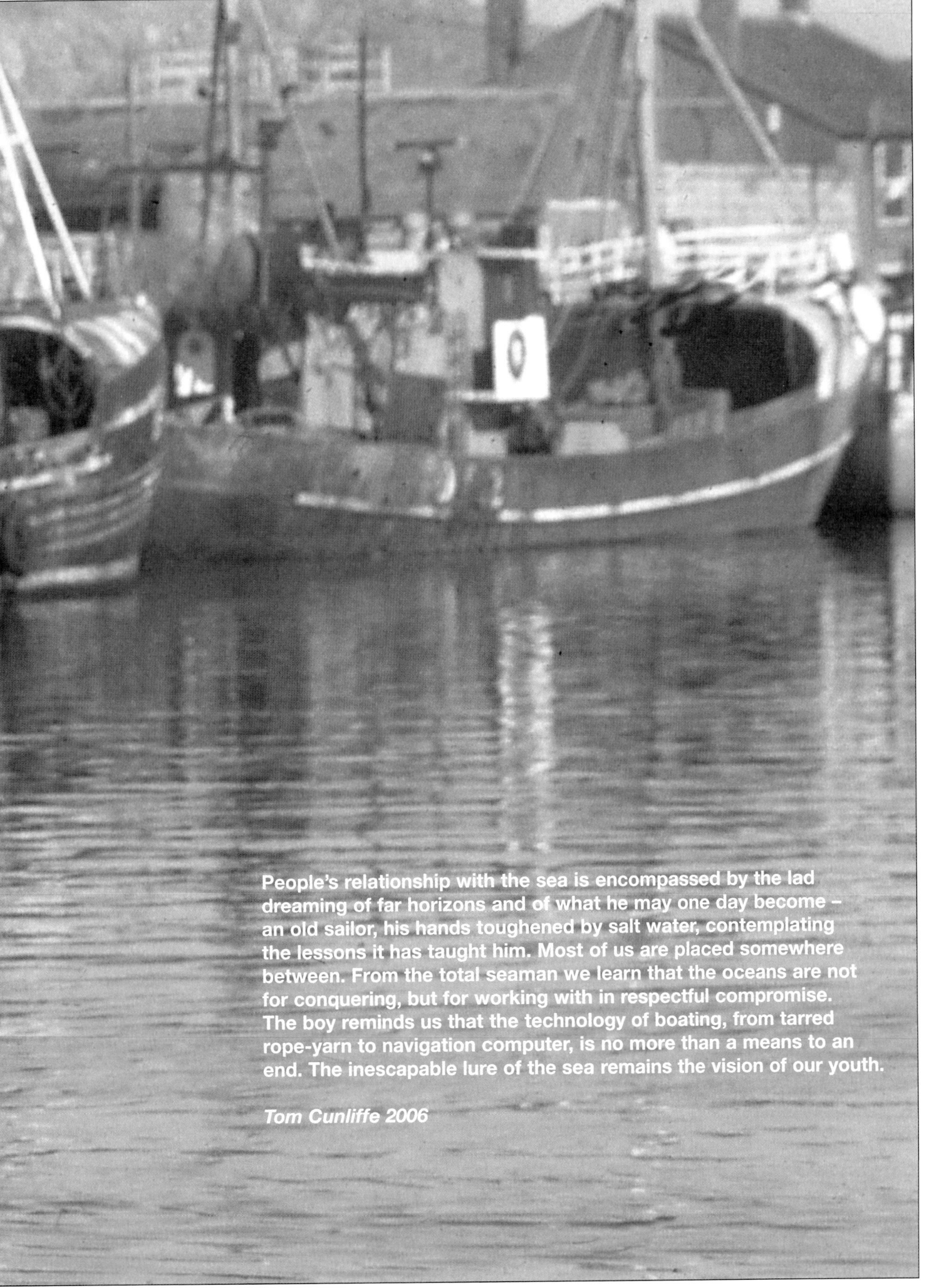

People's relationship with the sea is encompassed by the lad dreaming of far horizons and of what he may one day become – an old sailor, his hands toughened by salt water, contemplating the lessons it has taught him. Most of us are placed somewhere between. From the total seaman we learn that the oceans are not for conquering, but for working with in respectful compromise. The boy reminds us that the technology of boating, from tarred rope-yarn to navigation computer, is no more than a means to an end. The inescapable lure of the sea remains the vision of our youth.

Tom Cunliffe 2006

Glossary

Aback A sail sheeted 'aback' is hauled to windward so that it looks to be inside out. The effect is a powerful manoeuvring tool to shove the bow to leeward.

Aft Toward the stern.

Astern Behind the boat.

Athwartships Sideways.

Baby stay A small forestay running between the hounds and the centre of the foredeck. It has some function in general mast support but is also useful in generating pre-bend.

Backed headsail To back a headsail is to pull its clew to weather – see 'aback'.

Backstay The wire which supports the mast against falling forward. May be set up permanently, or may be 'running' and set up with tackles or winches, depending on whether it is fixed or adjustable.

Balloon spinnaker A downwind sail whose luff and leech are of equal lengths. The sail is set flying and boomed out with a removable pole.

Bare poles To sail 'under bare poles' is to sail downwind with no canvas set and the engine off. The number of masts is irrelevant, so sloops do not sail 'under bare pole'. The technique is used in heavy weather sailing.

Battens Light wood or composite strips slotted into batten pockets in the leech of a sail to support the roach. The battens of a 'fully-battened sail' run from luff to leech and are carried by cars (see below) in the mast track.

Beam Literally the width of the boat. The term originates from the deck beams which run across any vessel of wooden or metal construction.

Bear away Turn away from the wind.

Belay Make fast. Usually used for sheets and halyards.

Belaying pin Vertical pin to which halyards and other parts of the running rigging are belayed.

Bend (n) A knot for tying two ropes together or for attaching a rope to an object semi-permanently. (v) To tie to something ('Bend on the sheets') or to attach a sail to a stay or boom for hoisting.

Bight The section of a rope between the load and the point at which it is made fast. An unloaded bight often takes up a curving form reminiscent of a wide bay, so the term is also used in coastal topography to describe such places.

Bilge keel A keel bolted to the 'turn of the bilge' – the place where the bottom of the boat curves round from its undersection to approach the vertical topsides. A bilge-keeled yacht has two such keels of substantial proportions instead of a single central keel.

Bitt A heavy post on the foredeck used for securing anything, including shorelines. Traditionally of timber and in pairs, these are sometimes seen singly and made of metal (see below – 'Samson post').

Bitter end The very end of a rope. On a traditional boat, it might have been secured to the bitts.

Block A pulley.

Bobstay Chain or wire rigging running from the forward end of a bowsprit to the hull just above the waterline. The bobstay supports the bowsprit against the all-important upward pull.

Bollard A strong securing point, sometimes in the form of a squat, waisted cylinder, sometimes single, often double. Bollards may be found on deck or at the dockside.

Boom The spar attached to the foot of a fore-and-aft sail to hold its clew aft.

Booming-out pole A fully rigged spar used to hold the genoa or spinnaker out to windward on a run to keep it from being blanketed by the mainsail.

Bottle screws Also called 'rigging screws' or 'turnbuckles' (USA), these are permanently fitted double-ended screws that tension standing rigging, usually at the lower end.

Bow The forward part of the vessel. The starboard or port bows are the area on that side abaft the stem.

Bower anchor Main anchor.

Bowsprit A spar extending forward from the bow from which a jib is set.

Broaching Swinging sideways out of control in a strong following wind or sea.

Bulldog grip A specialised U-bolt used for making a temporary eye in wire rope.

Bunting Flags, or the light, traditional cloth used to make them.

Burgee Small, triangular flag flown from a stick at the masthead. It can swivel with the wind and is a useful indicator of wind direction. Usually, but not always, signifies membership of a specific yacht club.

Cable The rope or chain on the anchor.

Cap Shrouds Shrouds supporting the top of the mast athwartships. They often lead to the deck or chain plates via spreaders at the hounds.

Car A movable fairlead for a sheet. Typically found on a metal track on the side deck for the genoa sheets, or athwart the cockpit for the mainsheet.

Catenary The curve made by chain cable between the stem and the anchor.

Caulking The compound or other material forced between wooden planks to make them watertight.

Centre of effort The centre of an area of sail, from which its power can be thought to originate when considering its effect on manoeuvring.

Centreboard A board or metal plate lowered through the bottom of the hull to control leeway in a boat with no keel.

CEVNI An endorsement to the ICC (see below) permitting the holder to operate on European inland waterways. It is an acronym for Code European de Voies de la Navigation.

Chain Plate A metal plate set strongly into the deck or topsides to attach shrouds or stays.

Cheek block A block with one side flattened so it can be fitted permanently to a spar or to the deck.

Chine The angular joint where the topsides meet the bilge in a flat or v-bottomed boat.

Cleat A strong, universal fitting shaped like a truncated 'T' with long arms for securing ropes.

Clevis pin The removable strong steel pin (usually stainless) which carries the weight of a rigging terminal. Not to be confused with the split pin which secures it in place.

Clew The aft lower corner of a sail. The sheet is bent on here if the sail is not set on a boom.

Closehauled Sailing to windward steering to the sails rather than on a free course.

Coachroof The cabin top above the deck.

Coaming Permanent vertical protection around a hatch or cockpit.

Cockpit The area below deck level but open to the weather from which a small vessel – power or sail – is controlled.

Colours The national ensign.

COLREGS The International Regulations for Prevention of Collision at Sea.

Companionway An entry point to the accommodation which can be accessed without undue clambering, usually at the forward end of the cockpit.

Coriolis Force The force generated by the Earth's rotation which accelerates moving objects to one side or other of a north-south trajectory. The effect is least near the equator and greatest at the poles. The Coriolis Force was named after a French physicist and is used mostly in understanding weather systems.

Counter A form of stern which extends above the waterline beyond the rudder. A 'reverse counter' extends the boat's natural lines above the waterline, but instead of continuing these to a logical conclusion with a long overhang it turns back sharply on itself to mirror the bow profile.

Cracking off A colloquial term for 'bearing away'.

Cross-trees Secondary spars attached well up the mast running athwartships which serve to 'spread' the upper shrouds and give them a better angle of pull.

Cutter A single-masted boat with more than one headsail. Traditionally the outer sail, or jib, was carried on a bowsprit. Many modern cutters set both headsails inboard.

Dead reckoning Literally a position worked up from course steered and distance run through the water. 'Dead Reckoning Navigation' has come to mean all navigation done by traditional means in the absence of electronics or a visual fix.

Dinghy An open boat of diminutive proportions, often a yacht's tender.

Displacement The weight of water that would be displaced by a vessel were she to be lowered into a full open tank. It is the equivalent of her actual weight.

Downhaul A line which pulls down the tack of a sail or the forward part of a spar.

Draught The measurement between the waterline and the lowest outer skin of the keel.

Drogue A device to create drag streamed from a long rope in heavy weather. Streamed astern, it can slow a boat down and keep her stern to the weather. From ahead, it works as a sea anchor, in theory holding the boat's head up to the wind.

Eye splice A loop worked into the end of a rope by passing the strands through one another.

Fairlead A fitting which leads a rope 'fair'. Among other places, it may be found on the rail for mooring lines, or on deck to lead sheets onto a winch where it may take the form of a cheek block.

Fall The hauling end of a rope rove through a tackle.

Fender Board A plank used to augment fenders when lying against pilings.

Fluke The part of the anchor which ploughs into the bottom.

Fore-and-aft Running between bow and stern rather than athwartships. Fore-and-aft rig is the yacht or small-craft rig as opposed to the square rig used on ships, with yards running athwartships.

Forefoot Where the keel meets the stem.

Forestay The stay supporting the mast from forward, to which the jib, genoa or (traditionally) the staysail is hanked.

Freeboard The vertical distance between the deck and the waterline.

Gaff The spar which spreads the head of a four-cornered, old-fashioned, fore-and-aft rigged mainsail. Vessels using such sails are 'gaff rigged'.

Genoa A headsail whose leech overlaps the mast and mainsail.

Halyard A rope used for hoisting a sail.

Heads The universal name for a sea toilet, so-called because in sailing ships with no plumbing, all hands went to the bow where a hole was cut in the deck to accommodate the necessary.

Headstay Another name for the forestay.

Heave to Setting the sails to work against one another to take off way and allow a boat to look after herself with no helmsman.

Heel The leaning of a boat when wind blows into her sails.

Helm The tiller or wheel. Also a non-gender-specific person steering.

Hounds The point on the mast where the lower shrouds are attached.

ICC International Certificate of Competence.

Kedge A secondary anchor of no specific type.

Keel-stepped A mast whose heel stands through the deck onto the keel rather than standing on deck, when it is deck-stepped.

Ketch A boat with two masts, the forward one (mainmast) is taller than the after (mizzen). The mizzen is stepped forward of the rudder post.

Kicker See 'kicking strap'.

Kicking strap A tackle between the boom and the mast at deck level, serving to keep the boom down and supply leech tension to the mainsail.

Knot Speed measurement meaning one nautical mile per hour.

Lanyard A short, light line permanently attached to something.

Leadline A line with a lead weight for measuring depth of water – usually as backup for a malfunctioning echo sounder.

Lee berth A berth onto which the wind is blowing.

Lee shore A shore onto which the wind is blowing.

Leech The trailing edge of a sail.

Log An instrument for measuring speed and distance run through the water.

Luff (n) The leading edge of a sail. (v) To alter course closer to, or directly into the wind.

Lying a'hull 'Lying to' with no canvas set. The boat is not steered.

Midships/amidships The central area of the boat.

Mizzen The after mast on any multi-masted vessel, except on a schooner with more than two masts or a square rigger with more than three.

Neap tides The lesser tide experienced bi-monthly when sun and moon are pulling against one another at half-moon.

Painter The line for securing the bow of a small boat such as a dinghy or liferaft.

Peak The aft upper corner of a gaff sail.

Pile A post driven into the seabed, usually either for securing vessels or as a navigation beacon.

Pinch To sail too close to the wind.

Pitch-pole To be tumbled stern over bow by heavy following seas.

Pivot Point The point somewhere around the forward part of the keel around which a boat swivels when she steers.

Plumb stem A vertical stem (see 'stem') found mainly in traditional working craft.

Poop (v) A 'pooping' sea sweeps a vessel from aft forward.

Port The left-hand side of the boat looking forward.

Pounding The slamming as the bow hits the trough of a sea.

Pram A dinghy with a bow transom as well as a transom stern.

Pre-bend A healthy bend in the mast set by tensioning the standing rigging. Pre-bend stiffens the spar and assists mainsail shape.

Preventer A line rigged from the end of the main boom to the bow to steady the spar in light weather and to prevent gybing in heavy going.

Quarter The side of a vessel between amidships and the stern. 'Over the quarter' means around 45° forward from dead aft or 45° abaft the beam.

Reaching Any sailing heading between closehauled and running.

Reefing Shortening sail as wind increases.

Reefing pennants The lines used for hauling and holding down the clew of a boomed sail when reefing.

Roach The area of a fore-and-aft sail which extends beyond the straight line between two corners, most frequently applied to the leech.

Rudder post The rudder shaft.

Running backstay Temporary backstays used to tension the jib or staysail luff on yachts whose rig cannot carry a standing backstay.

Samson post A single bitt.

SAR Search and Rescue.

Schooner A fore-and-aft rigged boat with two or more masts that is neither ketch nor yawl.

Seacock A valve on a through-hull skin fitting which can close off the hole when required.

Sections The athwartships slices through the hull in the body-plan part of a vessel's drawings.

Shackles A horseshoe-shaped metal fitting closed with a screw-thread pin, used for semi-permanently attaching anything on board that will take serious load.

Shaft The steel rod that connects the engine to the propeller.

Sheave Pronounced 'shiv'. The 'wheel' inside a pulley block or set into a spar to lead a rope or turn its direction of pull.

Sheet The rope which controls the set of a sail.

Shroud Wire rigging which supports the mast athwartships.

Skeg A built-up extension of the lower hull either forward of and supporting the rudder, or protecting a salient propeller.

Skin fitting Through-hull fitting.

Sloop A single-masted vessel with one headsail.

SNAME/USYRU The Society of Naval Architects and Marine Engineers/United States Yacht Racing Union, (USYRU is the predecessor to US Sailing).

Snatch block A block that can be opened to admit the bight of a rope, rather than having to feed the end through.

Spade rudder Rudder with no external support save the through-hull bearing.

Spar General term for all the items on board that would traditionally have been wooden poles of various sizes involved with the rig in some way. Eg: the mast, or a booming-out pole. A boat hook is not a spar.

Sponson Platform projecting outboard from the hull.

Spreaders The struts used to spread the shrouds to a wider staying angle.

Spring line A shore line led forward from the stern or aft from the bow either to stop the boat surging fore-and-aft, or to assist in manoeuvring.

Spring tide The larger tides experienced bi-monthly when sun and moon are pulling together at full and new moon.

Square-rigger An early form of rig where the rectangular sails are bent to yards braced athwart the masts.

Stability A vessel's ability to resist capsize.

Stanchion Stainless steel or bronze rods providing support for the guardrails at the deck edge.

Standing rigging The wire rigging which supports the mast.

Starboard The right-hand side of the boat looking forward.

Staysail A sail set on a stay. Used especially in boats with more than one headsail, or more than one mast. In common parlance for modern yachts, the staysail is generally the inner headsail of a cutter.

Steerage way The minimum way required for a vessel to answer her helm.

Stem The actual bow, or cutwater. In a wooden vessel it is the vertical timber to which the planks are attached.

Stern The aft, or back end of a boat.

Stern post The structural member at the aft end of a wooden hull on which the rudder is often hung.

Stern tube The tube in the hull abaft the engine through which the propeller shaft and associated watertight glands are fitted.

Strop A loop of rope forming a sling around a spar or a block – can be permanent or temporary.

Swedish fid A fid with a 'hollow' blade open on one side. Used for splicing modern ropes whose lay tends to disintegrate under the trauma of making the tucks.

Tabernacle An open-topped box-like structure firmly fixed to the deck in which the heel of a deck-stepped mast is secured.

Tack (v) To go about, or change course in such as way as to bring the bows through the wind. (n) The lower corner of a sail's leading edge.

Tackle Pronounced 'taykul', although in the form 'block and tackle' it is 'tackul'. An arrangement of pulley blocks and rope used to gain mechanical advantage. Typical application is a mainsheet. Ground tackle (pronounced 'tackul') is the name given to anchors and their associated cables.

Taffrail The section of toerail or bulwark capping running athwart the stern.

Terminals
Standing rig: A proprietary fitting worked into the end of a wire rope by which a shroud or stay can be attached to the mast or the ship.

Electrical: A fitting crimped or soldered to the end of an electrical wire to make a connection.

Tide-rode A boat moored or anchored in a tidal stream will head up to either the wind or the tide, whichever is stronger. If she opts for the tide, she is tide-rode.

Tiller A wooden or metal bar connected to the rudder to steer a vessel.

Toerail Raised ledge around the outer deck edge. It may be of wood (traditional), aluminium, plastic or some other compound. Some toerails are finished by a wooden capping.

Toggle U-shaped metal link with a clevis pin used to allow universal movement at the end of a wire.

Topping lift A line running from the masthead to the boom to support the spar when the sail is lowered.

Topsides In English as spoken in Britain, this term means the sides of the boat between the waterline and the deck. In American English, used without a definite or indefinite article, it can also mean 'on deck' ('I'm going topsides').

Transducer A through-hull or in-hull sensor for an echo sounder or other instrument.

Transom A form of stern. A transom runs athwartships in a flat section and the rudder is hung outboard of it. In wooden craft it is planked athwartships rather than fore and aft.

Traveller The athwartships track to which a boom is sheeted.

Trice Haul up.

Trip To break out the anchor. A tripping line is a light line dedicated to this purpose.

Trysail A storm sail set boomless abaft the mast when the mainsail is stowed.

Turning block A block which alters the direction of a lead.

Vang In American English, a vang can be a kicking strap (technically known in the US as a 'center boom vang'). In either form of the language it also means a strop controlling a main boom when reaching or running, as well as a line controlling a gaff or sprit.

Wake Disturbed water left astern by a moving boat.

Warp (n) Another word for a heavy rope, often a shoreline. (v) To move a vessel using only ropes.

Waterline The fore-and-aft line at which a vessel floats.

Weather berth A berth with the wind blowing off it.

Weather helm The tendency of a sailing vessel to come head to wind.

Weather shore A coast that lies to windward of a boat.

Weather side The side of the boat facing the wind.

Wetted area The total immersed area of the boat.

Whisker pole A small spar used without rigging to hold a headsail out to windward on a run to keep it from being blanketed by the mainsail (cf 'Booming-out pole').

Windlass A dedicated winch for controlling anchor cable and lifting the anchor. A windlass may be powered manually, electrically or hydraulically.

Wind-rode A boat moored or anchored in a tidal stream will head up to either the wind or the tide whichever is stronger. If it's the wind, she is wind-rode.

Yaw To veer continually from one side of the course to the other.

Yawl A two-masted sailing craft whose mizzen is stepped abaft the sternpost. A yawl's mizzen is generally smaller than a ketch's.

Index

abandoning ship 122-123
anchor, weighing 83
anchor bends 41
anchor 'scope' 76, 78, 80
anchor warps 76, 78, 80
anchor weights 80
anchorage, choosing 79
anchoring 76-83
  'Bahamian Moor' 82
  chain or warp for 78
  fore-and-aft 82
  setting up a sheer when 83
  tidal height 79
  warp or chain for 78
  wind-against-tide 81-82
  wind-rode 81
anchors
  in dinghies 139
  dragging 81
  fouled 83
  how they work 76
  'kedge' 81, 82, 142, 146, 147
  laying 80
  lying to two 81-82
  types of 77
autopilots 97, 99 see also self-steering arrangements

backstays 20, 21, 23
  jury-rigged 118
'Bahamian Moor' anchoring 82
bare poles 104, 109
  performance 63
barometers 150
batteries 36
batteries, flat 37-38
battery charging 39
beaching 'legs' 57
bearings, cutless 34
belaying pins 48
berthing 62-63
berthing under power 64-75
  alongside 64-73
    blowing off 73
    blowing on 73
    dynamics of 68-70
    fendering 65
    helming techniques 72-73
    'midships shortie' 70
    pivot point 72
    propeller torque 72
    rafting up 71
    rope handling 66
    short docks 64-65
    short-handed 69
    tidal walls 67
    tide and current 73
    what can go wrong 70
berths, leaving 74-75
  lee berths 75
bights 41
bilge pumping/pumps 112, 136, 145
boarding other boats in harbour 71, 136
bobstays 85
bollards, securing to 49
booms, stowing and reefing sail in 26
bosun's chairs 55
bottle screws 21, 22
bottoms, clean 17
bow lines (mooring lines) 64, 65, 68
bow springs 64, 74
bowlines (knots) 42, 49, 68, 85, 120
bowsprits and bull ropes 82, 85
breast lines 64, 65, 71
breezes, land and sea 151
broach, gybe 98
broach to windward 98
broaching 89
  anatomy of 98
  prevention against 99
bull ropes 82, 85
bungs 112, 113
buoyancy, centre of 101-102
buoys, anchor 83
buoys, mooring 84
buoys, 'pickup' 84
'burgee sticks' 134, 135
burgees, club 132, 134-135
  setting up 135

cap shrouds 20, 21, 22
Cape Finisterre 150-151
capsize resistance factors 101-102
  angle of vanishing stability 102
  beam 102
  coach roof 102
  displacement 102
  freeboard 102
  long-short keel 102
  roll inertia 102
  static stability 101
car systems 24
Caribbean Sea 152
centre of buoyancy 101-102
centre of gravity 101
chains, anchor 78, 80, 85
charts, anchorages on 79
children in dinghies 135
chines, 'lifting' 15
cleats, securing to 48
closehauled sailing 14
clove hitches 41, 49
collision regulations (COLREGS – International Regulations for Prevention of Collision at Sea)
  in fog 130
  for rivers 140, 141-142
Contessa 32: 102
Coral Sea 149
Coriolis Force 151
cotter pins 23 see also split pins
crew overboard 119-121
  in fog 129
  recovering a casualty from water 120-121
    horizontal lifting 121
    power for the lift 121
    vertical lifting 120
  search patterns 119
crown knots 43
Cruising Club of America, Technical Committee 102
current, spotting 62
customs of the sea 132-137
cutless bearings 34
cutter, pilot 107
cutter rig 18, 92

detergents 137
'dew point' 129
dinghies
  anchor and cable in 139
  boarding 139
  children in 135
  hard 138
  inflatable 122, 138
  rowing 138
  life jackets in 139
  loading 139
  painters 139
  propulsion 138
  types of 138
  used to recover casualty from water 120
displacement speed see speed, displacement
distress as safety issue or genuine emergency 110
diurnal variation 150
drogues 89, 104, 105
  offset 116
  series 105
drying out 56-57
drying out, selecting a berth 56
drying out alongside 57
Dyneema ropes 40

echo sounders 141, 144-145
electrical tool kits and spares 39
emergency equipment 111, 112 see also bungs; EPIRBs; fire extinguishers; flares; liferafts
Emergency Position Indicating Radio Beacons (EPIRBs) 114, 123
engines see power units
English Channel 129, 148
ensign warrants 132
ensigns
  courtesy 134
  defaced 132, 134
  illegal 133
  national 132-133
  position to wear 133
  when not to fly 134
environment, care for 136-137
Environment Agency 136
EPIRBs (Emergency Position Indicating Radio Beacons) 114, 123
eye splices 44

Fastnet Race (1979) 106, 112, 148
fender boards 65
fender lanyards 65
fendering/fenders 65
'fetch' 148
figure of eight knots 42
filters, seawater 31, 32
fire 113-114
fire extinguishers 113, 114
fisherman's bends 41
Flag, Union 133
flag signals 134
flares 122

types 123
flooding 112-113, 145
fog 128-131
being seen and heard in 129
collision regulations (Colregs) 130
conduct on deck 129-130
forecasts, interpreting 128-129
interpreting sound signals in 130
land 128
lookouts in 129-130, 131
radar in 130, 131
safe speed in 130
sea 129
signs of impending 129
strategies for 130-131
forestays 20, 21, 23, 94, 118
fuel
economy 16, 17
factors in planing craft 17
filters 29, 30, 33, 117
lift pumps 30
problems 33
running out of 117
system 29-30
tanks 29, 100
fuelling up 137

gaff cutters 19, 106
Norwegian pilot-boat type 109
gaff rig 19
gaffer's quickie 46
gasket coil hitches 52, 70
gearboxes and couplings 30
generators, running, in harbour 136
'gennakers' 26
GMDSS (Global Maritime Distress and Safety System) 110
GPS (Global Positioning System) 81, 107, 119, 123, 128, 131
Great Lakes 152
ground speed 13
grounding 144-147
damage, checking for 145
dangerous 145
deep-keeled monohulls 147
echo sounder use 141, 144-145
getting off under power 146
getting off under sail 147
on lee shore 147
in rivers 142
'safe' 145
towing off 146
on weather shore 147
weight, shifting or dumping 146
what to do 145-147
Guernsey 129
Gulf Stream 87, 149

harbour speed limits 135
harbours of refuge, assessing 87
harnesses 120
headstays see forestays
heaving to 95, 106-107
heaving to, theory 107
heaving to in practice 107
heel bolts 145
holding tanks 137
'hounds' 20
'huffling' 143
hull failure 113
hull forms 8-11
power boats 11
displacement 11
planing 11, 15, 17
semi-displacement 11, 15, 17
sailing craft 8-10
keel length 8
long-keeled variants 9
short-keeled variants 10
hull speed 12
modifying factors in sailing boats 13
net effect of factors on sailing boats 14
hypothermic aftershock 120

impellers, seawater pump 32
injector pumps and injectors 30, 33
Inter-tropical Convergence Zone 152

jammers 49
Jersey 129
'Joshua' 104

keel, types of see hull forms
keels and grounding 145, 147
ketch rig 19
knots, essential 41-42, 48, 49, 52, 68, 70, 82, 85
Knox-Johnston, Sir Robin 104

lazy jacks 25
leaks, 'fothering' 113 see also flooding
lee-bowing 143
lee shore 87
grounding on 147
in rivers, avoiding 142
length-beam ratio 15
life jackets 111

and dinghies 139
in fog 129
liferafts 114, 122-123
lift pumps, fuel 30
lightning strikes 153
lines, securing 48-49
to a cleat 48
to a post, bollard or winch barrel 49
locking hitches 48, 70
log books 127, 131
lying a'hull 103, 109

mainsheets, hanging 52
man overboard see crew overboard
manners of the sea 71, 132-137
manoeuvring 62-63
marlinespike seamanship 41-47
masts
alignment of 23
climbing 55
losing 118-119
mizzen 19
rake of 22
setting up 21-22
stowing and reefing sail in 26
MAYDAY call 110, 114, 122
meals on time 125
Ministry of Defence (Navy) 132
mizzen masts 19
mizzen sails 89
Moitessier, Bernard 104
mooring 84-85
anatomy of 84-85
between piles 85
chafe when 85
picking up 84
with lasso 85
securing to 84-85
wind-against-tide 85
Motor Fishing Vessel 11
multihull stability 103
multihulls, hull speed 13
multimeters 36

navigating an uncharted or marginally charted river 141
night orders 127
noise pollution 136
Norfolk coast 130
North Sea 149
Norway, West 151

O'Brien, Conor 104
Offshore Racing Council 112
oil pollution, preventing 136-137
orders, night 127

painters 139
PAN-PAN call 110, 114, 117, 118
para anchors 100, 108
'parbuckling' 121
Pardy, Lin and Larry 108
parties in harbour 136
piles, mooring between 85
pitch-poling 101, 104
pivot point 72
planing 13, 15
posts, securing to 49
power, creating 53-55
power consumption 38-39
power units 29-39
drive chain troubleshooting 31-35
fuel problems 33
liquid cooling 31-32
overheating 31-32, 117
stern tube leaks and failures 34-35
engine failures 117
engine refuses to start – electrical failure 36-38
flat battery 37-38
nothing happens 36-37
turns but does not fire 36
engine spares 117
engine stop toggles/solenoids 36
inboard engine drive chain 29-30
running, in harbour 136
propeller shafts 30
propeller torque 72
propellers, damaged 145
propellers, fitting 30
pump impellers, seawater 32

racing sail craft, hull speed 13
radar in fog 130
radios, handheld VHF 114, 123
rafting on piles 85
rafting up 71, 136
reef knots 42
RIBs (rigid inflatable boats), small 138
rig failures 118-119
rigging, standing 20-23
age-induced failure 23
care of 23
setting up masthead sloop rig 21-22
rigging spares 119
rigid inflatable boats (RIBs), small 138
rigs, sailing 18-19
rivers 140
bars 141
collision regulations (Colregs) 140, 141-142

depth, controlling 140
navigating uncharted or marginally charted 141
sailing yachts in 141-143
collision regulations (Colregs) 140, 141-142
exit strategy 143
grounding 142
huffling 142
keeping way on 142
lee-bowing 143
lee shore, avoiding 142
masthead, keeping an eye on 143
thinking ahead 143
transits, use of 143
windward, keeping to 142
tidal considerations 140
RNLI (Royal National Lifeboat Institution) 113, 117
roll inertia 102
rolling hitches 41, 82
rope handling when berthing 66
ropes
anchoring ('rode') 76, 78, 80
coiling 50-51
Dyneema 40
slip 75
Spectra 40, 118
stowing 51-52
types of 40
round turn and two half-hitches 41, 49, 85
Royal Cruising Club 134
Royal National Lifeboat Institution (RNLI) 113, 117
Royal Yacht Squadron 132
rudder failures/losses 114, 115
when grounding 145
power boats 115
sailing boats 115-116
spade 113, 115
rudders, jury 115
rigging 116
rudders, 'spade' 10, 113, 115
running off 95, 103

safety equipment 111-112
safety harnesses 111, 112
in fog 129
safety practice 111
sail combinations in heavy weather 91-92
sail makers' whippings 46
sail systems 24-28
asymmetric downwind 26-28
emergency drops 28
setting 27
'snuffer' system 26-28
trimming 27-28
headsails (jibsails) 24, 91, 92, 95, 107, 115-116
changing at sea 24
'gennaker' 26
hanked-on 24
roller genoa 24
storm jib 94
'yankee' jib 91
mainsails 25-26, 92, 95, 107, 115
in-boom stowing and reefing 26
in-mast stowing and reefing 26
lazy jacks 25
mizzen 19, 106, 115
staysails 92
trysails 92, 94, 103
sailing boats' abuse of searoom 136
sailing rigs, common 18-19
sailmaker's palms and needles 47
sails, steering with 115-116
salt and standing rigging 23
Samson posts 49
'Saoirse' 104
schooner rig 19
sea cocks 31, 113
seals, 'face' 34
seaman's eye 62
searoom, sailing boats' abuse 136
seasickness 124-125
meals on time 125
securing lines 48-49
to a cleat 48
to a post, bollard or winch barrel 49
self-steering arrangements 116 see also autopilots
'sheet, cracking the' 54
sheet bends 42
shrouds, lower 20, 22, 118
signal flags 134
skegs 10
skin-fitting failures 112, 113
slings, helicopter-style 120
slip ropes 75, 85
sloop rig 18, 20
masthead, setting up 21-22
SNAME/USYRU committee 106, 112
'snubbers' 80
'snuffer' system 26-28
Society of Naval Architects and Marine Engineers
(SNAME)/USYRU committee 106, 112
Solent, the 129
Spectra ropes 40, 118
speed
displacement 14, 16
and fuel economy 16
modifying factors in power boats 15

and fuel economy 16, 17
ground 13
hard driving 14
hull see hull speed
limitations in sailing boats 14
limits, harbour 135
sailing boats under auxiliary power 14
stalling 63
water 13
splices 43-44
split pins 23, 30, 118-119
spreaders 20, 71
spring lines 64, 65, 68, 71, 74
squalls 152-153
stability, multihull 103
stability, static 101
stability, vanishing, angle of 102
StackPack 25
stalling speed 63
starter motors/solenoids 37
steering failures 114-116
see also rudder failures/losses
steering sailing craft in waves 96-99
downwind 98
upwind 96-97
steering with sails 115-116
stern glands 34, 112
stern lines 64, 65, 68
stern 'overhang' 13
stern springs 64, 68, 74
stern tubes 30
leaks and failures 34-35
storm survival 100-109
see also weather, heavy
capsize resistance factors 101-102
angle of vanishing stability 102
beam 102
coach roof 102
displacement 102
freeboard 102
long-short keel 102
roll inertia 102
static stability 101
multihull stability 103
options in open water 103-109
bare poles 63, 104, 109
drogues 104 see also drogues
extreme running 104-105
heaving to 95, 106-107
keeping end-on 103
lying a'hull 103, 109
motorsailing to windward 106
para anchors 100, 108
power craft 103
running off 95, 103
trailing warps 89, 104
power boats 101
sailing boats 101
static stability 101
stowage in heavy weather 90
stream, spotting 62
stuffing boxes 34, 35
'Suhaili' 104
surfing 13, 99, 104
Swedish fids 43

tackles 54-55
friction in 55
tanks, holding 137
thunderstorms 153
tidal considerations in rivers 140
tidal height when anchoring 79
tidal walls, securing alongside 67
tide races 149
tides and waves 149
tiller failures 115
toggles 23
toilets, sea, use of 137
towing 58-61
alongside 61
chafe when 58, 60
in harbour 61
heaving lines 58
off a shoal 146
snatch when 58, 60
under way 60-61
towlines, passing 58
towlines, securing 59-60
transits 73, 143
'Tribuckles' 121
trim, fore-and-aft 90, 91
trim tabs, steering by 115
tugboat hitches 49
turnbuckles 21, 22

Union Flag 133
United Kingdom Shipping Register 132
United States, Eastern Seaboard 87, 129, 149, 153
United States Coast Guard 139
United States Yacht Racing Union (USYRU)/SNAME committee 106, 112

velocity ratio 53, 54
visibility, poor 128 see also fog
volt meters 39

walls, tidal, securing alongside 67
warps, anchor 76, 78, 80

warps, trailing 89, 104
wash, manners regarding 135
watch, changes of 127
watch systems 125-127
  four-hour watch-on-watch 126
  living with 127
  longer passages 126
  rolling watches 126
  short daytime passages 125
  single-night passages 125
watchkeeping 112, 127
water speed 13
waterspouts 153
watertight integrity 88, 103
wave generation in non-displacement hulls 17
waves 148-150
  anatomy of 148-150
  breaking in open water 150
  composite 149
  'fetch' 148
  inside 150
  land-based obstructions 150
  length 90
  shoaling water 149
  steering sailing craft in 96-99
    downwind 98
    upwind 96-97
  tides and races 149
  time factor 148
weather, heavy 86-99 see also storm survival
  definition 86
  handling power craft in 88-91
    beam sea 88-89, 90
    dodging 89
    downwind 89, 91
    faster power craft 90-91
    head sea 88, 90
    slow-speed motor boats without trim adjustment 88-89
    stowage 90
    trim 90, 91
    upwind 88, 90
    watertight integrity 88, 103
    wave length 90
  handling sailing craft on passage in 91-99
    apparent and true wind 92-93
    apparent wind, controlling for safety 93
    broach, prevention against 99
    broach to windward 98
    gybe broach 98
    heaving to 95
    making life easier 95
    rig, 'cutter' 92
    running off 95
    sail combinations 91-92
    shortening sail 93
    'spilling' off way 93
    steering downwind 98
    steering in waves 96-99
    steering upwind 96-97
    storm canvas 94
    true and apparent wind 92-93
    weatherliness 91, 106
  harbours of refuge, assessing 87
  and lee shore 87
  strategic options 87
weather gauge, maintaining 87
'weatherly' boats 91, 106
wheel steering failures 114, 115
whippings 45-47
winch barrels, securing to 49
winches
  loaded, easing rope around 54
  loading 53
  powered 54
  to recover casualty from water 120
  riding turns on 54
  self-tailing 53
  winding 54
winching 53-54
wind, apparent 62, 92-93
wind, true 92
wind awareness 62
wind phenomena 150-153
  and barometers 150
  disturbance to leeward of an obstruction 152
  'falling' winds 152
  gale-force winds, predictable 150-151
  gusts in lee of high ground 152
  katabatic winds 152
  land breezes 151
  sea breezes 151
  squalls 152-153
  isolated thunderstorms 153
  waterspouts 153
windlasses, anchor 78, 83
  for recovering casualty from the water 121
workboats, traditional straight-stemmed 9

yachts
  bilge-keeled 10
  classic long-keeled 9
  fin and skeg/spade 10
  modern long-keeled 9
yawing 99
yawl rig 19

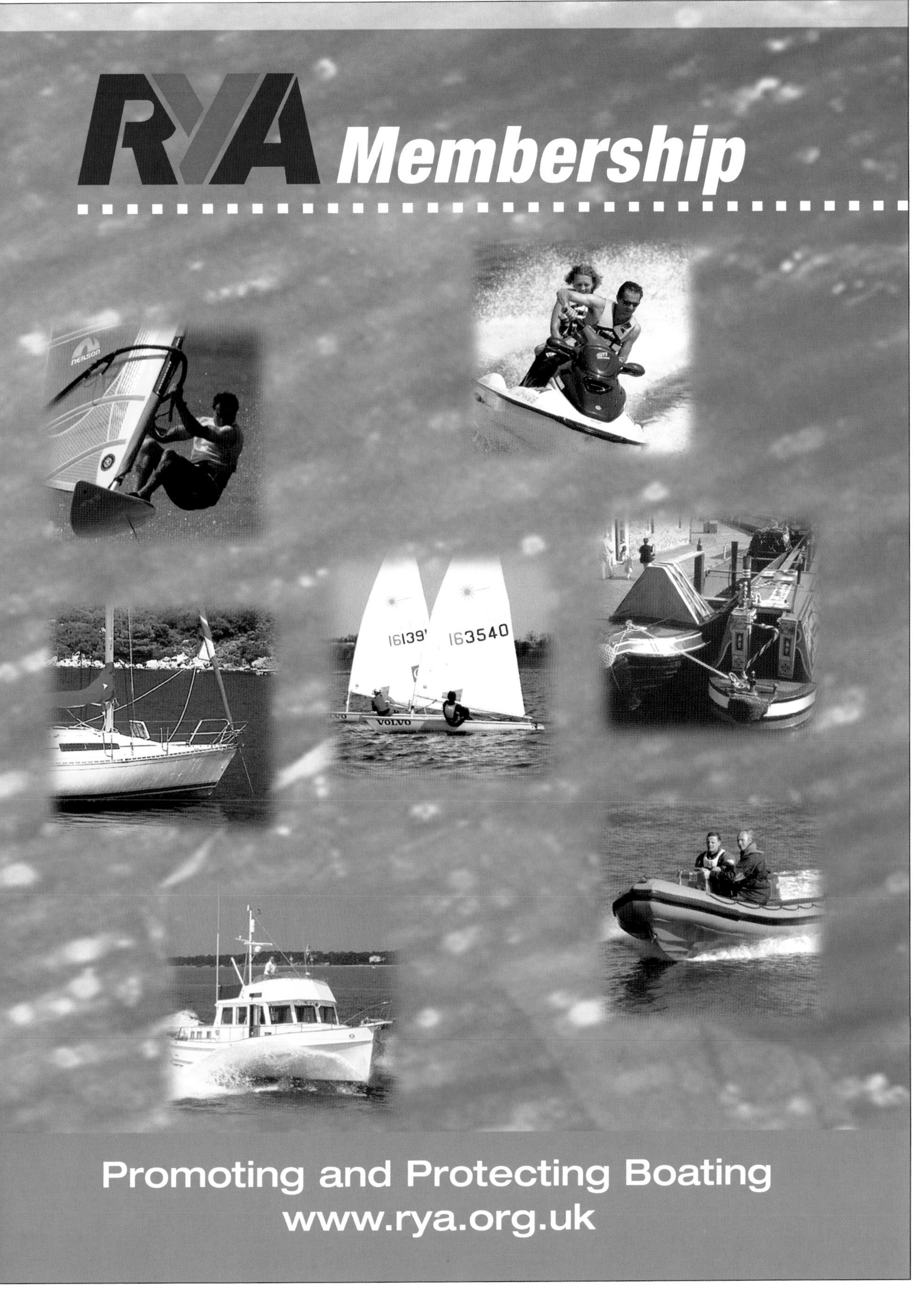
RYA Membership
NEILSON
161391
163540
VOLVO
Promoting and Protecting Boating
www.rya.org.uk

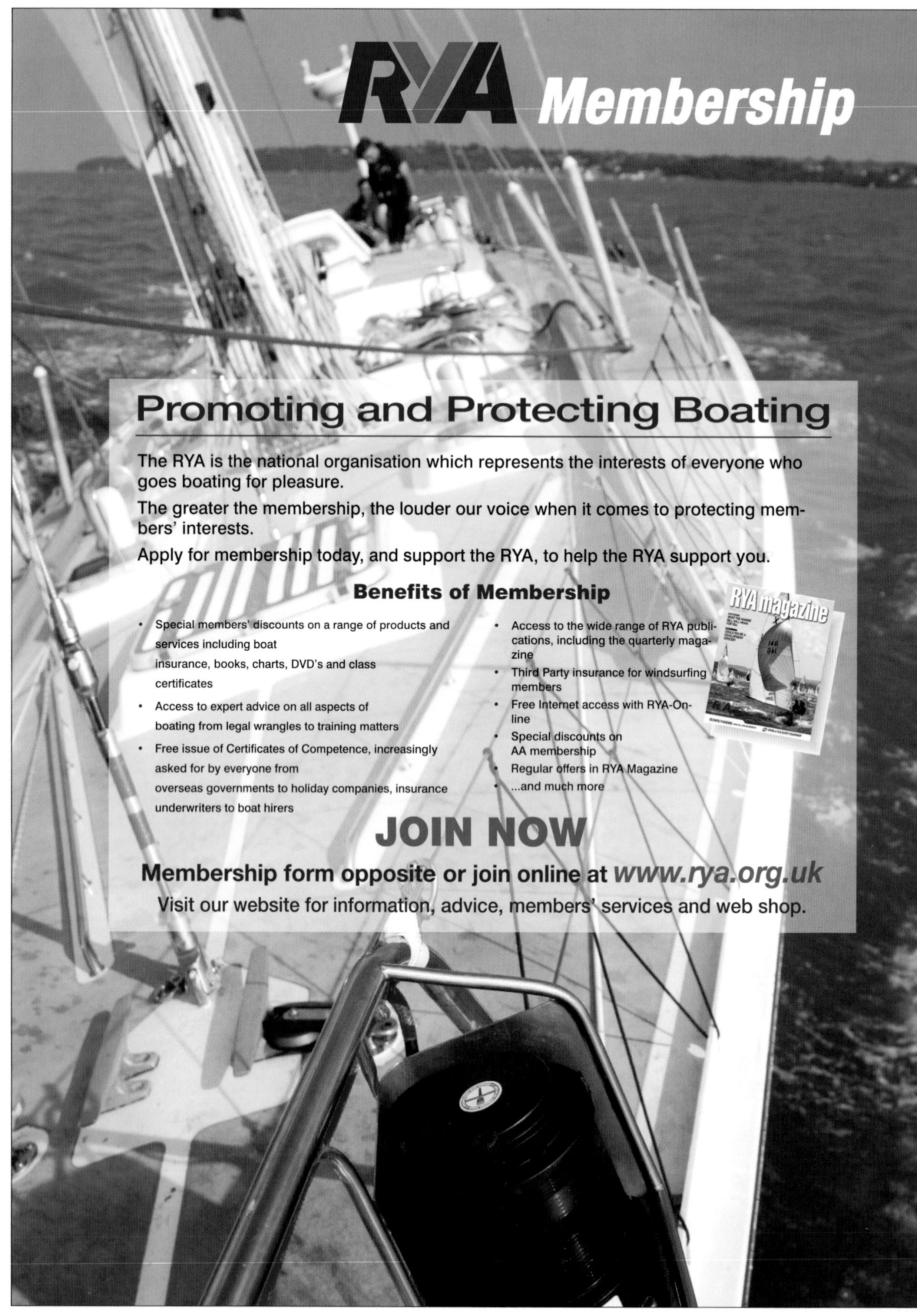
RYA Membership
Promoting and Protecting Boating
The RYA is the national organisation which represents the interests of everyone who goes boating for pleasure.
The greater the membership, the louder our voice when it comes to protecting members' interests.
Apply for membership today, and support the RYA, to help the RYA support you.
Benefits of Membership
Special members' discounts on a range of products and services including boat insurance, books, charts, DVD's and class certificates
Access to expert advice on all aspects of boating from legal wrangles to training matters
Free issue of Certificates of Competence, increasingly asked for by everyone from overseas governments to holiday companies, insurance underwriters to boat hirers
Access to the wide range of RYA publications, including the quarterly magazine
Third Party insurance for windsurfing members
Free Internet access with RYA-On-line
Special discounts on AA membership
Regular offers in RYA Magazine
...and much more
RYA magazine
JOIN NOW
Membership form opposite or join online at www.rya.org.uk
Visit our website for information, advice, members' services and web shop.

IT'S ALL ABOUT YOU AND THE BOATING YOU DO

RYA MEMBERSHIP APPLICATION

One of boating's biggest attractions is its freedom from rules and regulations. As an RYA member you'll play an active part in keeping it that way, as well as benefiting from free expert advice and information, plus discounts on a wide range of boating products, charts and publications.

To join the RYA, please complete the application form below and send it to The Membership Department, RYA, RYA House, Ensign Way, Hamble, Southampton, Hampshire SO31 4YA. You can also join online at www.rya.org.uk, or by phoning the membership department on +44 (0) 23 8060 4159. Whichever way you choose to apply, you can save money by paying by Direct Debit. A Direct Debit instruction is on the back of this form.

	Title	Forename	Surname	Gender	Date of Birth
Applicant ❶					/ /
Applicant ❷					/ /
Applicant ❸					/ /
Applicant ❹					/ /

E-mail Applicant ❶		Address	
E-mail Applicant ❷			
E-mail Applicant ❸			
E-mail Applicant ❹		Post Code	

Home Tel | Day Time Tel | Mobile Tel

Save money by completing the Direct Debit form overleaf

Type of membership required (Tick Box)

☐	**Junior (0-11)**	Annual rate £5 or **£5 if paying by Direct Debit**
☐	**Youth (12-17)**	Annual rate £14 or **£11 if paying by Direct Debit**
☐	**Under 25**	Annual rate £25 or **£22 if paying by Direct Debit**
☐	**Personal**	Annual rate £43 or **£39 if paying by Direct Debit**
☐	**Family***	Annual rate £63 or **£59 if paying by Direct Debit**

Please number up to three boating interests in order, with number one being your principal interest

☐ Yacht Racing	☐ Yacht Cruising	☐ Dinghy Racing	☐ Dinghy Cruising
☐ Personal Watercraft	☐ Sportboats & RIBs	☐ Windsurfing	☐ Motor Boating
☐ Powerboat Racing	☐ Canal Cruising	☐ River Cruising	

* *Family Membership: 2 adults plus any under 18s all living at the same address. Prices valid until 30/9/2011 One discount voucher is accepted for individual memberships, and two discount vouchers are accepted for family membership.*

IMPORTANT In order to provide you with membership benefits the details provided by you on this form and in the course of your membership will be maintained on a database. If you do not wish to receive information on member services and benefits please tick here ☐. By applying for membership of the RYA you agree to be bound by the RYA's standard terms and conditions (copies on request or at www.rya.org.uk)

Signature

Date / /

Source Code

Joining Point Code

GET MORE FROM
YOUR
BOATING
SUPPORT THE
RYA

PAY BY DIRECT DEBIT – AND SAVE MONEY

Instructions to your Bank or Building Society to pay by Direct Debit

Please fill in the form and send to:
Membership Department, Royal Yachting Association, RYA House, Ensign Way, Hamble, Southampton, Hampshire SO31 4YA.

Name and full postal address of your Bank/Building Society

To the Manager Bank/Building Society

Address

Postcode

Name(s) of Account Holder(s)

Branch Sort Code __ – __ – __

Bank/Building Society Account Number

Originator's Identification Number

9	5	5	2	1	3

DIRECT Debit

RYA Membership Number (For office use only)

Instructions to your Bank or Building Society
Please pay Royal Yachting Association Direct Debits from the account detailed in this instruction subject to the safeguards assured by The Direct Debit Guarantee. I understand that this instruction may remain with the Royal Yachting Association and, if so, details will be passed electronically to my Bank/Building Society.

Signature(s)

Date: D D / M M / Y Y Y Y